# 趣读 MOVIE COMMENTARIES
# 英文影评

English Garden | 卫禹兰 编著

外文出版社
FOREIGN LANGUAGES PRESS

图书在版编目（CIP）数据

趣读英文影评/卫禹兰编著．-北京：外文出版社，2008
（英文花园）
ISBN 978-7-119-05509-1

Ⅰ．趣…　Ⅱ．卫…　Ⅲ．①英语－语言读物②电影评论－
世界　Ⅳ．H319.4：J

中国版本图书馆 CIP 数据核字（2008）第 118717 号

选题策划：蔡　箐
责任编辑：葛　欣　王　欢
装帧设计：奇文云海
印刷监制：冯　浩

**英文花园**
**趣读英文影评**

作　　者：卫禹兰

ⓒ外文出版社
出版发行：外文出版社
地　　址：中国北京西城区百万庄大街 24 号　邮政编码：100037
网　　址：http：//www.flp.com.cn
电　　话：(010) 68995964/68995883（编辑部）
　　　　　(010) 68995844/68995852（发行部/门市邮购）
　　　　　(010) 68320579/68996067（总编室）
印　　制：保定市新华印刷厂
经　　销：新华书店/外文书店
开　　本：880mm×1230mm　1/32
印　　张：8.5
字　　数：227 千字
装　　别：平
版　　次：2009 年第 1 版第 2 次印刷
书　　号：ISBN 978-7-119-05509-1
定　　价：18.00 元　　　　　上架建议：英语读物

# 序

这是一本英汉对照的电影评论集萃。

影评是指点电影，激扬文字的事业。我一直以为，好的影评是电影鉴赏力和文字表达力的互相成全。阅读它是一个充实和启发的过程。如果仅当电影是娱乐消遣倒也罢了，而若不愿辜负电影作为艺术的那一面，就不能只是爱看，还得会看。读影评很大程度上是看一个老练于看电影的人如何看电影，从而增加积累，培养感觉，提高眼光。当然，阅读本身也是一件痛快过瘾的事。影评作为文艺评论中的一种，向来是漂亮文字的演练场，见证种种犀利、泼辣、幽默、俏皮的语言精华，激发我们对文字的感受力。因此，我怀着一种一举两得的愿望编译了这本书，希望它能让读者在看电影和学英语这两件事上都能有所获益。

我选择了近年来一些很有说头的影片。为了呈现一种丰富性，选择时努力涵盖尽量多的电影种类和出品国家。即使对一部影片的评论，也尽量选择多个视角，多种声音。评论段落主要选自欧美各大报刊或网站。这些闪亮的文字除了好看，还很昂贵。我指的不只是稿费，而是说这些评论严重到可以影响一部影片的世界口碑和票房收益。之所以有如此的影响力，这与它们品格独立，性格鲜明，文风独特密不可分。如果本书能让读者在看电影和学英语之外，还能对影评有所认识，则幸甚至哉。

能力有限，编译过程中的疏漏和错误在所难免，在此诚恳致歉。

卫禹三

# 目 录

# The Devil Wears Prada

# 时尚女魔头

**导演**：大卫·弗兰科（David Frankel）

**原著**：劳伦·魏丝博格（Lauren Weisberger）

**主演**：梅丽尔·斯特里普（Meryl Streep）

　　　安妮·海瑟薇（Anne Hathaway）

**片长**：106 分钟

**发行**：20 世纪福克斯（20th Century Fox），2006 年

# 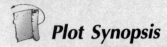 *Plot Synopsis*

In New York, the simple and naive just – graduated in journalism Andrea Sachs is hired to work as the second assistant of the powerful and sophisticated Miranda Priestly, the ruthless and merciless executive of the Runway fashion magazine. Andrea dreams to become a journalist and faces the opportunity as a temporary professional challenge. The first assistant Emily advises Andrea about the behavior and preferences of their cruel boss, and the stylist Nigel helps Andrea to dress more adequately for the environment. Andrea changes her attitude and behavior, affecting her private life and the relationship with her boyfriend Nate, her family and friends. In the end, Andrea learns that life is made of choices.

## 剧情简介

纽约。天真单纯的安德丽娅·桑切丝（安妮·海瑟薇饰）刚刚从新闻专业毕业，被数一数二的时尚杂志《Runway》雇佣，成了主编米兰达·普雷斯特丽（梅丽尔·斯特里普饰）的第二助理。米兰达精明强干又冷酷无情。梦想着做一名记者的安德丽娅把这个机会当成一份练手的临时工作。她得到了第一助理艾米丽和设计师奈杰尔的帮助。前者教她在工作中如何适应她们严酷的主编，后者教她如何穿着得体。安德丽娅的为人处世在逐渐地改变着，同时这影响着她的私人生活，影响着她与朋友、亲人以及男友内特的关系。最终，安德丽娅认识到，生活原来是由选择构成的。

# Critique

This clever, funny big-screen adaptation of Lauren Weisberger's best-seller takes some of the snarky bite out of the chick lit book, but smoothes out the characters' boxy edges to make a more satisfying movie. There's no doubt *The Devil Wears Prada* belongs to Meryl Streep, who turns in an Oscar-worthy (seriously!) strut as the monster editor-in-chief of Runway, an elite fashion magazine full of size-0, impossibly well-dressed plebes. This makes new second-assistant Andrea (Anne Hathaway), who's smart but an unacceptable size 6, stick out like a sore thumb. Streep has a ball sending her new slave on any whimsical errand, whether it's finding the seventh (unpublished) Harry Potter book or knowing what type she means when she wants "skirts". Though Andrea thumbs her nose at the shallow world of fashion (she's only doing the job to open doors to a position at *The New Yorker* someday), she finds herself dually disgusted yet seduced by the perks of the fast life. The film sends a basic message: Make work your priority, and you'll be rich and powerful... and lonely. Any other actress would have turned Miranda into a scenery-chewing Cruella, but Streep's underplayed, brilliant comic timing make her a fascinating, unapologetic character.

—*Ellen A. Kim from Amazon. com*

电影把劳伦·魏丝博格的畅销书做了一次聪明而风趣的改编，它剔除掉了这本女性流行读物中的那些犀利成分，磨圆了人物棱角来成全一部恰到好处的电影。《时尚女魔头》无疑是属于斯特里普的，她扮演这个大魔头主编所表现出的精湛演技足以平了奥斯卡。说到电影的故事，时尚界的精英杂志《Runway》

的编辑部里满是身材苗条、衣着考究得不可思议的员工，新任的第二助理安德丽娅头脑比她们机敏，身材比她们臃肿，怎么看都和环境不搭调。斯特里普喜欢安排反复无常的差事来消遣她，不是命她去拿裙子却不说明哪一款哪一型，就是让她去找还没有出版的《哈里·波特》第七卷。虽然安德丽娅极端鄙视这个肤浅无聊的时尚界（就像她只是把《Runway》当作进入《纽约客》的敲门砖），但她发现自己还是掉进了一个两难的陷阱：她既厌恶，又被这种快节奏的风光的生活方式俘虏了。电影传达出这样一个基本信息：如果你生活中的一切都为工作让位，你将会拥有财富、权力，还有孤独。再回到表演，如果米兰达这个女魔头换了其他演员来诠释，估计会成为一道残酷的摆设，多亏了斯特里普的克制和分寸感，让米兰达这个角色魅力四射、无可争辩。

—*Ellen A. Kim*, *Amazon* 网站

In "The Devil Wears Prada", Meryl Streep, as the invincible fashion editor Miranda Priestly never raises her voice. To snarl or shout would be to imply that some resistance to her authority exists. Streep, a brilliant comedienne, pushes the terror tactics into satire, but the comedy moves in a shrewd direction: Streep's every gesture says that fashion is multibillion - dollar business in which civility has become a disposable luxury. "The Devil Wears Prada" tells a familiar story, and it never goes much below the surface of what it has to tell. Still, what a surface! The movie turns dish into art. Tells about the novel of the same title, which was written by Lauren Weisberger after she had worked for less than a year as an assistant to Anna Wintour of Vogue. The screenwriter, Aline Brosh McKenna has shaped Weisberger's breathless iterations into a reliable plot - a primal Manhattan success story in the form of a fairy tale. The movie delivers an inordinate amount of pleasure, and, in the end, Miranda escapes our censure. "The Devil Wears Prada" presents the heroine's career options as a simple choice between power and honor. Someday I'd like to see a film suggesting that you can be the boss without giving up your intellectual ideals, and that the alternative rejecting power has its corruptions, too.

*—David Denby from The New Yorker*

　　在《时尚女魔头》中，梅丽尔·斯特里普作为天下无敌的时尚编辑米兰达，从不提高嗓门说话，因为咆哮或大喊大叫有损她的威严。斯特里普是一个才华横溢的喜剧演员。她用讽刺的风格来化解表演难题，但是却把这部喜剧片导向了这样一个尖锐的方向：斯特里普的举手投足都在告诉人们，时尚归根结底其实是价值亿万的生意，教养对于时尚而言是一种随意的奢侈。《时尚女魔头》只是讲了一个老故事，而且也没有越过故事表层把它讲得更深入一些。再说了，即使浅薄都浅薄得不像样，这部电影简直是把快餐包装成了艺术。与电影同名的小说，是作者劳伦·魏丝博格在给《时尚》赫赫有名的安娜·温特尔做了不到一年的助手后写就的。电影编剧麦肯纳把魏丝博格絮絮叨叨的讲述转化成了一个情节可信的曼哈顿灰姑娘如何成功的童话故事。影片拉拉杂杂地释放了大量愉悦和快感，于是在影片结尾，米兰达躲过了我们的谴责。《时尚女魔头》把女主角的职业选择简化成权力和尊严之间的选择。我倒希望有一天能看到这样的电影，它能让你在做老板的同时保持你的个人主见，而且告诉人们，彻底选择拒绝也不是没有弊端的。

*—David Denby*，《纽约客》

　　Some self-appointed critics pin "Devil's" visual shortcomings on a misapprehension of what truly counts as "fabulous" in the realm of style. It is not summed up by a parade of Gucci, Pucci, Dolce & Gabbana and Prada, they say, but by breezier labels like Chloé, Marc Jacobs and Marni, which are coveted by young trendsetters but are in scant evidence on screen. In their place are masses of wool bouclé power suits, double-C logo pearls, tweed newsboy caps and thigh-high boots that threaten to sink the film under their weight.

Those costumes are "a caricature of what people who don't work in fashion think fashion people look like," said Anne Slowey, the fashion news director of Elle. Conceived and styled by Patricia Field, who assembled the wardrobe for "Sex and the City", "the clothes are a little too head-to-toe perfect," Ms. Slowey said. For Ms. Field, the costumes were never intended to match reality. "Did Holly Golightly represent reality in a Givenchy dress? I was in that zone," she said. "My job is to present an entertainment, a world people can visit and take a little trip". If they want a documentary, they can watch the History Channel.

"The hair, the clothes, the furs, the handbags, the editor's apartment, it's very much the heyday of the 80's, which was our flashiest moment to date," said Tiffany Dubin, a former curator of vintage fashion for Sotheby's. Those elements prompted Ms. Dubin to dismiss the film's style with the fashionista's ultimate putdown: "The people in it are trying a little too hard."

The first hint that "Devil" may go over the top arrives in the form of a wardrobe montage in which Miranda stalks into the office on a series of mornings, flinging onto her assistant's desk enough status bags and lavish furs to clean out the Bronx Zoo. They are just the beginning of a brazen outpouring of $12,000 handbags, $30,000 furs and $1,000 over-the-knee boots assembled by Ms. Field with a budget of $100,000 and a little help from designers and friends who, she said, provided access to about $1 million worth of clothes. "I find it astounding that all these people in the movie have so much time to change," said Hal Rubenstein, the fashion director of *InStyle* magazine. "By and large, if you go from work to an event in the evening, you change your shoes, your jewelry and your bag, the same way that the magazine editors tell their readers to do." Mr. Rubenstein objected as strenuously to the filmmakers' tendency to pile on the goods. "For the most part women in fashion fiercely edit what they wear," he said. In contrast, the movie offers much too much in the way of furs and gold bangles, he said, reflecting "a weird desire for abundance for the sake of abundance."

Ms. Dubin said: "It's costume. People now are more subdued."

——*Ruth La Ferla from New York Times*

一些自封的批评家认为本片其实误解了什么才是时尚王国的"极品",正是这种误解导致了影片的一些视觉缺陷。他们认为,好并不意味着非得是 Gucci、Pucci、、Dolce & Gabbana 和 Prada 的狂轰烂炸,而应该是风格轻盈一点、像 Chloé、Marc Jacobs 或者 Marni 这样被主导潮流的年轻人所垂涎的品牌,可惜这些在影片中并不多见。我们满眼都充斥着厚重的毛料套装、双 C logo 的珠宝、斜纹的报童帽和高筒靴,似乎这些东西要用它们的重量把影片坠沉了去。

Elle 杂志的新闻主管安妮·思露薇说,这些服装绝妙地讽刺了一帮并非在时尚界工作的人对时尚的想象。《时尚女魔头》的服装设计师帕特丽夏·菲尔德当年还曾设计过《性与城市》。但是在思露薇看来,"那些衣服有点太装模作样了"。

菲尔德争辩道,影片中的那些服装本就不是用来和现实匹配的。"难道霍莉·戈莱特丽穿着纪梵希的衣服是为了表现现实吗?我的电影也是这样,"她说,"我的工作是提供娱乐,让人们到一个乌托邦的世界中做一个短暂旅游。""要是他们想看纪录片,那可以去看历史频道。"

苏富比复古馆的一个前馆长蒂芙尼·杜彬说,"影片中的那些发型、衣服、毛皮、手提包、主编的公寓,像极了全盛时期的上世纪 80 年代,那个历史上最浮华的时刻。"这些元素最终使杜彬唾弃该片的品味:"影片里的人物的确有点过于刻意了。"

影片第一个暴露了它财务超支的地方是那个服装秀的蒙太奇段落,在无数个早晨,米兰达盛气凌人地走进办公室,把大批名贵的提包和皮衣摔在助手的桌子上。这算什么,炫耀才刚刚开始，还有价值 12,000 美元的包，30,000 美元的毛皮，1,000 美元的高筒靴，菲尔德在 100,000 的预算之外，还拉来了其他设计师和朋友的援助，总之，整部电影的服装支出高达一百万美元。

"令我惊讶的是，电影里所有的人都有那么多的时间来换衣服，"《InStyle》杂志的时尚主管霍尔·鲁宾斯坦感叹道。"基本上，你要是下了班去参加一个晚间活动，你得换鞋、换首饰、换包，就像杂志编辑引导读者去做的那样。"鲁宾斯坦极力反对电影制作人这种像成批地展销商品一样的疯狂做法。"时尚女性主要是费尽心思地搭配衣服。"但是电影却截然相反，竭尽所能地炫耀贵重毛皮和珠宝，他说，这反映了"一种扭曲的对穷奢极欲的穷奢极欲。"

杜彬说："只是服装而已，如今人们过分受控于它了。"

—*Ruth La Ferla*，《纽约时报》

---

### Note

Chick lit：时尚女性流行读物。Chick 的意思是年轻女孩子，Lit 是 literature 的缩写，顾名思义就是年轻女孩子的文学。一般不外乎讲爱情、讲是非、讲怎么穿衣打扮。

# Babel *

# 通天塔

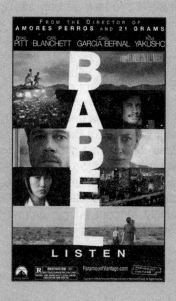

**导演**：亚历桑德罗·冈萨雷斯·伊纳里图
（Alejandro González Iñárritu）

**编剧**：吉勒莫·阿里加（Guillermo Arriaga）

**主演**：布莱德·彼特（Brad Pitt）

凯特·布兰切特（Cate Blanchett）

盖尔·加西亚·伯纳尔（Gael Garcia Bernal）

役所广司（Koji Yakusho）

菊地凛子（Rinko Kikuchi）

**片长**：143 分钟

**发行**：派拉蒙优势（Paramount Vantage），2006 年

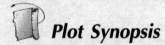 *Plot Synopsis*

4 interlocking stories all connected by a single gun all converge at the end and reveal a complex and tragic story of the lives of humanity around the world and how we truly aren't all that different. In Morocco, a troubled married couple are on vacation trying to work out their differences. Meanwhile, a Moroccan herder buys a rifle for his sons so they can keep the jackals away from his herd. A girl in Japan dealing with rejection, the death of her mother, the emotional distance of her father, her own self-consciousness, and a disability among many other issues, deals with modern life in the enormous metropolis of Tokyo, Japan that is literally the size of the state of California. Then, on the opposite side of the world the married couple's Mexican nanny takes the couple's 2 children with her to her son's wedding in Mexico, only to come into trouble on the return trip. Combined, it provides a powerful story and an equally powerful looking glass into the lives of seemingly random people around the world and it shows just how connected we really are.

## 剧情简介

一只枪串起了四个连锁的故事，你会发现到影片结尾这四个故事汇聚到了一点上。这是一个关于天下芸芸众生的复杂悲剧，它让你觉得你、我、大家其实并没有什么不同。在摩洛哥，一对旅行中的问题夫妻正试图解决他们之间的分歧；与此同时，一个摩洛哥牧羊人给儿子们买了一只枪，以便保护他们的羊群不受豺狼的侵袭；一个日本女孩正被诸多烦恼如影随形地包围着，她无法正视母亲的死、与父亲的感情距离、不足为外人道的自我感觉以及她那牵连着很多问题的残疾，总之，她要应付的是在一个和加州一样大的超级大都市东京里的现代生活。此时在世界的那一头，那对夫妻的保姆带着他们的两个孩子去墨西哥参加儿子的婚礼，不料在回来的路上遇上了麻烦。经过组合后，这些小故事呈现出了一个有力的故事和一个有力的视角：原来世界上看似随机的人们真实是如此地彼此攸关。

# *Critique*

I feel that the connection that I want to make is not a physical or coincidental connection, nor a plot connection. I think as human beings, what makes us happy is very different; it depends on cultures or races. What makes us sad and miserable is exactly what we share, and that thing is basically the impossibility of love, the impossibility to be touched by love, the impossibility to touch with love and express it. That is one of the most painful things that every human being has experienced, as well as feeling vulnerable to love. I think those two things are the most tragic things that bring us together. This film and the connections to the characters is about that, all of them on different levels, no matter which culture, no matter which country, religion, age, social class... All of these people are at an inability to express themselves, with their husbands, with their wives, with their kids. When you cannot be touched by words, and when you cannot touch people with words, then the body becomes a weapon, an invitation, and that is what is tremendous about the story. I feel that you saw a story about human beings and not about Moroccans, Mexicans, or Americans.

—*Director Ínárritu said at Cannes Film Festival when being interviewed*

我觉得我在影片中想要表现的联系既不是物理的或巧合的那种联系，也不是情节上的联系。我想作为一个人，我们快乐的原因可能千差万别，它会受到文化或种族的影响。然而我们难过或痛苦的原因却是一致的，这基本可以归结为缺乏爱的能力、缺乏感受爱的能力、缺乏把握爱和表达爱的能力，这是每个人都曾经历过的最痛苦的事情之一。而与此同时，人在爱面前总是很脆弱。正是这两种最具悲剧性的事实把我们联系到了一起。这部影片和人物之间的那种联系所要传达的是，无论他们的生活是多么不同，无论他们的文化、国籍、宗教、年龄、社会阶层是多么不同……他们都同样地没有能力去表达自己，没有能力与丈夫、妻子和孩子沟通。当你不能被语言打动，或者你不能用语言去打动他人，你的身体就带上了攻击或是诱惑的信息，这就是这个故事的主旨。我觉得这个故事是关于整个人类的，而不是具体的摩洛哥人、墨西哥人或者美国人。

——导演伊纳里图在戛纳电影节接受采访时如是说

My friend Herbert was rude to his mother last spring, and, some time later, Mt. St. Helens* erupted. And three girls I met on the Central Park carrousel were kicked out of school for smoking, and the price of silver dropped by forty thousand rupiah in Indonesia. With these seemingly trivial events from my own life, I illustrate the dramatic principle by which the Mexican-born director Alejandro Gonz lez I rritu makes his movies. I rritu, who made "Amores Perros" (2000), is one of the world's most gifted filmmakers. But I had the same reaction to "Babel" that I had to his most recent movie, "21 Grams" (2003): he creates savagely beautiful and heartbreaking images; he gets fearless performances out of his actors; he edits with the sharpest razor in any computer in Hollywood; and he abuses his audience with a humorless fatalism and a piling up of calamities that borders on the ludicrous.

—*David Denby*, *from New Yorker*

去年春天，我的朋友赫伯特曾经粗暴地对待自己的母亲，过了些天，圣海伦火山爆发了，我在中央公园的旋转木马上遇到的三个女孩因为吸烟被学校开除了，还有印尼的白银价格下降了四万印尼卢比。这些都是我生活中看似无关紧要的琐事，但我用它们可以阐明墨西哥裔导演亚历桑德罗·冈萨雷斯·伊纳里图创作影片的基本戏剧原理。曾经拍过《爱情是狗娘》（2000 年）的伊纳里图可以说是当今世界上最有天才的导演之一。然而,我对《通天塔》的感觉和对他最近的影片《21 克》的感觉一样:虽然他拍出了美得令人心碎的影像;他调动演员们完成了勇敢无畏的表演;他做出了好莱坞最凌厉的剪辑;但是他却用毫无生趣的宿命论和一连串荒谬可笑的灾难残忍地折磨了观众。

—*David Denby*,《纽约客》

To judge from audience reactions at the Cannes and Toronto film festivals, many people find "Babel" deeply moving. A lot of people felt that way about "Crash", which also seemed as if it had been conceived on a diagram board, from the outside in, rather than the inside out. "Babel" reaches its nadir at the Mexican-American border, when a drunken Bernal makes the stupidest choice possible (as you know he will), putting the poor Mexican nanny and her charges in dire peril. I know I was meant to be devastated, but at this point I just wanted to cry foul. If "Babel" were a football game, I'd flag it 15 yards for piling on*. Others may want to give it an Oscar. To each his own.

—*David Ansen*, *from Newsweek*

从戛纳和多伦多电影节观众的反应来看,很多人都被《通天塔》感动了。有很多人发现了它和影片《撞车》的相似之处,仿佛构思的起点都是一张图表,思路是由外向内,而不是相反。《通天塔》最糟糕的地方莫过于喝多了的伯纳尔在墨西哥与美国的边境上做了一个最愚蠢的选择(好像我们知道他一定会这么做),从而使可怜的墨西哥保姆和她照顾的孩子陷入可怕的危险境地。我知道我本来是打算让内心被它震动一番,但恰恰在这个时刻我想破口大骂:太拙劣了。如果《通天塔》是一场橄榄球比赛,我会判它 15 码的犯规罚球。当然,也有人想把奥斯卡颁发给它。那就各买各的账吧。

—*David Ansen*,《新闻周刊》

For a film named after miscommunication on a biblical scale, *Babel* is surprisingly easy to follow; the challenge lies in caring. Individual characters jump to life in individual scenes—García Bernal popping his cork in one desert, Pitt popping his in another—and Barraza might break your heart at the end. Stylistically, yes, the director takes risks that pay off, such as muting a few scenes to convey Chieko's deafness.

But he doesn't give much cause to care about her story, which incorporates flashy editing, bored nudity and many a stone-faced close-up. It seems tangential to the film's Moroccan axis, which isn't, in any case, as epic or profound as I rritu intends.

He remains as entranced as ever by fate, loss and the interconnectedness of humankind, and I admire him for it. But *Babel* isn't the last or best word on that subject. It's just a lot of talk.

*—Amy Biancolli, from Houston Chronicle*

作为一部以《圣经》中表达人类沟通之难的典故来命名的影片，《通天塔》令人惊讶地轻松接下了这一主题，它的挑战主要是对同情心的表达。影片中每个角色个体都在一个孤零零的环境中独自面对生活——加西亚·伯纳尔在一片沙漠中突然爆发了，皮特是在另一片沙漠中，而巴拉萨在片尾能让你伤透了心。在影片的文体风格上，导演的确冒了风险并且付出了代价，比如他消去了一些场景的声音来表现千惠子耳聋的感受。

但是导演没有给我们足够的理由来关注千惠子的故事，我们只是被花哨的剪辑、无聊的裸体和很多没有表情的面部特写搞晕了。这条线似乎只是和摩洛哥那个故事的轴线相切，无论如何，它配不上伊纳里图那宏大的史诗般的意图。

伊纳里图仍旧像往常一样对人类的命运、失落和宿命的联系着迷，我为此尊敬他。但是《通天塔》并不是对这个主题最终的或最好的表述。它只是一堆口水而已。

*—Amy Biancolli,《休斯敦时报》*

Babel has the material of greatness—vast scope, humane vision, fine actors—but sadly not the ability to make it all into something beyond mildly pretty and pretentious blather. In striving to recreate the chaotic din of a God-cursed global humanity, it succeeds only in making noise.

—*Chris Barsanti, from Filmcritic. com*

《通天塔》堆砌了一堆"伟大"的材料，比如宏伟的视角、人文的关怀，精良的演员团队。但是很遗憾，它没能超越它那种温吞吞的美和自命不凡的喋喋不休。虽然它努力重现那种被上帝诅咒的人性的普遍混乱和喧嚣，但结果仅仅是成功制造了噪音而已。

—*Chris Barsanti, Filmcritic* 网站

## Note

*Babel*：即 *The Tower of Babel*，通天塔又称巴别塔。典故出自《圣经》旧约全书中的《创世纪》第 11 章，大洪水以后诺亚的后人来到一个叫西纳的地方居住，突然间心血来潮想建一座高可通天的宝塔，以纪念人类在地球上所创下的丰功伟绩。上帝得知这个消息后很不高兴，于是就变乱了他们的语言（这之前地球上的人们只会讲一种语言，这种语言后来失传）。由于每个人说的话其他人都听不懂，所以人们根本无法把塔盖起来，这座塔也就永远地停工了。这些人就此觉得再也没有生活在一起的必要，于是分道扬镳，分散到了世界的各个角落，分别成为七大洲的祖先。

*Mt. St. Helens*：圣海伦火山，它是美国大陆唯一仍在爆发中的火山。

*pile on*：一般指堆积的意思。但也是橄榄球比赛的术语，特指一种犯规行为，一般会判罚 15 码罚球。

# Volver

# 回 归

**导演/编剧：**佩德罗·阿尔莫多瓦（Pedro Almodóvar）

**主演：**佩内洛普·克鲁兹（Penélope Cruz）

卡门·莫拉（Carmen Maura）

劳拉·杜纳丝（Lola Duenas）

尤汉娜·柯博（Yohana Cobo）

布兰卡·波提罗（Blanca Portillo）

**片长：**121 分钟

**发行：**20 世纪福克斯阿根廷分公司

（20th Century Fox de Argentina），2006 年

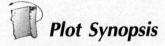 *Plot Synopsis*

Three generations of women survive wind, fire and even death, thanks to goodness, audacity and a limitless vitality. They are Raimunda (Pénelope Cruz), who is married to an unemployed labourer and has a teenage daughter (Yohana Cobo); Sole (Lola Due as), her sister, who makes a living as a hairdresser; and the mother of both (Carmen Maura), who died in a fire along with her husband. This character appears first to her sister and then to Sole, although the people with whom she has some unresolved matters are Raimunda and her neighbour in the village, Agustina (Blanca Portillo).

## 剧情简介

三代女性从大风、大火和死亡的威胁中存活下来，这得感谢上帝、感谢她们的无畏的胆量和顽强的生命力。她们是蕾木达（克鲁兹饰），她嫁给了一个失业工人并有一个十几岁的女儿（柯博饰）；索欧（杜纳丝饰），蕾木达的妹妹，靠做理发师维持生计；她们两个人的母亲（莫拉饰），与丈夫一起死于一场大火。这个角色很神秘，虽然她起初只在自己的姐姐，其次是二女儿索欧面前现身，但她其实是和蕾木达以及村里的邻居奥格斯蒂娜（布兰卡·波提罗饰）有着无法释怀的事情。

 *Critique*

Not many directors could take a film built around the theme of death and make it as funny, thoughtful, and deeply meaningful as Pedro Almodóvar has with *Volver*, now officially Spain's nominee for the Oscar for Best Foreign Picture.

*Volver* is a strong effort by Almodóvar, who won the Oscar for Best Original Screenplay for 2002's *Talk to Her*. The story revolves almost exclusively around the female characters, and Almodóvar's writing and direction indicate a deeply innate understanding of women and their relationships. The characters in *Volver* are complexly drawn, with intricate relationships and motivations. Even the theme of death is more than it seems on the surface. While there are surreally funny moments in the film, there is emotion and drama woven around the comedy. More than death, though, *Volver* is a film about women, family, and motherhood: The ties that bind, the sacrifices a mother will make for her child, the misunderstandings that can tear mother and daughter apart——and the healing that can come, even beyond death, from the resurrection and reburial of the past.

—*Kim Voynar, from Cinematical. com*

并非是个电影导演就可以驾驭死亡这个题目，并能把它拍得像阿尔莫多瓦的《回归》一样有趣、深刻、意味深长。现在这部影片正被西班牙正式提名去角逐奥斯卡最佳外语片奖。

2002 年以《对她说》获得奥斯卡最佳原创剧本奖的阿尔莫多瓦对《回归》一片付出了巨大的努力。故事几乎统统围绕着女性角色，阿尔莫多瓦的写作和执导显示出了他对女性和女性关系的理解天赋。《回归》中的人物设置是出类拔萃的，兼有复杂的人物关系和动机。即便是死亡主题也比我们表面看到的要复杂得多。虽然影片中不时有超现实的滑稽可笑的片断，但这是一出渗透着感情和戏剧精神的喜剧。当然，《回归》说的不仅仅是死亡，它更是一部关于女人、家庭和母性的影片：关于把她们联结在一起的纽带，关于母亲为孩子所做的牺牲，关于可以疏远母女关系的误解——还有最终会到来的谅解和弥合，它来自于过去记忆的复苏和重葬，甚至能够超越死亡。

——Kim Voynar, Cinematical 网站

Pedro Almodóvar is one of the only directors who, a quarter-century into his career, remains an international brand name, his every new film anticipated and talked about the way Bergman's or Godard's or Antonioni's used to be. Volver ( "To Return") is his latest in a long run of wonderful pictures. In it, his once-kitschy* obsession with color and surface continues to deepen into a big, bold, almost painterly style.

The director hasn't completely left camp* behind, in that you have to have a high tolerance for melodrama to see past the apparent corniness of his plot twists. But even if you're allergic to clich , don't roll your eyes too soon. This is lush, fertile, emotionally rich filmmaking: No matter how jaded a viewer you are, the idea of a dead mother-or any lost object of love-reappearing out of the past to make peace with the living has an archetypal force that's hard to get around. When Irene's ghost (who's hiding from Raimunda because of an old quarrel* between the two), overhears her daughter singing a gorgeous Gardel tango that she used to sing to her as a child, I guarantee you will not care that the director's trying to get you to cry. You'll just do it.

——Dana Stevens, from Slate. com

佩德罗·阿尔莫多瓦是那种凤毛麟角的导演，他的国际盛誉在将近四分之一世纪的导演生涯中历久弥新，他的每一部新片都不逊于伯格曼、戈达尔、安东尼奥尼所曾受的赞誉。《回归》是他最新的也是能够被时间证明的作品。在这部影片中，他过去对俗艳色彩和外表的迷恋已经发展成一种壮丽的、大胆的、油画般的风格。

导演也没有完全放弃坎普风格，因此你一定要忍受住影片中那种情节剧结构，忍受住那种明显粗鄙夸张的情节转折。即便你对陈词滥调高度敏感和反感，也千万不要过早地转移你的注意力。这就是那种大喜大悲、感情浓烈的电影：不管你观看的时候多么疲倦，但是让一个已经死去的母亲（或任何失去爱的人）为

了与生者和解而重现人间，这个情节中有一种我们熟悉的难以逃避的生活原型。当艾琳的鬼魂（因为旧日宿怨而躲避着蕾木达）无意中听到她的女儿唱着她在她童年时教的歌，一首华丽的 Gardel 的探戈小调，我敢说你不会介意导演就是要赚你的眼泪。看，你马上就要落泪了。

—*Dana Stevens*，*Slate* 网站

The true heart and soul of "Volver" comes from Penelope Cruz, for whom Almodovar specifically wrote the role of Raimunda. Although Cruz has received more attention in recent years for her high-profile romances and her largely unsuccessful attempts to break through in the American film industry (where her most convincing turn was in "Vanilla Sky" and even that found her playing a role she had already done in the original Spanish version), the fact is that she has always shown herself to have strong acting chops lurking behind the heart-stopping beauty when she has been given a strong role to play. In "Volver", she gets just that kind of role the kind of feisty earth mother that Anna Magnani used to play a few decades ago and tears into it with evident relish. The result is not only one of the year's strongest performances funny, tragic, heart-rending, angry and sexy all at once in a rare year with a surplus of significant female roles but far and away the best and most convincing work that she has ever done.

—*Peter Sobczynski*，*Efilmcritic. com*

佩内洛普·克鲁兹是《回归》实际上的核心和灵魂，阿尔莫多瓦正是根据她才创造出蕾木达这个角色的。克鲁兹近些年受到了越来越多的关注，因为她恋爱得相当高调，因为她努力在美国电影工业中有所突破却难获成功（《香草的天空》是她最受肯定的好莱坞作品，然而人们遗憾地发现，这不过是她早期西班牙影片的翻版）。事实上，她一直是那种表演的激情在让人心动的美丽外表下暗涌的演员，尤其是当她遇到一个厉害的角色时。在《回归》中，她刚好得到这样一个角色——一个安娜·麦兰妮几十年前曾经扮演过的精力旺盛的大地母亲的角色，她激烈地进入这个角色，把它诠释得津津有味。她融滑稽、悲惨、令人心碎、愤怒和性感于一体，结果这不仅当之无愧地成为这个重量级女性角色过剩的年度中最厉害的表演，也毫无疑问地是她创造的所有

角色中最出色的。

——*Peter Sobczynski*, *Efilmcritic* 网站

Red, in every conceivable shade, is, not surprisingly, a key color in *Volver*, a movie about the indomitable power of good old 35mm celluloid. (David Lynch may have gone digital, but this director never will.) About a half-hour into the film, Almodóvar's effortlessly gorgeous shot of blood saturating two sheets of paper towel—you'd think you were watching time—lapse images of a rose in bloom—momentarily suggests a tonal shift for the entire movie, white turning to a crimson so deep it's practically noir. Channeling Hitchcock even in this, Almodóvar isn't what he used to be (who is?), but he's a master of the medium nevertheless, deploying color and light and shadow not merely to express emotions but to tap into ours, directing the blood flow of the audience as much as he directs the movie.

——*Rob Nelson*, *from The Village Voice*

各种各样你能想象出的红色无疑是《回归》的基调，尤其是在这样一部精良的老式 35 毫米胶片的魅力大放光彩的影片中。（大卫·林奇或许会采用数字拍摄，但是阿尔莫多瓦绝对不会。）在影片进行大约半小时的时候，阿尔莫多瓦自如地呈现给我们那个鲜血渗透两层纸巾的视觉华丽的镜头——你最好想象着你看到的是一朵怒放的玫瑰的延时拍摄画面，当它渐渐暗红和发黑时，它立刻暗示出整部影片调子上的转化——这部影片实际上很黑色。你甚至能发现希区科克的痕迹掺杂其中，阿尔莫多瓦已经不是过去的自己（但谁又是呢？）。无论如何，阿尔莫多瓦是运用媒介的大师，他操纵着色彩、光线和阴影不只表达自己，还感染着我们。他导引着观众的血流，就像他导演电影一样。

——*Rob Nelson*，《乡村之音》

Almodóvar has reached a point in his development at which he can shake such baroquely plotted, psychologically dense movies out of his sleeve with what looks like astonishing ease. He's able to keep us off balance by radically shifting tones without interrupting the organic flow of the narrative. One moment Raimunda is working out the details of a grisly criminal cover-up, the next she's cheerfully whipping an abandoned restaurant into shape. With all its unexpected twists and turns, the story still unfolds naturally, like some gaudy Mediterranean flower.

—*Thomas Peyser, from Style Weekly*

阿尔莫多瓦已经抵达这样一种境界，他可以把一部充满巴洛克情节和心理张力的影片挥洒自如到让人惊异的程度。他可以通过急剧地转调来颠覆观众心理，同时却并不打断影片自然的叙事流。这一刻蕾木达还埋头于掩盖一桩血腥罪行的种种细节中，下一刻她已经兴高采烈地忙着将一个废弃餐馆变废为宝。虽然这些曲折和扭转总是不期而至，但故事仍然自然而然地展开着，就像一些华丽的地中海之花。

—*Thomas Peyser*，《风格周刊》

## Note

Kitschy, camp：camp、trash、kitsch 三个概念可以放在一起说，指西方现代文化中的一种艺术风格。它故意欣赏某一类人为的造作，顾名思义，它是华丽的、夸张的、戏剧化的、充满激情的、过度铺张的，甚至匪夷所思的，以这种眼光对待作品，实际上是要消除将艺术分为高低雅俗的成见。作家陈冠中曾在《西方现代文化札记》中说，若是西洋文化不好理解，那么华语世界的例子有央视春节晚会、靳羽西本人的发型和面部化妆、电视台大型节目主持的声调和套句、武侠小说里的怪异女高手如李莫愁、灭绝师太等等。

Gardel：指 Carlos Gardel，1890 年出生于法国，2 岁时随母亲来到阿根廷，1935 年 6 月 24 日在空难中丧生。他开启了阿根廷探戈歌声的时代，被誉为"布宜诺斯艾利斯的夜莺"，"拉丁世界的猫王"，"探戈之父"。他的作品经常出现于电影之中，包括《真实谎言》、《辛德勒名单》，《女人香》和《魔鬼大帝》里都曾用过 Carlos 演唱的《POR UNA CABEZA》。

# Sill Life

# 三峡好人

**导演/编剧：**贾樟柯

**主演：**赵　涛　韩三明

**片长：**108 分钟

**发行：**西河星汇，2006 年

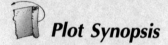 *Plot Synopsis*

Two stories are interweaved in connection with the geographical transformation of the Three Gorges Hydro Project area: in the first, Han Sanming plays Han Sinming, a miner from northern China, who revisits the vicinity after a sixteen-year absence and attempts to find his wife and his adult daughter—trying to locate them at addresses that now exist underwater. In the second story, nurse Shen Hong (Zhao Tao) also returns to the site of Fengjie and scours the area for her husband, who has been estranged from her for two years, and who, it seems, has become consumed by the work and lifestyle of an executive. The marriage, it turns out, is irreparable. Meanwhile, as a documentary-style backdrop to these stories, the old structures of Fengjie are continually destroyed—walls brought to crumbling heaps, towers blown to bits—and new, makeshift structures installed as replacements.

## 剧情简介

影片由两个故事交织而成，它们都和三峡工程引起的地理变迁有关：在头一个故事中，来自中国北方的矿工韩三明重访已阔别 16 年的奉节地区，试图找回他的妻子和已经成年的女儿，然而他发现旧址已经淹没在水下。第二个故事中，护士沈红（赵涛饰）也来到奉节遍寻她的丈夫，丈夫已有两年不归，而且似乎已经沉迷于一个经理的工作和生活方式。显而易见，他们的婚姻已经无可挽回。与此同时，观众可以看到故事有一个记录片似的背景，奉节的老建筑正陷在持续的摧毁中——那些老墙和老塔逐渐灰飞烟灭，被临时建筑所取代。

 *Critique*

## Chinese Wasteland

Sometimes film festival juries actually get it right. Jia Zhangke has been making films for ten years, but, until now, a major festival prize (from the "big three" of Cannes, Venice, and Berlin) has excluded him. Finally, though, the Golden Lion bestowed in Venice on his newest feature *Still Life* acknowledges what students of international cinema already knew: Jia is one of the leading film-makers of our time. His works advance the art of cinema in ways that are dazzlingly innovative, while also being precisely attuned to the radical new demands of 21st century society. Each of Jia's films articulates an abstract structure of time and space, and a more sensual structure of feeling, through which we can see and feel our way to coming to grips with a new, changing world.

Jia's camera has two key preoccupations: physical bodies and landscapes. The bodies are male, copiously presented, and frequently half nude. This is something completely new in Jia's work. His camera slowly, repeatedly, pans over groups of ruddy skinned workers as they rest, eat, play, or hammer away at the infrastructure of Fengjie that they are slowly pounding into rubble. These tableaux of bare-chested men are not movie-beautiful: they are natural, tough, work-honed bodies, with a tangible sense of weight, of taking up space, containing a wiry potential for endless physical labour. One might even detect something like an eroticized gaze in the film's obsessive, close, lingering pans.

It is precisely in the intersection of these two obsessive imageries that the film generates its own particular beauty: namely that of bodies walking through wastelands. Both main characters pick their way, without comment, through this post-disaster landscape, two individual lives persisting within an absolutely inhospitable environment. One of the things the film celebrates is this miracle of human persistence: how the necessary-survival-trumps the impossible.

Miracles are on offer, too, in a wry, understated mode. Jia offers visions of flight and some strange magic. An impossibly shaped building takes off like a rocket before the men with the hammers can get to it. A flying object streaks before Sanming's and Shen Hong's eyes: Is it some embodiment of their need to move through impossible barriers, their ability to imagine how to change their worlds? They never meet, but an angel ties them together: a young singing boy who smokes and strolls in and out of their worlds, singing at the top of his voice. In the end, another symbolic linkage: a high-wire artist appears, in the distance, suspended between two buildings that are destined no doubt to topple over some time soon.

*Still Life* incorporates a complex symbolic system that suggests possible meanings without fixing them definitively. Most prominently displayed are the set of four ambiguous symbols of consumption and enjoyment that the film underlines with titles onscreen: cigarettes, wine, tea, and candy. They stand in as replacements for the standard four household items (fuel, rice, cooking oil, and salt) that represent the daily necessities of life in a set Chinese expression. Jia's update replaces survival with pleasures, even addictions.

That high-wire act is another symbol, one of a series of spectacular linking images that includes the new suspension bridge over the Yangtze lit spectacularly by order of an official for his assembled VIPs. The Three Gorges Dam itself appears at the end of Shen Hong's story, both linking and separating the two sections of the river: the massive upstream reservoir with its disappearing strata of devastation and the downstream section leading to Shanghai. This ambivalent signifier of construction/destruction serves as an ironic backdrop to Shen's announcement that she herself is leaving her husband.

Jia shot *Still Life* in some of the same locations and at the same time as the documentary *Dong* and the relationship between the two is provocative. *Dong* records the painter Liu Xiaodong as he prepares two large-scale works, one of half-naked male workers in Fengjie lounging with the river as a backdrop, the second of female entertainment workers in Bangkok lounging en deshabille amidst fruits and furniture. In *Dong*, we are supposed to be seeing documentary truth, as the artist Liu paints real people in a real place. But Sanming is in *Dong*, as are some of the other characters from the movie. Yet he is not really a worker in Fengjie, he only plays one in *Still Life*. So what is he doing in *Dong*? Similarly, shots are shared between the two films: the creepy disinfectant team in their moon suits, the bare-chested men hammering in syncopated rhythms at the city ruins, the collapsing wall of one wrecked building.

As Jia maps it, cinema does not divide neatly into fiction and documentary. *Dong* creates a subjective world, as much inside the mind of the artist Liu as outside in objective space. *Still Life* digs deep to reveal an underlying reality, mobilizing sophisticated formal strategies to create images of truth. These same strategies demand-or, rather, construct, during the process of watching-viewers who are ready to watch, absorb, and feel this vision. It is a vision of a man-made hell, of the monumental and limitless destruction left behind by a society rushing to tear up its foundations and gut its history. And it is a vision of embodied resistance-an individual, physical resilience that can spark an impossible, miraculous, but tangible hope in a world that seems to offer none.

—*Shelly Kraicer, from Cinema-scope. com*

# 中国的荒原

某些时候电影节的评审团还是很有眼光的。贾樟柯已经拍了十年的电影，但是主流的电影节奖项（世界"三大"影展的戛纳、威尼斯和柏林）却一直躲避着他。然而今天，威尼斯金狮终于选中了他的最新故事片《三峡好人》，这揭开了那些关注世界电影的人心中一个不言而喻的事实：贾樟柯是我们这个时代的电影领袖之一。他的作品闪耀着创新之光，提升了电影艺术，而且对21世纪社会新的根本需求保持着恰如其分的敏感。贾樟柯的每一部作品都提供给我们一个关于时空的抽象结构，以及一个更具体可感的生命经验，我们借此可以观察和体验人们是如何把握这样一个变化不定的新世界的。

身体和风景构成了贾樟柯镜头的两个主要对象。那些身体是意味丰富的、时常半裸的男性身体。在此，贾樟柯的这部作品中散发出一种几乎全新的东西。他的摄像机缓慢地、来来回回地摇过那些正在休息、吃饭、游戏，或者在奉节的残骸中埋头缓慢锤打的一群群皮肤发红、肌肉结实的工人。这些形体沉默、胸膛裸露的男人并不是上镜的电影尤物：他们的身体是自然的、粗糙的、经受劳动打磨的、在重量和空间上都切实可感的，蕴涵着一种强韧的可以承受无休止的体力劳动的力量。你甚至可以在那些着迷的、仔细的、流连的摇移镜头中察觉出一种类似于色情凝视的东西。

恰恰是在这两种迷人的意象的交汇处，这部影片产生了它独特的美：也就是身体穿行于废墟之中的那种美。两个主人公沉默无言地各自走在这个灾难后的荒原中，两个个体坚持不懈地活在一个绝对荒凉的环境中。这种人类坚持的奇迹，一种必须如此的生存意志战胜了不可能，正是影片力图赞美的东西之一。

影片还以一种古怪的克制的方式呈现着种种奇观。贾樟柯让我们看到了诡异的飞行或一些奇异的景象。比如一个形状不寻常的建筑物像火箭一样倏地自己飞走了，虽然并没有人对它抡起过大锤。一个不明飞行物从三明和沈红的眼前滑过：这难道是象征着他们希望突围出障碍吗？或者他们想象着如何改变世界的能力？这两人从未相遇，但是影片让一个天使把他们联系在一起：

一个吸着烟的小男孩一边在他们的世界中走进走出，一边用他最高的声音的唱着歌。另一处隐喻性的联系体现在结尾处：我们远远地看到一个在高空中走钢丝的艺人，那钢丝悬在毫无疑问即将倒塌的两座楼之间。

《三峡好人》掺进了一套复杂的象征系统，它提示着一些可能的涵义，但拒绝将其明确化和固定化。最醒目的是那一组四个以字幕标明的关于消费和享乐的意义含混的象征物：烟、酒、糖、茶。它们替代厨房的标准四大件（柴、米、油、盐）走上舞台，用一组中国人的习惯修辞来表现人们的日常需要。由此，贾樟柯以愉悦感甚至沉溺感替代了生存感。

那个高空走钢丝表演是另外一个象征符号，那是一个象征着联系的壮观景象。这联系还包括那座横跨长江的吊桥，一个官员专门为他的 VIP 队伍按了电钮，桥上的灯分外壮观地依次亮起来。三峡大坝出现在沈红的故事结局中，既联系又分离着河流的两部分：上游是巨大的水库，地层因为受到破坏正在消失；另一半是流向上海的下游。这个意义矛盾的所指像是一个既建构又解构的颇具讽刺意味的背景，当时沈红正声明她将离开她的丈夫。

一定程度上，贾樟柯的《三峡好人》是和纪录片《东》同时同地摄制出来的，两者的联系显而易见。《东》纪录了画家刘小东两部篇幅庞大的作品的准备过程。一幅作品画的是一个在奉节打工的半身赤裸的工人，背景是河流。另一幅是曼谷一群从事娱乐服务的衣着随便的女孩子，背景是水果和家具。在《东》中，我们期待看到的是纪录片的真实，就像艺术家刘小东在一个真实的地方画真实的人。但是我们在《东》中看到了韩三明，以及《三峡好人》中其他的一些人物。韩三明的实际身份并不是奉节的工人，那是他在《三峡好人》中所扮演的角色。那么应该如何解释他在《东》中的所作所为呢？同样地，一些镜头在两部影片中是共享的：那些身着制服在废墟上匍匐的消毒队员们，那些在城市的断壁残垣上有节奏地敲打着的胸膛裸露的男人，那些建筑残骸中正在坍塌的墙。

正如贾樟柯所言，电影并不能被断然地分成故事片和纪录片。《东》创造了一个主观世界，艺术家刘小东的脑子里有多少构思，客观的空间就会相应地改变多少。而《三峡好人》则是深入地挖掘出一种潜在的真实，用一种复杂精妙的策略创造出关于真实的影像。这种相似的策略都要求着，确切说是建构着这样一种观影过程，观众在其中要凝视、吸收和感觉那些影像。那是一个人造地狱的影像，一个社会在前行中无所顾忌地粉碎着它的基础和历史，留下了无尽的永久的毁灭。那也是关于具体抵抗的影像，一个个体的、本能的适应力可以在一个几乎一无所有的世界中点燃一种本来不可能、但又奇迹般确实存在的希望。

—*Shelly Kraicer*，*Cinema-scope* 网站

Jia has always been interested in the dislocation of contemporary Chinese existence (his last film was "The World," set at a theme park outside Beijing), but as his movies have gradually broadened in scope they've also developed a current of wry comedy and even tenderness.

One critic friend of mine has suggested that "Still Life" is a comedy of sorts, and he may be right. The missing husband and wife are found, after much effort, but their presence doesn't really resolve anything. Instead, the story moves forward as a series of remarkable images and tiny human encounters, almost meaningless in themselves. A man and woman dance on a riverfront promenade that will soon be submerged; another man does bad impressions of Chow Yun-Fat movie dialogue. In between workdays spent destroying their own city, demolition crews drink, stage fights with each other, wax rhapsodic about the beautiful Chinese scenery (as seen on banknotes).

It would be too easy to describe Jia's tone as ironic; it can be wistful or whimsical or deliberately obscure (I'm not sure what the spaceships are doing in this otherwise naturalistic film, frankly). One thing I'm confident about is that one viewing is not enough to absorb "Still Life". It strikes me as Jia's finest film yet, both a docudrama with obvious social and historical relevance and a subtle, slow, quietly powerful chronicle of human loss. It never seems inaccessible or willfully arty, but it won't yield all its secrets on the first date.

*—Andrew O'hehir, Salon. com*

贾樟柯一直关注着当代中国生活的断裂状态（他的上一部影片《世界》以一个北京郊外的主题公园为背景），随着视野的不断扩大，他的影片也越来越涌动着一种幽默甚至柔软的东西。

我的一个评论家朋友认为《三峡好人》是一部喜剧，他可能是对的。经过许多努力，失散的丈夫和妻子终于重逢，但是他们的出现实际上没有解决任何问题。除此之外，故事流动中充满了惊人的意象和人与人之间微不足道的邂逅，微不足道得连他们自己都觉得无聊。一对男女在即将被淹没的河边跳舞；另一个人对着周润发电影中的对话东施效颦；在拆除他们自己城市的工作之余，这些拆迁民工在一起喝酒、打闹、为人民币上美丽的风景而狂喜。

用讽刺来形容贾樟柯的风格太轻巧了。它时而热切，时而反常，时而会有存心的障碍（坦白说我不太明白在这部现实主义影片中为什么出现宇宙飞船）。我有把握的一点是，要真正理解《三峡好人》，只看一遍是不够的。这部贾樟柯最优秀的影片让我的心为之一动，它既是一部和社会与历史紧密关联的具有文献意义的电影，又敏锐地、静静地、缓慢有力地记录下了人性的失落。它绝对不是那种装蒜的、难以接近的东西，但也不可能让你一眼看穿。

*— Andrew O'hehir，《沙龙》网站*

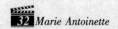 

# Marie Antoinette

# 玛丽王后

**导演/编剧**：索菲亚·科波拉（Sofia Coppola）

**原著**：安东尼娅·弗雷泽（Antonia Fraser）

**主演**：克里斯滕·邓斯特（Kirsten Dunst））

里普·托恩（Rip Torn）

朱迪·戴维斯（Judy Davis）

**片长**：123 分钟

**发行**：哥伦比亚公司（Columbia Pictures Corporation），2006 年

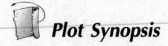
# Plot Synopsis

Born to Austrian nobility, Marie Antoinette (Kirsten Dunst) is only 14 years old when she's pledged to marry Louis XVI (Jason Schwartzman), the 15-year-old king of France, in an alliance that has everything to do with politics and nothing to do with love. Sent to France and literally stripped of her former life, Marie weds Louis. Young and more than a bit out of step with the new life that's been thrust upon her, Marie gives herself over to the pleasures of life in Versailles, knowing and caring little of the political intrigue that surrounds her. In time, Marie's trusted older brother, Joseph, is brought in to coach Louis on the finer points of marital relations, and before long the couple is finally blessed with a child. However, as Marie tends to her children in her palace and enjoys an affair with a Swedish nobleman, political power plays are throwing France into chaos, and the growing ranks of the poor rebel against the royals and their life of privilege.

## 剧情简介

　　出身奥地利贵族的玛丽·安托奈特（克里斯滕·邓斯特饰）在年仅14岁时被安排嫁给15岁的法国王储路易十六（杰森·史瓦茨曼饰），这是一场为了奥法联盟的不折不扣的政治婚姻，完全无关爱情。她被送到法国，然后被彻底地剥夺了过去的生活方式，并和路易完婚。年幼的玛丽很难适应强加于她头上的新生活，她开始沉湎于凡尔赛的花天酒地，对围绕在她周围的政治阴谋一无所知也漠不关心。玛丽信任的哥哥被派到路易身边传授给路易婚姻生活的奥妙，不久后这对夫妻终于幸运地有了一个孩子。然而，就在玛丽安心在凡尔赛宫照料孩子并享受着与一个瑞典贵族的私情时，法国陷入政治斗争的动荡中，壮大中的社会底层正要推翻王室和他们的特权。

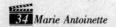

# Critique

Pouring Coca-Cola in the cabernet, Sofia Coppola's dazzling "Marie Antoinette" couldn't be more anachronistic if it showed the queen of France saying, "Let them eat sushi." Coppola works in weird ways, but the real Versailles was so much weirder.

Just as Tobey Maguire proved that the superhero is about the vulnerability, Kirsten Dunst nicely unveils the innocence in the doomed queen of France. The story follows Antonia Fraser's biography, and the crazy flourishes simultaneously blast away the musty mists of history and make the audience feel, as the Austrian-born queen must have, lost in translation.

Coppola's command of the language of cinema is a delight. Again and again, she creates character and story without a word of dialogue. The death of a child is rendered by the mere switch of a portrait, and the queen realizes her approval ratings are in the tank when she applauds at an opera, but no one else joins in.

—*kyle Smith*, *New York Post*

就像把可乐掺入红酒中一样，如果索菲娅·科波拉把玛丽王后那句著名的话改成"他们可以吃寿司（原话是：老百姓没有面包吃，他们可以吃蛋糕）"，那么这部让人眼花缭乱的《玛丽皇后》就时代错乱得可以了。科波拉的创作确实是疯狂的，但实际上的凡尔赛宫比这还要疯狂和荒谬。

如同托比·马奎尔（《蜘蛛侠》的主演）证明了超级英雄其实也脆弱，克里斯滕·邓斯特给我们细腻地揭示出了这个身不由己的法国王后无辜的一面。故事基本忠于安东尼娅·弗雷泽的传记原著，同时那种极度的奢华把历史的阴霾一扫而光，它让观众感觉到，这个来自奥地利的王后一定在在文化差异中失落了什么。

科波拉对电影语言的运用值得称道。一次又一次，她无声地创造着人物和故事，不用一句对白。比如她用一幅肖像的转换来表现一个孩子的死亡。比如当玛丽再次为一部歌剧带头鼓掌时，四面悄然，无人响应，由此这个王后意识到她的人气已经在下滑了。

——*kyle Smith*,《纽约邮报》

In Sofia Coppola's revisionist fairy tale, it's all about the celebrity. Coppola uses the quaint narrative shell of the Hollywood costume drama (perhaps she even intends this film as a tribute to Hollywood's Depression-era spectacles) to tell a very public private story: the dilemma of the poor little rich girl, born into the unrelenting celebrity spotlight of Hollywood royalty.

Perhaps the most curious, and anachronistic, aspect of this film is its utter lack of any historical contextualizing. Some have sought to argue this film, and Antonia Fraser's biography which it is based on, as resetting the historically harsh judgment of the historical personage. This Marie Antoinette emerges as fully American, a poor little rich girl who just wants to have fun, a McMansion* suburban housewife and mother, living the Malibu Barbie* lifestyle totally to the max.

Why some French people speak with an American accent, while others with a British one, is never explained. When Marie Antoinette's daughter occasionally lapses into actual French it only muddies the question. But it is very easy to imagine this Marie Antoinette brushing off the rabble with a cheerleaderly callow. When the angry, starving, long-deceived mob finally comes for Marie and Louis in this two-hour movie, it isn't a moment too soon.

As a serious film, only an American could love Marie Antoinette. To the French, it must be gravely insulting. As an unwitting camp, it may have a great future. Taken ironically, Marie Antoinette suddenly becomes an eerily portentous parable of the Bush regime. The subtext reads: poor little Georgie W gets married off and has to live in poisonous Beltway society, when all he really wants is a simple life playing oil baron cowboys in Texas and grouse-hunting with his fellow good old boys.

——*Les Wright*, *from Culturevulture. net*

实际上，在被索菲娅·科波拉修正过的这个童话故事中，所说一切都是关于名利场的。科波拉用好莱坞古装剧的精巧叙事结构（或许她甚至有意以此视觉奇观来刺激一下低迷期的好莱坞）讲了一个非常大众化的私人故事：一个可怜的富家女在好莱坞名利场严酷的聚光灯下进退两难。

或许该片最奇怪、最错乱的方面在于它全然不交代任何历史背景。一些关于这部影片以及安东尼娅·弗雷泽的原著传记的争议因此而起，该传记努力纠正历史成见，重新评价历史人物。影片中的这个玛丽王后看起来完全像个美国人，一个只是想寻开心的可怜的富家女，一个住在郊区千篇一律的毫宅中，过着彻底的马利布芭比生活的主妇和妈妈。

该片也从不解释为什么要让这些法国人有的带着美音，有的带着英音。而当玛丽的女儿偶尔失误一般发出地道的法音时，我们却被弄得更加糊涂了。但是很容易想象这个玛丽·安托奈特那种啦啦队队长般的闹腾和天真惹火了下层社会，当愤怒、饥饿、被欺骗已久的暴民在这部两小时影片的结尾冲向玛丽和路易时，这个结果当然不意外。

如果把该片看成一部严肃之作，那么估计只有美国人会喜欢它。对法国人来说，这简直是一次严重的污蔑。而如果将它看成是无心的游戏之作，说不定它前途无量。讽刺地来看，《玛丽王后》忽然间成了关于布什执政的一个奇特寓言。它的潜台词是：不幸的小布什被嫁进了万恶的美国国会，而他实际上渴望着这样一种简单生活，去德州做石油大王和西部牛仔，去和老伙计们一起打松鸡。

—*Les Wright*，*Culturevulture* 网站

Read into that what you will. Coppola has provided a blank slate to give her audience the opportunity to derive modern meaning from her movie ( Marie = Paris Hilton ) , and supporters have been working overtime to find significance in the filmmaker's inscrutability. But really, "Marie Antoinette" is simply a movie about the beauty that can be found in blankness.

Coppola wants us to empathize with Marie. Her excesses are barely mentioned, her lack of intelligence translated into a beguiling innocence. When Bow Wow Wow's "I Want Candy" is cued ( one of many new wave, post-punk songs featured in the film's impeccably anachronistic soundtrack), Coppola is telling us we all want a sugar (or caffeine or shopping spree) high, and that we'd indulge, too, if we were hermetically sealed and unaware of the suffering around us.

Such an attitude makes you long for the arrival of the sharp blade of the guillotine. Coppola is only able to maintain the energy and wit of her vision for about an hour of the movie's two-hour running time.

Coppola may have failed here, but her aesthetic instincts remain strong. The movie is perfectly cast. The palace world is a wonder to behold. Can you make a meal out of bonbons? Coppola thinks so.

—*Glenn Whipp*, *Los Angeles Daily News*

想怎么理解就怎么理解吧。科波拉给她的观众提供了一张白纸，观众乘机可以自由发挥影片的现代涵义（玛丽＝帕丽斯·希尔顿，希尔顿集团创始人康拉德·希尔顿的曾孙女，典型的豪门千金），还有一些支持者一直不遗余力地想在艺术家的善变和难解中找出意义来。但实际上，《玛丽王后》是一部很简单的影片，它要说的只是，美丽可能是浮华和虚无的。

科波拉希望我们用玛丽的故事来领会这一点。她的放纵无度几乎不被提及，她的智力欠缺被转化成了一种供人消遣的天真。当乐队宝哇哇的《我想吃糖》响起时（影片中许多新浪潮和后朋克的插曲之一，这使影片的声道又完美又显得时代错乱），科波拉暗示我们其实都想甜（咖啡因或者购物狂欢）一把，而且如果我们被密封起来对周遭痛苦一无所知，我们不如就纵容自己吧。

这种观点和态度会激发你对断头台那一幕的期待。对于这部片长两小时的影片，科波拉的能量、才华和想象力只能维持一个小时而已。

科波拉或许在这一点上败走麦城了，但是她对美的敏感和直觉却维持地相当强烈。该片的演出阵容堪称完美。那宫殿的布景也美得令人称奇。你能用一堆小糖果做出一顿饭来吗？科波拉就认为可以。

—*Glenn Whipp*，《洛杉机日报》

Coppola's third feature is all surface and no substance, leaving you as undernourished as the French in the bread-shortage months preceding the revolution. The Academy-Award winning writer-director assumes that an Austrian teenage princess of 1768 is no different from an American girl today. If you can accept Coppola's take on the "real" Marie Antoinette over the many portraits painted and written about the beleaguered queen, then you may be able to swallow this seriocomic, candy-colored confection.

—*Susan Tavernetti*, *Palo Alto Weekly*

科波拉的第三部长片浅薄至极，毫无实质可言，搞得你就像大革命前没有面包吃的法国人民一样营养不良。在这个曾经摘下奥斯卡桂冠的编剧和导演眼中，一个1768年十几岁的奥地利公主和今天一个美国少女没有什么区别。你要是能够接受科波拉这一版的"真实"的玛丽·安托奈特胜于那个在传统绘画和写作中备受谴责的王后，你就能吞咽下这套亦庄亦谐、花里呼哨的糖果餐。

—*Susan Tavernetti*,《帕洛阿尔托周报》

## Note

McMansion：指一种大小和风格与周围房子完全不一样的或格格不入的制式豪宅。McMansion 这个字由英文 McDonalds（麦当劳）和 mansion（大厦）组成。麦当劳的口号是全球统一的风味，因此 McMansion 指一种格调统一的建筑。它丧失风格，毫无个性。

Malibu Barbie：Malibu 是美国加州南部的某海滩之名。Malibu Barbie 是一款经典的加州夏日风情芭比娃娃造型。

# Curse of the Golden Flowers

# 满城尽带黄金甲

**导演：**张艺谋

**编剧：**张艺谋/吴楠/卞智洪

**主演：**周润发、巩俐、周杰伦、刘烨、陈谨、
倪大宏、李曼、秦俊杰

**片长：**115 分钟

**发行：**北京新画面影业有限公司，2006 年

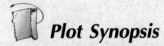

# Plot Synopsis

China, later Tang Dynasty, 10th Century. On the eve of the Chong Yang Festival, golden flowers fill the Imperial Palace. The Emperor (Chow Yun Fat) returns unexpectedly with his second son, Prince Jai (Jay Chou). His pretext is to celebrate the holiday with his family, but given the chilled relations between the Emperor and the ailing Empress (Gong Li), this seems disingenuous.

For many years, the Empress and Crown Prince Wan (Liu Ye), her stepson, have had an illicit liaison. Feeling trapped, Prince Wan dreams of escaping the palace with his secret love Chan (Li Man), the Imperial Doctor's daughter. Meanwhile, Prince Jai, the faithful son, grows worried over the Empress's health and her obsession with golden chrysanthemums. Could she be headed down an ominous path?

Against a moonlit night, thousands of chrysanthemum blossoms are trampled as blood spills across the Imperial Palace.

## 剧情简介

中国，十世纪的晚唐。重阳节前夕，皇宫中菊花遍地。皇帝（周润发饰）带着二皇子杰（周杰伦饰）出人意料地归来，宣称要与家人共度佳节。但是看他与久病不愈的皇后（巩俐饰）关系疏远，这个意图显得并不纯粹。

皇后和作为太子的继子元祥（刘烨饰）有多年的不伦之恋。泥足深陷的元祥终于想逃出皇宫，带上他的秘密情人蒋婵（李曼饰）远走高飞。蒋婵是御医的女儿。与此同时，性格忠诚的杰王子日益担心母后的健康，母后对菊花的过分迷恋也让他隐隐不安。难道她已经预感到要发生什么事吗？

中秋月圆之夜，遍地菊花尽遭践踏，皇宫中血流成河。

 *Critique*

It's a safe bet that most of the people who snickered through the screening I attended of Zhang Yimou's *Curse of the Golden Flower* had never seen a grand opera performance. Even that frame of reference might not have been enough to make them love the movie: All told, Zhang's latest is a lavishly overdecorated period melodrama with a lot of meaningless, bustling energy. It tries frenetically hard to convince us it's overheated and thunderously emotional, but it has a cold heart.

Zhang has always had an operatic sensibility: At his best he uses everything in the frame expressively—color, rippling fabrics, and especially headlong movement. Everything becomes an extension of the characters' passions. But in *Curse*, his 15th feature since the former cinematographer made his directorial debut with *Red Sorghum* in 1987, Zhang's trademark pulsating style has finally spilled over into mannerism. What Curse links up with in his past work isn't the muscular romanticism of *Ju Dou* (1990) or *House of Flying Daggers* (2004), but the dazzling orientalist pageantry of *Turandot*.

*Curse* also looks alarmingly like a dry run for the opening and closing ceremonies Zhang has been hired to direct for the Beijing Olympic Games in 2008. The meaning recedes and all that's left is the sheer bludgeoning spectacle of perfectly aligned phalanxes of thousands of real soldiers, trotting, jogging and running in lockstep in rattling golden armor, creating an unholy Dolby Digital din.

—*David Chute*, *L. A. Weekly*

张艺谋的《满城尽带黄金甲》可谓一场胜算，我看到尽管观众们在看电影时窃笑不止，但他们中的大多数都确实没有见识过这么豪华的演出。然而这个理由并不足以使那些观众爱上它：一言以蔽之，张艺谋的这部新作是一部装修过度的情节剧，那些精力消耗得过于无谓而混乱。它发疯一般要说服我们它是热血澎湃、感情汹涌的，然而它的心却是冷的。

　　张艺谋的身上一直有一种戏剧性的敏感：他极致地充满表现性地运用构图中的所有可用的元素——色彩、起伏的织物、还有尤其是那些一往无前的运动，把这一切都变成对人物内在激情的延伸。《黄金甲》是这个摄影师出身的导演自 1987 年以《红高粱》闪亮登场以来的第 15 部剧情长片，然而，张艺谋那鲜明的美学商标至此终于变味成了一种怪癖。《黄金甲》能让我们联想起来的旧作并不是《菊豆》（1990）或《十面埋伏》（2004）的那种阳刚的浪漫主义，而是《图兰朵》那种眩目的东方盛典，《图兰朵》是张艺谋 1997 年执导的普契尼歌剧，指挥是祖宾·梅塔，先后在佛罗伦萨和北京紫禁城上演。

　　令人惊愕的是，《黄金甲》还像是张艺谋被指定执导的 2008年北京奥运会开幕式和闭幕式的预演。意义彻底隐退了，剩下的唯有单调的、压迫感重重的奇观。那些成千上万的军人组成整齐划一的方阵，步伐一致地或走或跑，身上的黄金甲咔咔作响，制造出一场惹人反感的杜比数字噪音。

—*David Chute*，《洛杉矶周报》

In "Hero" (2003), "House of Flying Daggers" (2004) and now "Curse of the Golden Flower", director Zhang Yimou has transformed Hong Kong martial arts/fantasy movies into grand, international spectacles. Some critics have worried about his obsession with visual dazzle and digitized effects, but the stories and fights in the first two films more than measured up to the sumptuous design. "Curse", though, feels disappointingly inert. "Curse" does dazzle the eye, but its story plays like a bad soap opera. This emperor's family is so treacherous as to make Hamlet seem like a fairly well-adjusted member of an easygoing household.

Zhang makes the chrysanthemum the film's visual leitmotif. In a statement, he quotes an old Chinese saying, "Gold and jade on the outside, rot and decay on the inside," to explain his determination to smother his characters and sets with gold. In his story, he finds plenty of rot and decay. It starts with the Emperor (Chow), who decides to add poison to the multiple daily doses of herbal medicine he has prescribed for the Empress (Gong). One would like a clearer understanding for this act. True, the Empress has conducted an illicit affair with her stepson, Crown Prince Wan (Liu Ye). But this has been going on for three years so why does Emperor take action only now?

Zhang devotes considerable screen time to the details of the palace's daily rituals as if scrutiny of these formalized routines involving maids, courtiers and eunuchs will reveal something about the malevolent rot beneath the surface. This greatly adds to the running time but not to insight into character motivation.

Despite Zhang's collaboration with action director Ching Siu-Tokng, the film's few fights are cluttered and undistinguished, in direct contrast to the clarity of the terrific stunt work in the director's previous action films. Zhang over-relies on CGI, but the level of success in no way matches the battles of the "Lord of the Rings" trilogy, the high bar to which any film attempting vast battles must now aspire. In the hand-to-hand combat, the action is often jarring and even confusing.

—*Kirk Honeycutt*, *Hollywood Reporter*

从《英雄》(2003)、《十面埋伏》(2004)到如今的《满城尽带黄金甲》,张艺谋导演将香港的功夫和武侠电影转化成了盛大的、国际性的奇观。一切批评家担心他在视觉盛宴和数字效果中沉迷过多,不过头两部影片的故事和打斗至少是匹配那奢华设计的。然而《黄金甲》却了无生趣,让人失望。它确实看得人眼花缭乱,可是它的故事却像一出劣质肥皂剧。这个皇帝的后院叛乱得有些夸张了,相形之下,哈姆雷特倒像是个来自和睦家庭的恪守本分的乖孩子。

张艺谋将菊花作为此片的视觉基调。某次发言他引用中国老话"金玉其外，败絮其中"来解释他为什么将人物和布景掩抑在重重金色之中。他在他的故事中找到了诸多"败絮"，这始于皇帝决定在皇后每日服用数次的中药里下毒。观众可能希望这个举动的意图能够更明白点儿。是的，皇后的确与她的继子——太子元祥有染，但这事儿都已经持续三年了，为什么皇帝到现在才采取行动？

张艺谋把影片大量的笔墨都花在宫廷典礼的细节上，似乎细密地展现这些紧紧束缚着侍女、大臣和太监的僵化的礼仪可以揭示出外表下某种腐烂的本质。这大大地增加了篇幅，却对洞察人物的动机毫无建树。

虽然这次张艺谋的武术导演仍是程小东，然而与他之前的动作片中那些令人叹为观止之处的清晰有致相比，这部影片中寥寥的几场打斗却失于混乱和平凡。张艺谋过于依赖电影特效，但其水准却远不能与《魔戒》三部曲的战争场面相媲美，而后者给所有试图创作大场面的影片设下了一座难以企及的高峰。我们看到即使在短兵相接的格斗中，那动作也常常不谐调，甚至让人困惑。

—Kirk Honeycutt，《好莱坞报道》

*Curse of the Golden Flower* offers more visual dazzle than any film this year, and its delirious melodrama is a certified hoot. Offering splashy, trashy fun in a high-class setting, *Curse of the Golden Flower* is as overheated as *Desperate Housewives*, and twice the fun. At least until Teri Hatcher starts doing wire fu*.

—Peter Canavese，*Groucho Reviews*

《满城尽带黄金甲》是今年最眩目的影片，而且这部夸张的情节剧也实在是虚张声势。这就好像是用一流的制作水平包装了花哨的、无意义的噱头，《黄金甲》如同《绝望的主妇》一样使我们的神经饱受刺激，而且比《主妇》还要可乐。除非泰瑞·海切尔（《主妇》中 Susan 的扮演者）也去吊钢丝。

—Peter Canavese，《格洛乔评论》

Fans of epics in the *Crouching Tiger*, *Hidden Dragon* tradition may be confused or annoyed by the intensely lurid tone of this movie. Well, all that means is that it's different——gorgeously garish, both in the color scheme ( bold tints against the chrysanthemums of the film's title) and in the splash of wild emotion.

This is high, and high-wire, melodrama. It's less soap opera than grand opera*, where matters of love and death are played at a perfect fever pitch. And grand this Golden Flower is.

—Richard Corliss, Richard Schickel, Time Magazine

喜欢《卧虎藏龙》那种传统叙事诗般作品的影迷可能困惑甚至反感这部电影的这种歇斯底里的品格。是啊，它是想与众不同——它过度虚华，不论是在色彩设计（和片名中的菊花相配的浓墨重彩）还是在狂野激情的宣泄上。

这是一出不折不扣的、甚至极端的情节剧。说它是肥皂剧，更不如说它是"大歌剧"，其中的生死爱欲被表现得如此狂热尖厉，一如这黄金之花般浮艳。

—Richard Corliss, Richard Schickel，《时代》杂志

"Curse of the Golden Flower", Zhang Yimou's strangest and most troubled film, abounds in hysterical, mannered Tang Dynasty-era palace intrigue and dehumanized CGI* battle sequences.

—Robert Koehler, variety

《满城尽带黄金甲》，张艺谋最古怪最糟糕的电影。其中泛滥的是歇斯底里和矫饰的唐代宫廷阴谋，以及没有人味儿的数字战争场面。

—Robert Koehler，《综艺》杂志

The Chinese director Zhang Yimou achieves a kind of operatic delirium, opening the floodgates of image and melodrama until the line between tragedy and black comedy is all but erased.

—*Jeannette Catsoulis*, *New York Times*

中国导演张艺谋到达了一种歌剧式的迷狂境地，影像和情节剧的洪流倾泻而出，几乎冲破了悲剧和黑色喜剧之间的界线。

—*Jeannette Catsoulis*，《纽约时代》

*Curse* is straightforward and solemn, lacking not for spectacle but for humor and a humanizing touch.

—*Terry Lawson*, *Detroit Free Press*

《黄金甲》直截了当、一本正经。它不缺奇观，缺的是幽默和人性关怀。

—*Terry Lawson*，《底特律自由报》

> ## Note
>
> Wire fu：由 Kung Fu（功夫）一词演衍生出的词。指吊钢丝加电脑将扳舞出来的花拳绣腿。虽然《黑客帝国》里洋人也可以打得花团锦簇，但毕竟不是真功夫，所以老外们把这类片子自嘲为"wire-fu"片。
>
> Grand opera：大歌剧，十九世纪盛行于法国的历史题材歌剧。不用说白，演出场面力求富丽豪华。
>
> CGI：Computer Generated Imagery，电脑数字制作的电影特效。

# The Lives of Others

# 窃听风暴

**导演/编剧**：弗洛里安·亨克尔·冯·多纳斯马克
（Florian Henckel von Donnersmarck）
**主演**：马蒂娜·戈黛特（Martina Gedeck）
塞巴斯蒂安·考奇（Sebastian Koch）
乌尔里希·穆埃（Ulrich Muhe）
**片长**：137 分钟
**发行**：博伟国际（Buena Vista International），2006 年

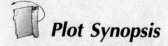 *Plot Synopsis*

The time is the Orwellian* 1984, five years before the fall of the Berlin Wall—and the major characters, all fictional, are a celebrated East German playwright, Georg Dreyman (Sebastian Koch), his actress-mistress, Christa-Maria Sieland (Martina Gedeck), some of Dreyman's dissident friends and the police who are watching them all. Dreyman is being persecuted not because he's a dissident, but because one of the government higher-ups, Minister Bruno Hempf, is crazy about Christa-Maria and wants to sleep with her. Wiesler's superior, the brutal and ambitious Stasi Lt. Col. Anton Grubitz (Ulrich Tukur), simply wants to get ahead by catching a big fish.

Wiesler is honestly suspicious of Dreyman. Unlike the other snoops, his motives are pure; he believes Dreyman a possible traitor. But the more he learns of them, the more he responds personally to the troubled pair. Their art and their lives touch him. He becomes increasingly protective—even as Dreyman, goaded out of his pragmatic silence by a persecuted friend's suicide, plots to send an anonymous critical article to West Germany's *Der Spiegel*.

## 剧情简介

故事发生在极权统治下的 1984 年，离柏林墙倒塌还有 5 年。所有虚构的主人公为东德著名的剧作家乔治·德莱曼（塞巴斯蒂安·考奇饰），他的演员妻子克里斯塔—玛丽娅·西兰德（马蒂娜·戈黛特饰），一些与德莱曼持不同政见的朋友以及监视着他们所有人的警察。德莱曼遭到迫害不仅是因为他有不同政见，还因为一位政府高官布鲁诺·赫姆夫部长迷恋玛丽娅并想和她上床。还有维斯勒的上级古比兹（乌尔里希·土库尔饰），他残忍而有野心，只是想钓个大鱼作为工作表现。

维斯勒发自内心地怀疑德莱曼，与其他特工不同，他的动机纯粹，他相信德莱曼是一个投敌卖国的嫌疑人。但是他对这对问题夫妇认识得越多，就越动了个人感情，被他们的艺术和生活所打动。于是他渐渐成了他们的保护人——一向对国事三缄其口的德莱曼因为一位遭迫害的朋友的自杀而拍案而起，开始密谋着在西德的《明镜》发表一篇匿名的批评文章。

# Critique

Mr. Donnersmarck, the 33-year-old writer-director, recalled the genesis of his project as follows: "Over the years, there were two things that led me to make the film. First were many childhood memories of my visits to East Berlin and the GDR (the German Democratic Republic). As a boy of eight, nine or ten, I found it interesting and exciting to feel the fear of adults. My parents were afraid when they crossed the border; they were both born in the East and thus were more closely controlled by the police. And our friends from East Germany were afraid when other people saw that they were speaking with us, Germans from the West. Without these early experiences I would have had trouble finding the right approach.

The idea for the film came to me as an image that just suddenly popped into my head: the close-medium shot of a man sitting in a bleak room, wearing headphones and listening to beautiful music even though he did not want to hear it. This man pursued me in my dreams and evolved over the years into Captain Gerd Wiesler."

*The Lives of Others* is a cautionary tale for all societies, not least our own, with its ominous mantras of secrecy for the sake of a conceivably endless war on terror. Though Mr. Donnersmarck hasn't editorialized excessively on the subject of state snooping, his narrative is damning enough in itself. Indeed, his film serves as a rebuke to the still-widespread nostalgia, in Germany and elsewhere, for the perceived social and economic idealism of the German Democratic Republic, despite its shameful suppression of all civil liberties.

This is not to say that the current globalization of capitalism is

producing heaven on earth for all the world's inhabitants. But whatever system we live by or under, the same problems arise. In the
writer-director's own words: "In the film, each character asks questions that we confront every day: how do we deal with power and
ideology? Do we follow our principles or our feelings? More than
anything else, *The Lives of Others* is a human drama about the ability
of human beings to do the right thing, no matter how far they have
gone down the wrong path."

—*Andrew Sarris, The New York Observer*

　　33 岁的导演兼编剧多纳斯马克是这样回忆他的创作动机的:
"多年以来,有两件事促成我拍这部电影。一个是我造访东柏林
和前东德的许多童年记忆。当时我还是一个将近十岁的小男孩,
对成人的恐惧只感到有趣和兴奋。我的父母在穿越边境时很紧
张:他们都出生在东德,也就更紧密地受到警察的控制。还有我
的东德朋友很害怕别人看见他们和我们这些来自西德的人讲话。
若是没有这些早年经验,我将难以找到正确的途径。

　　拍摄电影的想法随同一副画面突然地跃入我脑中:中近景镜
头里,一个男人坐在陋室中戴着耳机收听美妙的音乐,即使他可
能并不想听。这个人一直在梦中追逐着我,经过数年,他渐渐幻
化成了戈德·维斯勒上尉。"

　　不光对我们自己,《窃听风暴》对所有社会都有借鉴意义,
它揭露秘密的恐怖,而人类对恐怖的战争不会停止。虽然多纳斯
马克在国家秘密监控个人这个题目上没有发表过多评论,但是他
的控诉态度在电影叙事中表现得已然足够。事实上,他的影片可
以看作是对当前仍旧很泛滥的一种怀旧病的谴责,在德国或其它
地方,仍有人念念不忘德意志民主共和国那种社会和经济的理想
主义,哪怕这种制度对公民自由可耻地弃之不顾。

　　这并不是说当下的资本主义全球化对世界上所有人都是人间
天堂,其实不论我们生活于什么样的社会制度,同样的问题都不
可避免。用这位导演兼编剧自己的话说:"在影片中,每一个人
物问的问题都是我们每天都要面对的:我们应该怎样对待权力和

意识形态？我们能否尊重自己的原则和感觉？最重要的是，《窃听风暴》是一部关照人类的戏剧，它肯定人类做出正确选择的能力，无论他已在错误之路上走出了多远。"

—*Andrew Sarris*，《纽约观察》

Von Donnersmarck's notion is that good or great art has a humanizing quality that can triumph over the evils of an authoritarian society. Muehe, subtly and quietly, takes us through some of those changes—even as von Donnersmarck gives us a full picture of what life was like in the old East Germany. (He says his film is in part a reaction to amiable recent German comedies like "Goodbye, Lenin!" with their "ostalgie *" or nostalgia for the old East Germany.)

"The Lives of Others" works beautifully, both as a social and psychological drama and as a taut, tightly wired thriller. It was the big winner in last year's German film awards, winning "Lolas" for best picture, director, writer, actor (Muehe) and supporting actor (Tukur). And, considering that it marks von Donnersmarck's feature directorial debut—he previously made shorts and worked as Richard Attenborough's intern—it's a remarkably assured piece. The film spies on its characters as efficiently as the characters spy on each other.

At the center of the film, giving its key performance, is Muehe, whose face rarely betrays his thoughts, except to us, as he falls in love with the people on whom he spies. Muehe is a versatile actor; he played Dr. Mengele in Costa-Gavras' political thriller, "Amen". But Muehe's seemingly minimalist portrait here is touched with genius. We can see the functionary mask he presents to the world, as well as his resentments at being subordinate to the shallow opportunist Grubitz. We almost feel him softening as he sits riveted to his recorder.

In the end, von Donnersmarck, whose film is one of this year's five foreign-language Oscar nominees, succeeds in evoking both a vanished world and the people trapped in it. His is a world of mounting fear, institutionalized terror and people who reveal themselves, sometimes surprisingly, as human beings.

—*Michael Wilmington*, *Chicago Tribune*

在多纳斯马克的概念中，伟大的善的艺术有一种人道的品质，它可以战胜一个极权社会里的罪恶。穆埃微妙而沉静地带领我们感受那些变化的过程——甚至多纳斯马克本人也给我们展示了一幅前东德实际生活的全景。（他说，他的影片是对近年来像《再见，列宁》这样的德国喜剧的一种回应，所针对的是人们对前东德的那种怀旧病。）

不论把它当作社会心理剧，还是让人心里抓狂的恐怖片，《窃听风暴》都是一部杰作。它在去年的德国电影金罗拉奖中大获全胜，一举拿下了最佳影片、最佳导演、最佳男演员（穆埃）和最佳男配角（土库尔）。此外，这还是多纳斯马克作为导演的首部剧情长片——他之前只拍摄过短片，而且只是作为理查德·阿滕伯勒的助手，这更加说明了它的杰出。这部影片屏息凝神地监视着它的人物，就像影片中的人物互相监视那样。

作为影片的核心，穆埃的表演至关重要。他的面容从来不泄漏他的想法，但是当他爱上他所监听的人时，他的所思所想却对我们观众是敞开的。穆埃是一个万金油演员。他曾在科斯塔·加夫拉斯的政治恐怖片《阿门》中饰演曼哲鲁博士。而在《窃听风暴》中，他的"零度"表情简直是天才。我们可以看出他以一副功能性的面具去面对世界，并掩藏他对屈从于肤浅的机会主义者古比兹的怨恨。而当他着魔似的一动不动地听着录音时，我们几乎可以感觉到他正在变得柔软起来。

最终，多纳斯马克，这个其作品荣列今年奥斯卡五部最佳外语片提名的导演，成功地为我们唤醒了一个业已消失的世界和那些陷于其中的人们。这个世界中充满了受摆布的恐惧和制度性的恐怖，但是有人勇于揭露并且面对他们自己，这有时令人觉得不可思议，但正是我们的人性。

—*Michael Wilmington*，《芝加哥论坛》

Movies about moral wake-up calls, in which evil, conformist or misguided souls are shocked into realizing the error of their life choices, are tough nuts to crack. It's hazardous to try to pinpoint the tipping point of anyone's redemption, and even more difficult to effect such a deeply interior process dramatically. In "Schindler's List", Steven Spielberg dealt with that problem by simply sidestepping it: One moment a businessman goes along to get along, the next he does the heroically right thing.

Wiesler's concurrent metamorphosis is a little harder to swallow, particularly given the fervor with which von Donnersmarck paints him as a merciless fascist in the film's opening act. Whatever the cause, Wiesler softens in his mission. Is he guilted by the darling little boy in the elevator who innocently asks him if he is a Stasi member? Or does he get in touch with his humanity while overhearing Dreyman as he plunks out Beethoven on the piano and declaims, "Can anyone who has heard this music, truly heard it, really be a bad person?"

That question also signals the film's transformation from hard-nosed thriller to sentimental palliative. No wonder "The Lives of Others" has been nominated for a foreign-language Oscar. It has a facade of social consequence and moral nuance while sending us out with a feel-good balm for the heart. Just like, come to think of it, the cautious, crowd-pleasing plays of its reformed scribe, Dreyman.

—*Jan Stuart*, *Newsday*

那些关于呼唤道德觉醒的电影，即讲述罪恶、教条或误入歧途的灵魂如何震惊地意识到他们人生的错误抉择的影片总是有些顽固不化。试图找出个人获得救赎的转折点是虚妄且危险的，而且更加困难的是将这种内在的深层的过程戏剧性地表现出来。在《辛德勒名单》中，斯蒂文·斯皮尔博格用简单的一步跨越来解决这个问题：这一刻他还是个执迷不悟的商人，下一刻他已经做出了英雄般的正确选择。

维斯勒的突兀转变有一点让人难以消化，尤其是考虑到导演多纳斯马克在影片一开始把他狂热地描绘成一个无情的法西斯分子。不论是什么原因，维斯勒在执行任务中软化了。是那个电梯中可爱的男孩无辜地问他是否是安全局特工激起了他的廉耻？还是他的人性在无意中被触发，当听到德莱曼在钢琴上宣泄贝多芬并高声说："一个听到这音乐，真正听到它的呼唤的人，真的会是一个坏人吗？"

同样的问题体现在影片从那种坚硬的恐怖向柔软的感伤的过渡上。这就不奇怪《窃听风暴》为什么能被提名奥斯卡最佳外语片奖。它表现的是社会因果逻辑和道德细微差别的正面，它给我们炖了一锅安慰人的心灵鸡汤。想一想吧，这就像是被修正的作家德莱曼那谨小慎微的、取悦众人的剧本。

—*Jan Stuart， Newsday*

## Note

Orwellian：乔治·奥威尔（George Orwell）的作品的；属于或关于乔治·奥威尔的作品的或由乔治·奥威尔的作品联想到的，尤指其描绘未来极权主义国家的讽刺小说，如《一九八四》。

Ostalgie：德语里"东（Ost）"和"怀旧（Nostalgie）"两个词结合所创造的新词，意味"怀东"，怀念前东德。近年来，德国刮起了一阵怀旧风潮，人们借此释放多沉积下来的对于东德的怀念。影片《再见，列宁》可算是一个高潮。

# The Departed

## 无间道风云

**导演：**马丁·斯科塞斯（Martin Scorsese）

**编剧：**威廉·莫纳汗（William Monahan）

**主演：**莱昂纳多·迪卡普里奥（Leonardo DiCaprio）

马特·戴蒙（Matt Damon）

杰克·尼科尔森（Jack Nicholson）

马克·沃尔伯格（Mark Wahlberg）

维拉·法梅加（Vera Farmiga）

**片长：**149 分钟

**发行：**华纳兄弟（Warner Brothers），2006 年

*Plot Synopsis*

Two rats. Leonardo DiCaprio plays Billy, a trainee cop who has a bad family history. He is sent by Captain Queenan and Sergeant Dignam to infiltrate the Boston mob, run by Frank Costello. Matt Damon plays Colin, a policeman who rises fast through his ranks, but is secretly working for Costello. Both characters bounce off each other, while never actually meeting, while each tries to find the others identity, while coming unknowingly close (both are interested in the same woman).

## 剧情简介

两个卧底。迪卡普里奥扮演比利，一个家族史恶劣的警校学员。他被交给上尉奎因和迪格南警官，二人派他去波士顿黑帮老大弗兰克·科斯特洛那里做卧底。马特·戴蒙扮演柯林，一个升迁很快的警察，事实上却秘密地为科斯特洛工作。两人都曾互相试探，但从未正面相遇，当他们互相试图确认对方身份时，他们正不知不觉地接近彼此（都对同一个女人有兴趣）。

# Critique

*The Departed* is based on the highly successful 2002 Hong Kong crime thriller called *Infernal Affairs*, which starred Tony Leung and Andy Lau, and was directed by Andrew Lau and Alan Mak. The film did so well in Asia that it spawned a prequel and a sequel. Yet it only received a minimal release in the U. S. The Departed's screenwriter William Monahan says that he made an effort NOT to see *Infernal Affairs*, and instead worked from a translation of the Chinese script. In the press notes, Scorsese insists that his film is not a remake of the Hong Kong film. Well I don't know how he defines a remake but anyone who saw *Infernal Affairs* might think differently because in addition to the basic storyline that's lifted for *The Departed* there are other elements taken directly from the Hong Kong original-bits of business involving cell phones, elevators, a meet in a porn theater, rooftop encounters and more. Monahan and Scorsese lift these elements and tweak them yet they don't make them better or fully their own.

Monahan hails from Boston, which explains why he wanted to set the story their. But Scorsese never connects to the city the way he has with his home turf of New York. Similarly, we are constantly being reminded of the Irishness of the characters and the characteristics of being Irish yet a cultural flavor never flows through the film the way being Italian in New York came through in Scorsese's early films. Plus, Damon and DiCaprio never sell me on their ethnicity. In fact DiCaprio and Nicholson have a little trouble selling me on the fact that they're supposed to be from Boston. All this leads me to saying something that I never thought I'd say: when it comes to this particular story. Scorsese's been outdone by his

Hong Kong counterparts. Scorsese's *The Departed* doesn't improve in any way on *Infernal Affairs*, which served up a return to stylish Hong Kong action. Quit simply, Infernal Affairs delivered the goods, while *The Departed* just makes a partial shipment.

—*Beth Accomando*, *from Kpbs. org*

《无间道风云》翻拍自 2002 年大获成功的香港犯罪片《无间道》。出演《无间道》的明星是梁朝伟和刘德华，导演是刘伟强和麦兆辉。该片在亚洲反响很大，以至于又以它套拍出了前篇和后传。不过它在美国的发行量却非常有限。据《无间道风云》的编剧威廉·莫纳汗说，他努力地不去看电影《无间道》，而是从电影剧本的英译本中汲取需要。而斯科赛斯在声明中坚持说他的影片并不是那部港产片的翻版。当然我们也不知道他是怎么定义翻版的，然而看过《无间道》的人可能都会对此不以为然，因为《无间道风云》除了照搬基本的故事情节，还直接从这部香港原作中拿走了很多元素——小细节比如手机、电梯，在色情影院中相会，在屋顶上接头，等等。莫纳汗和斯科赛斯借用并改写了这些元素，但并没有改得更好些，也没有脱胎换骨成自己的东西。

莫纳汗是波士顿人，这大概可以解释他为什么把故事背景放在波士顿。然而斯科赛斯从来不能像对他的草根故乡纽约一样亲近地对待这个城市。同样地，我们不断地被提醒那些人物是爱尔兰人，有着爱尔兰特征，但影片却缺少那种文化味道，而在斯科赛斯早期的影片中，纽约的穷街陋巷里散发着浓浓的意大利味儿。此外，戴蒙和迪卡普里奥也没能让我们辨认出他们的种族身份。事实上，迪卡普里奥和尼科尔森也较难说服我们他们是来自波士顿的人。所有这些逼着我要说一些没能想过要说的话：对于这个特定的故事，斯科赛斯并没有他的香港同行做得好。斯科赛斯的《无间道风云》相对于《无间道》没有任何长进之处，而后者是向香港流行动作片的回归。非常明白，《无间道》是有料的，而《无间道风云》则是支离破碎的。

—*Beth Accomando*, *Kpbs* 网站

Director Martin Scorsese and screenwriter William Monahan

have taken the B-grade Hong Kong crime flick *Infernal Affairs* and re-imagined it as an American epic tragedy. The original film was gritty and entertaining; the new version is a masterpiece—the best effort Scorsese has brought to the screen since *Goodfellas* (ending a decade-long drought of disappointments and near-misses). In making *The Departed*, Scorsese has retained the essential plot structure of Infernal Affairs but has transformed the movie into something truly his own. Characters are better defined and situations are given an opportunity to breathe. None of this is done at the cost of pacing; *The Departed* is as suspenseful as anything the director has previously achieved. This movie deserves mention alongside Scorsese's most celebrated movies: *Taxi Driver*, *Raging Bull*, *Goodfellas*, and *The Age of Innocence*.

*—James Berardinelli, Reelviews*

导演马丁·斯科赛斯和编剧威廉·莫纳汗拿来《无间道》，将这部香港 B 级犯罪片改造成了一部美国悲剧史诗。原版影片是质地坚硬的娱乐片，而新版则是一部杰作——是斯科赛斯自《好家伙》以来献给银幕最优秀的作品（以此结束了长达十年的在失望和迷失中的沉寂）。在《无间道风云》中，斯科赛斯虽然保留了原作基本的情节结构，但是确实把它转化成了自己的东西。其中的人物得到了更好地定义，情景也更加值得回味。而这些并没有牺牲影片的节奏，《无间道风云》仍然像这位导演的旧作一样紧紧攥住了我们的神经。该片完全可以和斯科赛斯这些最负盛名的影片并驾齐驱：《出租车司机》、《愤怒的公牛》、《好家伙》以及《纯真年代》。

*—James Berardinelli*,《旋风景》

"The Departed" is not one of his greatest films; it doesn't use the camera to reveal the psychological and aesthetic dimensions of an entire world, as "Mean Streets", "Taxi Driver", "Raging Bull", and "Goodfellas" did. But it's a viciously merry, violent, high-wattage entertainment, and speech is the most brazenly flamboyant element in it. "The Departed" is a remake of the Hong Kong thriller "Infernal Affairs", directed by Andrew Lau and Alan Mak, and it has the speed and volatility of Hong Kong movies. But Scorsese and the screenwriter, William Monahan, have added weight to the cops-and-robbers plot by setting it in the Irish neighborhood of South Boston and by digging deep into urban tribal lore-the memories of loyalty and betrayal going back for decades, the nasty old jokes, the bullying insults and invective. The men commit obscene acts, and speak in cynical taunts, and the extreme violence and virtuoso cursing seem to feed off each other.

The story is highly improbable, although Scorsese and Monahan keep the complicated goings on clear and taut, and the entire movie is acted with spirit and conviction. DiCaprio, his mouth pinched in tension, his voice gravelly and low, holds his own against Damon, who has a charming and plausible line of patter as the calculating Colin. Scorsese also gets terrific work from Mark Wahlberg, as a combustible but honest Special Investigations Unit cop, and Vera Farmiga, as a police psychiatrist who is drawn to neurotic and violent men. All the characters are unusually intelligent, and the fast, scurrilous talk binds the tightly edited short sequences together. Scorsese, however, is trying to do with words what he used to accomplish with the camera, and he doesn't produce the kind of emotional involvement that once made his movies so exhausting and also so satisfying. At the end, he seems eager to dispose of his characters in order to fill out a pattern: one after another gets shot at point-blank range (there's hardly an actor who retains the back of his head), and shock gives way to disbelief and even laughter. "The Departed" is murderous fun, but it's too shallow to be the kind of movie that haunts your sleep.

—*David Denby, The New Yorker*

　　《无间道风云》并不是斯科赛斯最伟大的作品，它没有像《穷街陋巷》、《出租车司机》、《愤怒的公牛》和《好家伙》一样，用摄影机去揭示一个整体世界的心理和美学上的张力。但是它给我们提供了一种邪恶的快感和浓烈的娱乐，而语言是其中最具低俗之光的元素。《无间道风云》翻拍的是刘伟强和麦兆辉导演的香港犯罪片《无间道》，它带有港片的语言和味道。不过斯科赛斯和他的编剧莫纳汗在增加警匪情节的分量上做了努力，他们把背景改到南波士顿的爱尔兰区，深入挖掘城市深处的种族文化，挖掘出过去数十年关于忠诚和背叛的记忆，以及那些下流的老笑话，那些恫吓、侮辱和漫骂。其中的人们犯着恶行，说话愤世嫉俗，而那极度的暴力似乎与自我陶醉的咒骂相辅相成。

　　尽管斯科赛斯和莫纳汗把复杂的内容传达得清晰而紧张，但是故事本身仍然是非常不可思议的。整部影片是靠精神和信念贯穿支撑的。迪卡普里奥的嘴唇总是紧张地收敛着，声音沙哑低沉，他以此保持着他和戴蒙的对立，而戴蒙扮演的精明算计的柯林说话则是一种讨好人的、似是而非的喋喋不休。斯科赛斯对马克·沃尔伯格和维拉·法梅加的调教也让人惊讶，前者是一个脾气火爆但是品质忠诚的特别调查组警察，后者是一个要时刻应付神经质和有暴力倾向的病人的心理医生。所有的人物都才智非凡，而那快速的、粗鄙的台词则和快速剪切镜头浑然一体。然而，尽管斯科赛斯妄图像他过去自如使用摄影机那样使用语言，但是他并没有创造出其旧作中那种让人又疲倦又满足的情感张力。最终，他似乎迫不及待地要把他的人物安排进一种模式中：他们被直截了当地面对面一枪打死（几乎没有一个演员是把背影留给观众的），一个接着一个，但其制造的震惊只是引发了怀疑甚至嘲笑。《无间道风云》超级好玩，但是它过于肤浅而不能让你魂牵梦萦。

——David Denby，《纽约客》

# The Queen

# 女 王

**导演：**史蒂芬·弗里尔斯（Stephen Frears）

**编剧：**彼得·摩根（Peter Morgan）

**主演：**海伦·米伦（Helen Mirren）

迈克尔·辛（Michael Sheen）

詹姆斯·克伦威尔（James Cromwell）

阿历克斯·詹宁斯（Alex Jennings）

**片长：**97 分钟

**发行：**米拉麦克斯（Miramax），2006 年

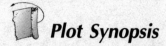 *Plot Synopsis*

The Queen is an intimate behind the scenes glimpse at the interaction between HM Elizabeth II and Prime Minister Tony Blair during their struggle, following the death of Diana, to reach a compromise between what was a private tragedy for the Royal family and the public's demand for an overt display of mourning.

## 剧情简介

《女王》像是一个居于幕后的老熟人。黛安娜王妃死后，她一直关注着女王伊丽莎白二世和首相布莱尔之间的矛盾和摩擦，以及他们最后终于达成妥协：将王妃的死定性为王室家族的私事，同时也允许公众公开哀悼她。

## *Critique*

History isn't supposed to repeat itself so quickly, but George W. Bush's tardy response last year to Katrina's devastation of the Gulf Coast echoed almost exactly the lethargy that enveloped the Royal Family of Britain eight years before, in the days following the car crash that killed Princess Diana. Like Bush in Crawford, the Queen stayed holed up in Balmoral, her country estate in Scotland, while her subjects, shocked by the violent death of the blond goddess whose flaws they cherished as much as her charms, sobbed their hearts out. Strange, isn't it, how the powerful get short-circuited from their power base. Too often, people whose job it is to lead by listening have the tendency to go politically deaf in times of crisis—to proceed as if nothing had happened, to sleepwalk in a state of bland or numb denial.

That, anyway, is the proposition of *The Queen*, an immensely entertaining and seemingly acute chronicle of the week Diana died, as dramatized through the very different reactions of stern, befogged Elizabeth II (Helen Mirren) and of Prime Minister Tony Blair (Michael Sheen), who was keenly attuned to public sentiment and how to manipulate it. The film, written by Peter Morgan and directed by Stephen Frears (best known for *Dangerous Liaisons*), won the screenplay and actress prizes at Venice this month.

The movie's patina of textual and textural accuracy comes from voluminous research by the BBC Films team, including interviews with Windsor insiders, a chatty crowd. Elizabeth might be expected to run a tight ship with tight lips; but because royal scandal is a marketable commodity and the tabloid press voracious and rapacious, Buckingham Palace regularly springs more leaks than the Titanic. So

you may take it as gossip gospel that Princess Margaret made the un-
generous observation quoted in the film that Diana was even "more
irritating dead than alive." Morgan also did a lot of asking around,
and people answered. He says, for example, that he based scenes of
the Prince of Wales' reaction to the crash on having talked "to someone who spoke to Prince Charles on the night of Diana's death."

Yet however accurate the portrait of the royals in *The Queen*,
the first impression the movie gives is one of cool, devastating satire. Or perhaps Elizabeth and her family really are as drab as the film
paints them! They don't aspire to glamour; they renounce it.
Cloistered at Balmoral, knitting and nattering in their plain wool
sweaters, caring more for their pets than for their children, the
Royal Family seems a parody of the pettiness and insularity of the
English middle class. It's as if the Windsors want to prove that although they're worth billions and practically define the term "idle
rich," they share the tatty taste and myopic world-view of Britain's
petty bourgeoisie. The grocer and the schoolteacher can look, not
up to, but over at Elizabeth and think, "She's one of us."

That's wishful thinking. Elizabeth has always struck me as a
crabby soul. Her job is, essentially, to smile in public, yet she's
never been good at it. The grin seems more a grimace, as if she
grudges the effort it takes to move those facial muscles. If warmth
and beauty are requisites of regality, she's flunked the test. Perhaps
because of the coldness I sense in Elizabeth, I've often felt a sympathy for Charles, whom I'm guessing didn't get a lot of it at home.
He works so hard at the game of ingratiation, and he's waited so
long for the position he was born to, that even his gaffes appeal to
me. That indiscreet love chat with Camilla Parker-Bowles—his
wish that he could be her tampon—had the clumsy tenderness of a
man not schooled in seduction but enslaved to it.

—*Richard Corliss, Time Magazine*

历史很少在短时间内如此迅速地重复自己，然而乔治·W·布什去年对海湾沿岸卡特里那飓风灾难的迟钝反应和八年前英国王室对黛安娜王妃车祸身亡的漠不关心几乎惊人地相似。就像布什待在克劳福德，女王则一直待在她在苏格兰的度假行宫巴尔莫罗堡里，而她的臣民正陷于那位金发女神的惨死而不能自拔。她在女王眼中的瑕疵恰恰成了公众眼中的魅力。有点儿奇怪是不是？她的权力基础是怎样突然短路的呢？我们见得太多了，以服从为天职的人们习惯于在危机面前保持政治上的沉默——仿佛什么都没有发生一样照旧前行，仿佛在冷漠和麻木不仁的国度里梦游。

总之，《女王》的意图就是这样，它分外有趣又貌似敏锐地再现了黛安娜死去后的那一周时间，戏剧性在严厉、困惑的伊丽莎白二世（海伦·米伦饰）和专注于照顾和控制公众情绪的首相托尼·布莱尔（迈克尔·辛饰）截然不同的反应中展开。这部由彼得·摩根编剧，史蒂芬·弗里尔斯导演（以《危险关系》成名）的影片在这个月的威尼斯影展上夺得了最佳编剧和最佳女演员奖。

该片在文本上的严谨和精确是以 BBC 摄制团队大规模的调查为基础的，他们采访了了解内情的温莎公爵以及很多爱说话的人。伊丽莎白在我们的期望中是一个严于律己，惜字如金的人。然而，王室丑闻向来是花边小报竞相争夺的卖点，白金汉宫持续出现的裂缝简直比泰坦尼克还要多。所以你可以把影片中引用玛格丽特公主的那句刻薄话——黛安娜"死了比活着还烦人"当作是善意的流言。摩根四下打听，人们解答了他的疑问。他举例说，影片中威尔士亲王对车祸的反应那场戏是有根据的，与他交谈的是"那个在黛安娜死亡的当夜曾与查尔斯王子说过话的人"。

然而不管《女王》中的王室肖像刻画得有多么精确，影片给人的第一印象却是冰冷致命的讽刺意味。或许伊丽莎白和她的家庭就像影片中所表现的那么单调乏味！他们和魅力绝缘，没有散发魅力的热情。他们隐居在巴尔莫罗堡，穿着朴素的羊毛衫，过着针织和唠叨的生活，关心宠物超过关心子女。这样的王室家庭就像是对琐碎狭隘的英国中产阶级生活的拙劣模仿。仿佛温莎公爵想证明坐拥亿万财产的他们虽然用实践诠释着"富贵闲人"这个概念，但是他们却在生活品位上敝帚自珍，对生气勃勃的资产阶级视而不见。甚至杂货店的人和中学教师都可以俯视着（而不是仰视）伊丽莎白并且想，"她跟我们一样"。

这不过是痴心妄想。伊丽莎白的固执一直让我印象深刻，虽然基本上她的工作就是对着公众微笑，但她从来没有做好过这一点。她的微笑总是一副苦相，好像她懒得活动那些面部肌肉似的。如果慈祥和美丽是我们对一个君主的要求，那么伊丽莎白是不及格的。也许是因为感到了伊丽莎白的冷漠，我总是对查尔斯心怀怜悯，我猜他在家里能得到的并不多。他努力做着讨好的游戏，那个天赋的位置也让他等了太长的时间，甚至他的过失都会吸引我。他对卡米拉轻率的情话——他希望可以做她的卫生棉——这显示的是一个被奴役而不是被诱惑的男人那种笨拙的温柔。

—*Richard Corliss*，《时代》杂志

"The Queen" was written by Peter Morgan, who has become a specialist in fanciful reconstruction. His other works include a television play, "The Deal," directed by Frears, which examined the early balancing act between Blair and Gordon Brown, his probable successor, and "Frost/Nixon", a stage play, just ending a run at London's Donmar Warehouse, about the interviews that David Frost conducted with the growling former President in 1977. Michael Sheen also played Blair in the first of these, and Frost in the second. Sheen is ideal for Morgan's purposes, in that he is engaged neither in exact facsimile nor, still less, in caricature. Both writer and actor, operating on the principle that well-known figures become less, not more, knowable with the passing of time, tend to fasten on what can be grasped—tics, expostulations, dates in a diary-and, thus armed, venture unabashed into speculation. I have no idea, for example, whether Blair actually threw poll statistics at Her Majesty over the phone, claiming that "seventy per cent of people believe that your actions have damaged the monarchy," but it sounds like the kind of thing that he (and he alone) would dare to say, braving the fact that, in earlier times, it would have led to ninety per cent of his body being sundered from the other ten.

As a director, Frears likes to stay on his feet, refusing to get bogged down in a dominant mood; his Roddy Doyle adaptations, "The Snapper" and "The Van", slip in and out of comedy as if rolling from one pub to the next. At the same time, there is, in Frears's homegrown work, an air of security—of shifting at his ease between familiar settings—that is never quite matched by his American projects, even in films as fruitful as "The Grifters" and "High Fidelity". And so it is with "The Queen", which bats back and forth* between a variety of camps: the shabby, thrusting enclave of Downing Street, the magnificent starch of the Palace, and the tweed-and-tartan heartiness of Balmoral, the Highland fastness to which the Royal Family retreats at regular intervals, and where it holed up in the week after the car crash. The Queen's decision to stay there and pull up the drawbridge, so to speak, was read by the public as evidence of a hard heart, and Blair's success in persuading her to return to London and address the nation on live TV was hailed as his finest hour. The movie digs up a news report from CNN, in which the anchorwoman suggests that the Royals failed to display "enough remorse over Princess Diana's death." A telling slip, throwing guilt at the Palace and hoping it will stick.

—*Anthony Lane*, *New Yorker*

《女王》的编剧摩根是一个能够奇思妙想地重构故事的专家。他的作品还有电视剧《交易》，也由弗里尔斯导演，讲的是早年布莱尔和戈登·布朗之间的博弈关系。刚在伦敦多玛仓库剧院上演了一轮的舞台剧《弗罗斯特/尼克松》可能是他的下一部电影作品。该剧围绕着 1977 年大卫·弗罗斯特采访暴怒的尼克松这件事展开情节。在前一部中扮演布莱尔的也是迈克尔·辛，而后者中弗罗斯特扮演他自己。迈克尔·辛对摩根来说很理想，他对布莱尔的刻画既不是太刻板，也不是太讽刺。不论编剧还是演员，他们一致认同的原则是，公众人物对时间的流逝感觉更麻木而不是更敏感，因此他们倾向于抓住一切能抓到的东西——人物面部的痉挛、劝谏、日记中的日期，然后既戒备又大胆地反省。我也不确定，比如说布莱尔是否真的在电话上用选票统计驳女王的面子，声称"70%的人民认为您的行为玷污了君主立宪制"，不过这听起来像是他（就他自己）敢说的那种话。事实上如果在早些时候，这能让他身首异处。

作为一个导演，弗里尔斯喜欢坚持自己，与主流情绪保持着清醒的距离。他所改编罗迪·道尔的《鲷鱼》和《发财专家》在喜剧中滑入滑出，就像从一个酒吧换到另一个酒吧。同时弗里尔斯的本土之作中有一种安全的气场，他可以自如地变换着熟悉的场景，而他在美国的作品则不免生硬，即使是像《千网危情》和《失恋排行榜》这样不错的影片也是如此。《女王》也同样没能幸免，影片来来回回地徘徊于多个"camp"之处：唐宁街领地的破旧和夺目，王宫的宏伟和僵硬，巴尔莫罗堡斜纹格子呢的温暖，王室定期逗留、并在车祸后那一周藏身的高原山庄。也就是说，女王停留的决定和那收起的吊桥被公众认为是硬心肠的明证，而布莱尔成功说服她回到伦敦并对全国做电视直播发言则被拥戴为他的最佳表现。影片里重播了 CNN 的一段新闻，其中主持人发表看法说，王室失于"未在黛安娜之死上表现出足够的怜悯"。这是一条用意明白的标签，它把王宫死死摁在负罪感中不得解脱。

—*Anthony Lane*，《纽约客》

**Note**

*bats back and forth*：美国俚语，详细考虑，反复讨论。

# The Wind That Shakes the Barley

# 风吹稻浪

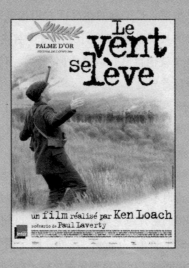

导演：肯·洛奇（Ken Loach）

编剧：保罗·拉弗蒂（Paul Laverty）

主演：斯里安·墨菲（Cillian Murphy）

　　　帕德莱克·德兰尼（Padraic Delaney）

片长：127 分钟

发行：百代电影公司（Pathé Distributors），2006 年

# *Plot Synopsis*

Ireland 1920: workers from field and country unite to form volunteer guerrilla armies to face the ruthless "Black and Tan" squads that are being shipped from Britain to block Ireland's bid for independence. Driven by a deep sense of duty and a love for his country, Damien abandons his burgeoning career as a doctor and joins his brother, Teddy, in a dangerous and violent fight for freedom. As the freedom fighters' bold tactics bring the British to breaking point, both sides finally agree to a treaty to end the bloodshed. However, despite the apparent victory, civil war erupts and families who fought side by side find themselves pitted against one another as sworn enemies, putting their loyalties to the ultimate test.

## 剧情简介

1920年,爱尔兰乡间的工人们组成自愿游击队来反抗英国为阻止爱尔兰独立而派遣来的残忍的"爱尔兰王室警吏团"。出于对祖国深深的爱和责任,戴米安放弃了他刚刚起步的医生职业,追随他的兄弟泰迪,共同不惧危险和暴力地为自由而战。这些自由战士的无畏之举刺激英国做出转变,双方达成了停战协议。然而,胜利只是表面的,内战爆发了,那些曾经并肩作战的亲人成了不共戴天的仇敌,将他们的忠诚推向最后的考验。

# Critique

Ken Loach's great, tragic "The Wind That Shakes the Barley" —which won the Palme d'Or at the 2006 Cannes Film Festival—takes its title from a 19th Century ballad by Robert Dwyer Joyce; one stanza of which ends: " The mountain glen/ I'll seek at morning early/ And join the brave united men/ While soft winds shake the barley. " Joyce's words, sung at a funeral in the film, seethe with a mix of pain and idealism, an undertow of plaintiveness and lament. And they distill the essence of Loach and writer Paul Laverty's film, which is set during a relatively brief time in the Irish guerrilla wars against the British, from late summer 1920 through the treaty signing of December 1921 and its aftermath. It's about the brave men in the rustling barley and morning light, and the bloodshed and fratricide that inevitably await them, especially the brothers Damien ( Cillian Murphy) and Teddy (Padraic Delaney).

"Wind" is a beautiful film, harrowing, tough and rife with grief, and it uses the cloud-veiled Irish countryside as a backdrop for a truly sad tale of the time when the battles were fought, the Irish Free State was formed, the British left part of the country and the Irish rebels, formerly united against the English, finally splintered into factions of various political hues and began killing each other.

What the film ultimately says is that the horrors of war cannot be assumed lightly—even though the Irish were right to revolt and the British wrong to occupy their land. It also says, typically for Loach, that the Irish and English working classes have more in common with each other than with aristocrats like the film's haughty informer Sir John Hamilton.

Loach ( "Land and Freedom", "Kes") is one of the finest

political filmmakers in the world, and an unusually stubborn one. He maintains a radical stance to this day, even as now, the prospects for peace, via a power-sharing agreement, are on the upswing. But "Wind" is no socialist tract. The movie is about the collision of political principles and human bonds and values, and it doesn't treat any of them lightly. Loach is on the side of the revolutionaries, but there isn't a moment of violence in the film that glorifies it or makes it exhilarating. Even though this is a period film, a grim, clear-eyed realism informs every scene. That's Loach's method. He's the master of the docu-drama or the realist social film, and "Wind" is one of his masterpieces.

—*Michael Wilmington*, *Chicago Tribune*

摘下了 2006 年戛纳电影节金棕榈桂冠的《风吹稻浪》是肯·洛奇伟大的悲剧作品,影片名称取自于 19 世纪罗伯特·威尔·乔伊斯所作的一首民谣,其中一节的结尾是:"……那山中幽谷/我将在清晨寻找/和勇敢的人们团结在一起/当微风拂过稻浪。"乔伊斯的诗句在影片中的葬礼上唱起,痛苦和理想一起在胸中翻腾,哀伤和悲悼阵阵袭来。这是洛奇和编剧保罗·拉弗蒂对这部影片的点睛之笔,该片的主体时代背景是爱尔兰和大英帝国的游击战争,从 1920 年夏末到 1921 年 12 月签订协议前后。它描写了在稻浪和晨光之中勇敢的人们,还有他们躲避不开的自相残杀,尤其是在戴米安(斯里安·墨菲)和泰迪(帕德莱克·德兰尼)两兄弟之间。

《风吹稻浪》是一部融合了悲惨、坚韧和忧伤的优美之作。云雾笼罩的爱尔兰乡村背景始终映衬着这个实在令人哀伤的故事——战斗过后,爱尔兰自由州建立,一度联合抵抗英国人的左翼政党和爱尔兰造反者最终四分五裂、互相残杀。

影片最终要表达的是,战争的恐怖不可能导向光明——虽然爱尔兰人有权利反抗,虽然英国人占领他们的土地是不义的。洛奇也想表达,和影片中的告密者约翰·汉密尔顿那种贵族相比,爱尔兰人其实和英国的工人阶层更能心意相通。

　　洛奇（《以祖国之名》、《小孩与鹰》）是世界上最优秀的政治片导演之一，也是一个少见的顽固分子。他始终保持着一种激进的姿态，即使今天权力分享的契约已在保障和促进着和平的前景。不过《风吹稻浪》并不是一张社会主义传单。影片探讨的是政治原则的碰撞以及人性的束缚和价值，而且对任何一点都没有轻薄待之。洛奇是站在革命者一边的，但是影片中丝毫没有赞美或粉饰暴力。虽然这是一部历史片，但那种无情的、清醒的现实主义照亮了每个角落，这就是洛奇的方法。他是文献纪录片和现实主义社会电影的大师，《风吹稻浪》就是其中的杰作之一。

　　　　　　　　　　　　　　—*Michael Wilmington*，《芝加哥论坛报》

　　The title does not exactly sing seductively: The Wind that Shakes the Barley. What are we talking about here—agronomy? Nor does its narrative—1920s Ireland in the throes of what we would now call an "insurgency" —provide the analogies to current events that it would have been easy to make. Then there's the Ken Loach problem. He is a mild-mannered English leftist who has been for years making earnest, naturalistic, rather conventionally mounted studies about working-class topics that do not make the cinephile's aesthete spirit leap in anticipation. He's the kind of guy who turns down decorations from the Queen because he loathes the evil—or at least twitish—company he would have to keep on her honor's list. Put it simply: Almodovar he is not.

　　Yet *Barley* won the Palme D'Or at last year's Cannes film festival and despite its length (over two hours) and some structural problems, it is an absorbing, worthwhile and often passionate movie. Yes, it has a certain medicinal virtue; it is not easy to take. But it also has extraordinary dramatic power and because Loach is an honest and honorable craftsman, it often betrays his own sympathies.

　　The "troubles"* that began in Ireland almost a hundred years ago, did not end with the response to the Free State election, even though the revolutionary answer to it was rather quickly put down. They have persisted into our own times and Loach's film is permeated with an unspoken acknowledgment of that fact. Nor can we ignore that other insurgencies, engendered largely by the stupidity and arrogance of imperialist powers, are everywhere present in our own world—though, again, Loach allows our thoughts to drift in that direction without guidance from him. Loach may not be a sockeroo filmmaker—I think he is a sufficient one in his slightly stodgy way—but he is manifestly a good and thoughtful man and *The Wind That Shakes the Barley* represents his gifts at something like their best. It is more than worth your while.

—*Richard Schickel, Time Magazine*

　　"风吹稻浪"这个名字并不诱人。我们在此讨论什么呢——农业学吗？叙事也一样——关于上个世纪 20 年代阵痛中（如今我们可能称之为"叛乱"）的爱尔兰，原本可以轻松地给当下的某些事件提供相似的参照。于是肯·洛奇的问题就来了。作为一个温和的英国左翼人士，多年来他一直一丝不苟地、自然主义地、甚至规规矩矩地关注着工人阶层这一主题，从来不曾超出影迷对他的审美期待。他就是那种会拒绝女王勋章的人，因为他憎恨罪恶——至少要嘲笑它，这罪恶与女王赐予的荣誉相伴而生。简单地说，他不是阿尔莫多瓦。

　　尽管如此，尽管《风吹稻浪》篇幅冗长（超过了两个小时）并存在一些结构上的问题，它还是夺得了去年的戛纳金棕榈奖，并不失为一部吸引人的、有价值的、激动人心的影片。是的，它是一剂苦口良药，它不易消化，但它也具备一种非凡的戏剧张力。因为洛奇是一位诚实可敬的艺术家，影片常常会不可避免地泄露他的怜悯心。

　　"爱尔兰问题"差不多起于百年之前，虽然它引起的反抗革命很快就被镇压下去。但是直到自由州选举时也没结束，一直持续至今。这在洛奇的电影中是一个不言自明的事实。同样我们也不能忽视其它的叛乱，它们由愚蠢和傲慢的帝国主义权力引起，遍布我们的世界——洛奇再一次让我们既向着这一方向思考而又不囿于他的看法。洛奇可能不是一个以才华著称的电影人，我认为他自足于自己那有些单调的方式，但他的确是一个有思想的好人。而《风吹稻浪》显现了这个人天分中最出色的一些东西，它绝对值得你看。

—*Richard Schickel*，《时代杂志》

A Ken Loach film about the British in Ireland always has the potential for controversy, but his historical drama "The Wind That Shakes the Barley" is unlikely to inflame passions on either side.

Atmospheric but pedestrian, it is a retelling of the classic trage-dy of all civil wars, from the U. S. to Vietnam to England, where brother is pitched against brother.

The film looks handsomely authentic, and the familiar charac-ters are engaging, but the story is predictable and the Irish accents are so thick that even English subtitles are required. Loach's human-ity is always in evidence, however, and the lack of histrionics will please many, so the film's conventionality could help make it acces-sible to general audiences.

—*Ray Bennett*, *Hollywood Reporter*

肯·洛奇关于英国和爱尔兰关系问题的电影总有引发争议的潜力，但这一次他的历史剧《风吹稻浪》在两边的反应都风平浪静。

这部大气却呆板的作品重述了所有与内战有关的经典悲剧，从美国到越南到英国的手足相残。

影片看起来真实可信，人物亲切动人，但是故事并不出人意料，那爱尔兰口音也过于浓重，以至于连英文字幕都必不可少。不过洛奇的人道关怀显而易见，而且它不做戏的态度博得了人们的好感，总之这种中规中矩的品格使它很容易被普通观众接受。

—*Ray Bennett*，《好莱坞报道》

**Note**

The Troubles：专指爱尔兰问题，指1920年开始的这场爱尔兰共和军在爱尔兰发动的游击战，以反对英国政府在爱尔兰的统治。

# Three Times

## 最好的时光

**导演：**侯孝贤
**编剧：**朱天文
**主演：**舒淇、张震
**片长：**129 分钟
**发行：**第一出版公司（First Distributors），2005 年

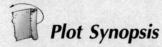 *Plot Synopsis*

Three Times is comprised of a trio of 45-minute shorts starring the same male and female leads (Shu Qi, Chang Chien), the mini-films look at romance in three different time periods: 1911, 1966, and 2005. The first segment, which transpires in 1966, has the leads meet in a pool hall then correspond by mail once he joins the army. When he's home on leave, he tracks her down so they can spend time together. The 1911 episode is a drama between a master and his favorite concubine. He has promised her freedom, but she is so important to him that he cannot bear to let her go. Finally, in 2005, the female character is an epileptic singer involved with another woman as well as the man. Eventually, she turns her back on the lesbian, but there is a price to pay.

## 剧情简介

该片是一部三段式影片，每段长约45分钟，由同一个男女演员主演（舒淇、张震），分别演绎了1911年、1966年、2005年的浪漫故事。第一个故事发生在1966年，主要相遇场景是在一个桌球厅，男孩参军离开后，两人靠写信联系。休假回家时，他费劲周折找到她共渡美好时光。1911年这段戏剧发生在一个文人和他所爱的青楼女子之间。他答应给她自由，但她对他太重要，以至于无法忍受别离。最后是2005年这段，女主人公是一个患有癫痫病的歌手，除了她的男朋友外还有一个同性恋女友。最终她抛弃了女友，并为此付出了代价。

# *Critique*

Seen in isolation, the first episode has the most satisfying plot and the last the least. But the film's achievement lies mostly in the beautifully articulated similarities and differences among the three—in their compositions and themes, in the way space is defined and camera pans connect characters, in their use of music and other means of personal expression ( snooker, pop tunes, and letters in 1966; poetry, singing, and letters in 1911; photographs, singing, and e-mails in 2005), and in the performances of the two stars. Chang, who was discovered by Edward Yang and played the lead in Yang's *A Brighter Summer Day* (1991) and *Mahjong* (1996), has become more identified with Wong Kar-wai, having appeared in *Happy Together* (1997), *2046* (2004), and "The Hand" ( Wong's episode in *Eros*, 2004). He's also in *Crouching Tiger, Hidden Dragon* (2000). Shu has appeared in more than 50 films, including *The Transporter* (2002).

Some aspects of *Three Times* evoke Hou's earlier films, beginning with his trilogy about Taiwan in the 20th century: *City of Sadness* (1989), *The Puppet Master* (1993), and *Good Men, Good Women* (1995, also set during three separate historical periods). The first segment also recalls his 1985 autobiographical film about his adolescence, *The Time to Live and the Time to Die*, the second recalls his 1998 *Flowers of Shanghai* (set in a ritzy Shanghai bordello during the 1880s), and the third his 2001 *Millennium Mambo* (a mainly contemporary film starring Shu Qi). But the structure of *Three Times* is new for him, which makes all these resemblances superficial.

—*Jonathan Rosenbaum, Chicago Reader*

在三段互相独立的故事中，第一段情节最令人满意而第三段最枯燥。不过影片最有成就之处在于三段之间美丽的相似和差别——在元素和主题上；在空间调度和镜头相对于人物的运动上；在音乐的运用和其它个人化的表达方式上（1966 年的桌球、流行音乐、书信往来；1911 年的诗词、唱曲、来信；2005 年的照片、唱歌和电子邮件）以及在两个明星的表演上。其中张震被导演杨德昌发现，并主演了他的影片《牯岭街少年杀人事件》（1991）和《麻将》（1996），后来越来越紧密地和王家卫相联，出现在《春光乍泄》（1997）、《2046》（2004）、《手》（王家卫《爱神》三部曲之一，2004）中，此外还出演了《卧虎藏龙》。而舒淇则出演过 50 多部影片，其中包括《非常人贩》（2002）。

《最好的时光》中的某些东西能让人联想起侯孝贤早期的作品。最早是他关于 20 世纪台湾的三部曲：《悲情城市》（1989），《戏梦人生》（1993）、《好男好女》（也以三段不同的历史时期为背景，1995）。影片的第一段还能让人想起他 1985 年的自传片《童年往事》和 1998 年的《海上花》（以 19 世纪 80 年代上海的一家奢华妓院为背景）。第三段能让人想起 2001 年的《千禧曼波》（舒淇主演，主要反映当代生活的影片）。但是《最好的时光》的结构对侯孝贤来说是新颖的，因而这些雷同之处则显得很肤浅。

——*Jonathan Rosenbaum*，《芝加哥读者》

This is undoubtedly one of the most beautiful films of the year. However, depending on your aesthetic predilections, it may also be one of the most boring. Hou Hsiao-hsien is a visual master, let there be no doubt, but his films always tend to be more steeped in evocative atmosphere than action. The camerawork of genius cinematographer Mark Lee Ping-bin is alive to the thrilling beauty apprehended in light reflecting into a simple pool hall, an ornately expensive brothel, lush with dark suggestiveness, or even the red taillights of cars making slow progress through traffic. If you are easily lulled into a sensuous rhythm of pure cinematic languor, this will satisfy. If not, you may be banging your head against the back of your seat.

Hou's disdain for dialogue is evident from the first episode, in which no one speaks for an eternity, and is at its most pronounced in the second, wherein he actually revives silent-movie titles to take the place of real speech. The nonverbal theme is carried into the final segment, which has its alienated characters forever texting each other on their cell-phones. Under these thinly plotted, unspoken circumstances, both lead actors do remarkably well, evince impressive histrionic range, and emerge as a charismatic, quite stunning couple to rival those of movie legend: Garbo and Gilbert, Cary Grant and Ingrid Bergman in *Notorious*, Elizabeth Taylor and Paul Newman in *Cat on a Hot Tin Roof*, or Tony Leung and Maggie Cheung in *In the Mood for Love*.

—*David Noh*, *Film Journal International*

这无疑是今年最优美的影片之一。但这还得取决于你的美学口味，否则它也可能是最闷的电影之一。侯孝贤无疑是视觉上的大师，但是他更沉浸于营造氛围而非情节营造上。天才摄影师李屏宾的摄影机自觉地捕捉着那些惊人的美，光线照射着一个简陋的台球厅，一个奢华的散发着黯淡意味的妓院，或者一个缓缓前行中的汽车尾灯。这是一部纯粹的闷片，如果你容易投入它那种感觉纤细的节奏，你会喜欢它。否则你恨不得用脑袋去撞你的椅背。

第一段故事能够很明显的看出侯孝贤对人物对话的不屑，其中谁也没有说一些山盟海誓的话。在第二段中顶多只是说出来，而且用无声电影的那种字幕形式取代了现实的表达。这种静默的主题一直延续到最后一段中，其中疏离的人物一直用手机短信互相沟通着。在这些稀少的情节和无言的氛围中，两个主演表现得相当出色，让人印象深刻的戏剧张力在他们身上蔓延，他们是一对魅力非凡的恋人，可以和以下这些电影神话中的恋人相匹敌：

嘉宝和吉尔伯特，《美人计》中的加利·格兰特和英格丽·褒曼，《豪门巧妇》中的伊丽莎白·泰勒和保罗·纽曼，《花样年华》中的梁朝伟和张曼玉。

—David Noh，《国际电影月刊》

Hou has never been an easy director to embrace. Earlier works like *Flowers of Shanghai*, *Good Men*, *Good Women*, and *The Puppet Master* deal in the kind of flat narratives filled with lush characters, muted emotions, and luminous colors that tend to be more like cinematic Chekhov. With last year's mesmerizing *Cafe Lumiere* and now this, Hou has somewhat opened up to a more familiar narrative drive that will garner him some much due attention.

All the magic in the world is in the first section. Hou takes a simple, unspoken love story and fills it with textures and colors that speak of all the great simplicity of just feeling right next to someone. It sounds cheesy, but see if you don't feel the same way. Hsiao-hsien has staked his claim as one of the last living lovers of cinema's ability to tell stories without much dialogue; the silence in his films says more than a thousand Rob Reiner movies.

——Chris Cabin, Filmcritic. com

侯孝贤向来都是一个不容易被消化的导演。比如他的早期作品《海上花》、《好男好女》和《戏梦人生》，扁平的叙事、丰富的人物角色、含蓄的情感、华丽的色彩使他看起来就像电影中的契诃夫。而从去年那部催人入睡的《咖啡时光》到现在这部《最好的时光》，侯孝贤在某种程度上找到了一种更熟悉的叙事动力，它值得我们关注。

世界上最奇妙的感觉都集中到了影片的第一段中。侯孝贤把质地和色彩赋予一个简单无言的爱情故事，那种极致的纯粹就像是我们和某个人的感觉对了。这听起来有点儿玄，可你不也是这么感觉的吗？如侯孝贤自己所说，他是世界上仅存不多的喜欢让电影不依赖对话来讲故事的人之一。其静默中的内涵甚至比罗布·赖纳的电影还要丰富上千倍。

—Chris Cabin，Filmcritic 网站

I'm as open to cinematic experimentation as the next person, but I often find that "offbeat" movies come across as more successful in concept than execution. So it goes with *Three Times*, a feature that arrived at last year's 2005 Toronto Film Festival riding the crest of a wave of positive critical buzz. And, while it's impossible to deny that the film is interesting and unique, it's not the kind of motion picture that will cause the average viewer to run out and urge his friends to make a trip to one of the obscure art houses where it's playing.

*Three Times* features minimal dialogue. It is mostly about mood and images, and it moves at a glacial pace. Hou is in no hurry to speed things along. He frequently holds shots, lingering for longer than a conventional director might. A side order of a caffeinated beverage is recommended. The middle segment is an homage to the silent era. Although in color, this part is designed like a pre-talkie movie, complete with intertitles. I don't claim to have enjoyed *Three Times* in a traditional sense. I appreciated its artistry and admired its intentions, but I found the characters to be unpleasantly cold, and the filmmaker's style to be distancing. This is the kind of film that would have benefited from the forging of an emotional bond between the audience and the protagonists. Still, if you have the chance and appreciate movies that stray from the straight-and-narrow*, you could find a worse way to spend 2 1/4 hours.

—*James Berardinelli*，*Reelviews*

我和别人一样对电影的实验性持一种开放的态度，但我也常常觉得那些"不规矩"的影片能获得成功，很大程度是因概念而非结果。《最好的时光》给我的感觉就是如此，这部剧情片在去

年2005年多伦多电影节上好评如潮。虽然我们不能否定它是有趣而独特的，但它不是那种能够吸引普通观众，能让他们鼓励自己的朋友进入晦涩的艺术影院去观看的电影。

《最好的时光》的特点是对话极少。它是关于情绪和影像的，而且节奏极缓。侯孝贤对速度没有兴趣。他频繁地让摄影机停住，逗留，时间长于一个传统导演可能使用的应有长度。因此我建议你看电影的时候用咖啡提提神。影片中间那一段是对默片时代的致敬。虽然它是彩色片，但它给我们的感觉却完全是有声片之前的电影，完全依赖字幕。当然我并不是说应该用传统的感觉来欣赏《最好的时光》。我欣赏它的艺术性，尊敬它的意图，但我觉得它的人物冰冷得让人不快，那种导演风格让人觉得有距离。这就是那种可能要依赖观众和主角之间的情感联系的电影。此外，如果你有机会欣赏那种偏离正道的电影，你会找到更糟的方式来度过这二又四分之一小时。

—*James Berardinelli*，《旋风景》

> ### *Note*
>
> Straight-and-narrow：固定短语，意为诚实正派，还可引申为严守道德戒律，循规蹈矩。《马太福音》第七章第十四节有"strait and narrow"，原文为"Because strait is the gate and narrow is the way which leadeth unto life, and few there be that find it."意思是"因为引到永生的那扇门是多么的窄，路是多么的狭，能找到它的人也就少了"。

# Pan's Labyrinth

## 潘神的迷宫

**导演/编剧：**吉尔勒莫·德尔托罗（Guillermo del Toro））
  **主演：**艾凡娜·巴奎洛（Ivana Baquero）
      道格·琼斯（Doug Jones）
      瑟吉·洛佩兹（Sergi López）
      艾瑞阿娜·吉尔（Ariadna Gil）
      马里贝尔·沃杜（Maribel Verdú）
  **片长：**119 分钟
  **发行：**华纳兄弟（Warner Bros. Picturehouse），2006 年

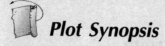

# *Plot Synopsis*

Set in rural Spain, circa 1944, Ofelia and her widowed mother, Carmen (Ariadna Gil), have just moved into an abandoned mill with Carmen's new husband, Captain Vidal (Sergi L pez). Carmen is pregnant with his son. Other than her sickly mother and kindly housekeeper Mercedes (Maribel Verd ), the dreamy Ofelia is on her own. Vidal, an exceedingly cruel man, couldn't be bothered. He has informers to torture. Ofelia soon finds that an entire universe exists below the mill. Her guide is the persuasive Faun* (Doug Jones). As her mother grows weaker, Ofelia spends more and more time in the satyr's labyrinth. He offers to help her out of her predicament if she'll complete three treacherous tasks. Ofelia is willing to try, but does this alternate reality really exist or is it all in her head?

## 剧情简介

背景是西班牙乡下,时间约 1944 年,奥菲莉娅和她寡居的母亲卡门(艾瑞阿娜·吉尔饰)刚刚搬进一座废弃的厂房,和卡门的新任丈夫维达上尉(瑟吉·洛佩兹饰)住在一起。卡门怀了他的儿子。除了陪伴有病在身的母亲和善良的女管家默西迪丝(马里贝尔·沃杜),爱幻想的奥菲莉娅大部分时间独自一人。继父维达是一个不能招惹的极端残忍的人,折磨拷打他的告密者。奥菲莉娅很快发现厂房之下有一个完整的地下王国,循循善诱的农牧神(道格·琼斯饰)充当着她的引导者。随着母亲日渐虚弱,奥菲莉娅在潘神的迷宫中度过越来越多的时间。他要求她完成三件背叛性的任务以此帮助她走出困境。奥菲莉娅愿意去努力,然而这到底是真实的还是只是她的幻想?

# *Critique*

We're often so entranced by the wonder of fairy tales that we overlook their horror. Even old folk tales that have been cleaned up and reworked over the ages still harbor relics from the days when we thought it was a good idea to rule kids by fear: Parents and step-parents with sinister hidden personalities; children who get baked into pies; winged or scaled creatures who demand impossible tasks of a hero, for reasons that are sometimes murky.

Fairy tales have their roots in very old, very deep human fears, fears that Guillermo del Toro teases out mercilessly in his ambitious, glorious and harrowing adult fairy tale "Pan's Labyrinth".

This is a somber, lovely picture, set in Franco's Spain a few years after that country's civil war. It's rich both in metaphorical terms and in literal ones. Del Toro's imagery is so vivid and concrete that it's likely to change the color of your sleep: A writhing, cooing root that's "almost" a human baby; a faceless creature with pale wrinkly skin draped over its willowy bones, its eyes located in the palms of its hands instead of in its head. Those far-side-of-sleep images (and the movie contains many others) can be read as symbols and stand-ins for other things—a nascent country that might have been; so-called leadership that's howlingly blind—but del Toro isn't playing a game of allegorical one-to-one matching here. The movie's meanings emerge from its visuals instead of being driven by them. Del Toro has mastered the delicate, difficult feat of using pure sensation to make us think.

—*Stephanie Zacharek*, *Salon. com*

　　我们常常过于陶醉在童话故事的美妙之中而忽略了它恐怖的那一面。甚至那些历经数十年被清理和改写过的古老民间传说仍然潜藏着幽暗之处,当我们喜欢用它来吓唬吓唬小孩子的时候就会明白这一点:父母或是继父母隐藏着邪恶的人格;小孩被烤进馅饼中;长着翅膀或鳞片的怪物出于阴暗的动机要求英雄去完成不可能的任务。

　　童话故事其实植根于非常古老而深远的人类恐惧中,而在《潘神的迷宫》这部宏大、沉重而悲惨的成人童话中,吉尔勒莫·德尔托罗狠心地揶揄了这种恐惧。

　　这是一部阴郁但吸引人的影片。故事发生在西班牙内战几年后的佛朗哥统治时期。无论在隐喻还是现实层面它都有着丰富的内涵。德尔托罗的想象是如此生动而具体以至于它能够改变你睡梦中的颜色:一个辗转反侧会咕咕叫的树根"几乎"就是一个婴孩;一个没有脸的怪物,苍白的皮肤堆在弯曲的骨架上满是褶皱,眼睛长在手心而不是额头上。这些睡梦中幽深的形象(影片中还有很多)可以当作是种种象征——一个本来会存在的初生国家;一个自大盲目的所谓的领袖——当然德尔托罗的讽喻不一定是一一对应的。影片的意义通过这些形象显现出来,但并不受其限制。德尔托罗精细地、高难度地用情感来促进我们思考。

—*Stephanie Zacharek*,《沙龙》

This is an exceptionally difficult movie to describe, never mind assess. On one hand, it has the simplistic charm of a old-fashioned fairy tale, with high stakes, magical and arbitrary rules, and an easily manipulated heroine. On the other hands, it is a depiction of a brutal despot's heartless greed for an heir and power over his countrymen in unstable 1944 Spain. Is the juxtaposition a statement on the importance of beauty, magic, hope, and wonder for a peaceful world, or are we witnessing an escapist fantasy of a traumatized child?

Visually (if you can get past horrors like men being punched to death with a bottle or someone stitching up his own face), the movie is darkly glorious. It's shot beautifully, even though some scenes seemed gratuitously amazing. For example, a creepy creature in one of Ofelia's mythic tasks seems only to have the purpose of starring in "freaky, dude, let's go see that" publicity photos. Pan himself is incredible. He's all bark and fairy circles, moss and goaty guile. The score by Javier Navarrette is delicious, very different and interesting, well in keeping with the rest of the film.

The real-life intrigues on the real world surface held more tension for me than the fantasy sections (if only because we know how they will turn out, even with obstacles), and there was much more of the mundane world's tense brutality than I expected. Certainly we fear for Ofelia in her quests, but at least the mythological world is predictable in its rules and behaviors (even when they trick you). The Captain is terrifying in his unpredictability and relentlessness.

It is hard to say, "I recommend this movie," despite its strong craft and unique style, if only because it is so rough, tragic, and e-motionally draining. It is excellently made, and I am very glad I saw it, but I could never see it again, no matter how cool the faun

was. Ivana Baquero（Ofelia）does a fantastic job carrying this movie, and Sergi Lopez is more than terrifying as a personage. It's true
that a life without magic is a cold one indeed, but this magic has a
terrible beauty to fear of its own.

*—Karina Montgomery, Cinerina*

这是一部极难描述的电影，更不要说评价它。一方面，它具有一个老式童话故事那种分外单纯的吸引力，比如那利害攸关、魔幻又专横的法则和那容易被操纵的女主人公。另一方面，它刻画了一个1944年西班牙动荡期的暴君，他残忍又贪婪地控制人民的权力以及一个继承人。这种双关究竟是为了强调美、奇迹、希望以及渴望和平的重要性，还是我们见证的是一个心灵遭受创伤的孩子逃避现实的幻想？

影片在视觉上黑暗血腥（除非当你看到某人被一只瓶子活活砸死或者某人自己缝自己的脸时，你能忍受那种恐惧）。影片拍得很美，虽然有些场景令人惊异得莫名其妙。比如说，奥菲莉娅的魔幻任务中有一只没有意义的爬行怪物，好像只为出现在宣传照片上招徕观众，"多么古怪的家伙，让我们去看看吧！"潘神这个形象不可思议。他为什么那么咆哮而扭捏，身上长着苔藓，阴阳怪气又奸诈呢。Javier Navarrette做的音乐很好听，陌生而有趣，与影片结合得很好。

对我来说，影片在现实层面的种种阴谋比幻想的层面更有张力（因为我们知道故事会怎样展开，即使它设置了障碍），而其中的观实世界甚至比我想象得还要残忍野蛮得多。我们当然也为奥菲莉娅的冒险担心，但是毕竟神话世界的规则和行为是可以预见的（即使遭受戏弄的时候）。而维达上尉的可怕则是不可捉摸和冷酷无情的。

"我推荐这部片子"这句话很难说出口，虽然它艺术性强、风格独特，但它实在太粗野、太悲惨，过于宣泄情绪了。该片确

实制作精良，我也很喜欢看，但不论那潘神有多酷，我也决不会
再看第二遍。艾凡娜·巴奎洛（奥菲莉娅）在该片中表现惊人，
而瑟吉·洛佩兹几乎可怕得不像人类。虽然说缺乏魔幻色彩的生
活是单调乏味的，但是这一魔幻的美却恐怖得连自己都难以面
对。

—*Karina Montgomery*，　*Cinerina*

　　Guillermo del Toro's "Pan's Labyrinth" is an adult fairy tale
where fantasy and reality are indistinguishable and can be read either
literally or as metaphor. But del Toro is very much pushing the "either" in the either/or equation, blurring the lines beautifully to
show that the boundaries between what we see as reality and make-
believe don't exist at all.

　　It's del Toro's sixth and most successful movie to date and can
be seen as something of a sibling to his previous career best, 2001's
"The Devil's Backbone". Both films are set during the Spanish
Civil War and feature children who venture into magical worlds to
retreat from the peril created by evil father figures.

　　As the film shuttles between the two worlds, del Toro introduces a host of creatures and situations straight from fairy tales and
children's literature, all of which are filtered through his own keen
sense of magic and horror. This isn't kids' stuff, though adventure-
some teens would find plenty here to engage them. It's dark poetry
set to startling images, a one-of-a-kind nightmare that has a soaring,
spiritual center. It's not to be missed.

—*Glenn Whipp*, *Los Angels Daily News*

吉尔勒莫·德尔托罗的《潘神的迷宫》是一部成人童话，幻想和现实在其中纠缠难辨，解读它的办法是既可以当作是真实的，也可以当作是隐喻。不过德尔托罗把这两个层面混淆得太漂亮了，它们之间的界线模糊难觅，这表明了真幻之间根本没有分别。

这是德尔托罗迄今第六部也是最成功的影片，也可以看作是他此前最优秀的影片《鬼童院》（2001 年）的姊妹片。它们都以西班牙内战为背景，讲一个孩子从邪恶的父亲所布下的危险中逃脱出来，在魔幻的世界中冒险的故事。

当影片在两个世界中穿梭时，德尔托罗直接从神话故事和儿童文学中引入了一大批怪物和经典情景，并用自己对魔幻和恐怖的敏锐感觉过滤了它们。即使那些热衷于冒险的青少年对影片中的很多地方会青睐有加，但这并不是小孩子看的东西。在那令人震惊的影像背后是一首黑暗之诗，一个有着飞升的精神核心的梦魇。你不该错过它。

—*Glenn Whipp*，《洛杉矶每日新闻》

> **Note**
>
> Faun：古罗马传说中半人半羊的农牧神，专门照顾牧人和猎人、以及农人和住在乡野的人，呈人形，有角、耳朵、尾巴，有时还有羊腿。

# Brokeback Mountain

# 断背山

导演：李安（Ang Lee）

原著：安妮·普露（Annie Proulx）

主演：希斯·莱吉尔（Heath Ledger）

杰克·吉伦哈尔（Jake Gyllenhaal）

米歇尔·威廉姆斯（Michelle Williams）

安妮·海瑟薇（Anne Hathaway）

片长：134 分钟

发行：焦点出品（Focus Features），2005 年

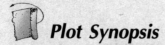

# *Plot Synopsis*

In the Summer of 1963 Wyoming, two young men, Ennis a ranch hand and Jack an aspiring rodeo bull rider, are sent to work together herding sheep on Brokeback Mountain, and what had otherwise been anticipated to be a rather uneventful venture, will soon turn into an affair of love, of lust, and complications that will spand through 19 years of their lives through marriage, through children, and through the mighty grip of societal confines and the expectations of what it is to be a man.

## 剧情简介

1963年夏天的怀俄明州，两个年轻人，农场帮工艾尼斯和有活力的牛仔杰克被派往断背山上一起放羊。这本来应是一段平静无波的生活，但不料两人却很快发展出一种爱欲情仇复杂纠缠的关系，并影响了他们此后19年的生活，与他们的婚姻、孩子、社会限制的重压，以及世俗对男人的期望做种种博弈。

# Critique

"Brokeback Mountain", Ang Lee's much-anticipated modern Western, is an extremely subtle and touching love story about two cowboys, splendidly played by Heath Ledger and Jake Gyllenhaal. A sweeping epic with the scope of George Stevens' "Giant" and the unabashed romanticism of "Wuthering Heights", "Brokeback Mountain" is at once a uniquely American and universal story, one that goes beyond the realm of queer romance or gay cowboy picture.

Lee has handled gay-themed satires (the delicious "Wedding Banquet"), violent Westerns (the ambitious but disappointing "Ride With the Devil") and literary romances (the accomplished "Sense and Sensibility"), but he has never before treated all these elements as delicately as he does in "Brokeback Mountain", his best work to date. It may be the first time that Lee shows such complete and commendable control over every aspect of his film, from the narrative to the mise-en-scene to the visual look and music.

Coming right after the failure of "The Hulk", the misconceived comic strip, "Brokeback Mountain" redeems Lee's reputation as a versatile director, one who continues to show impressive talent in depicting multi-nuanced relationships in various locales. Auteurist critics will have hard time to detect consistent themes or styles in the career of Lee, who hops effortlessly from genre to genre.

The movie is based on Pulitzer prize-winner Annie Proulx's 1997 short story, "Brokeback Mountain", first published in the *New Yorker* and later printed in her 1999 collection, "Close Range:

Wyoming Stories". For years, "Brokeback" was known in Hollywood as one of the "great unproduced" screenplays. Producers were simply afraid of its subject and strong emotions, which may explain why it took eight years for the story to reach the big screen.

It's a pleasure to report that the screenwriters, Pulitzer Prize-winner Larry McMurtry and his writing partner Diana Ossana, have met the challenge of taking a spare, brief tale and have vastly expanded its scope while still maintaining its spirit.

Even so, as powerful as the source material is, it's the direction, acting, and production values that give the movie shape and heart. "Brokeback Mountain" is one contemporary film that cannot be charged with being cynical or ironic. And though grounded in a specific historical era and locale, the movie has undeniable universal appeal. In many ways, it's an old-fashioned saga about two individuals (who happen to be cowboys and gay) fighting to preserve their love against great odds.

*—Emanuel Levy, Emanuellevy. com*

《断背山》是让人期待已久的李安眼中的现代西方，是两个牛仔之间细腻动人至极的爱情故事，希斯·莱吉尔和杰克·吉伦哈尔把它演绎得动人心魄。《断背山》兼有乔治·史蒂文斯《巨人传》（1957 年）的宏大史诗视野和《呼啸山庄》那种不顾一切的浪漫，这使它立刻超越了同性之谊和牛仔之恋的境界，而成为一个独特的关于美国甚至是世界性的故事。

李安曾经处理过的电影题材有同性恋讽刺（有趣的《喜宴》），西方暴力（有野心但却令人失望的《与魔鬼共骑》），浪漫文学（有造诣的《理智与情感》），但他从来没有把这些元素处理得像《断背山》这么细致，从而成就了他迄今最优秀的作品。这是他第一次把电影的叙事、调度、视觉、音乐等方方面面控制得滴水不漏，令人赞叹。

紧接着对漫画《绿巨人》差强人意的改编，《断背山》挽回了李安作为通才导演的盛誉，并再次展示了他在不同环境下多角度刻画复杂情感关系的那种惊人的天分。李安是那种可以在各种类型中自由出入的导演，以至于作者论的批评家们很难在他的电影生涯中找到一以贯之的主题和风格。

电影改编自普利策奖获得者安妮·普露 1997 年的同名短篇故事，首度发表于《纽约客》，后来收入她 1999 年的文集《近距离：怀俄明故事》中。多年以来，《断背山》在好莱坞是众所周知的不能碰的剧本。制片人纯粹是害怕它的题材和那种强烈的感情，因此它望穿秋水了八年才与大银幕结缘。

值得高兴的是，影片的编剧，普利策奖获得者拉里·麦克莫特里和他的搭档黛安娜·欧莎娜战胜了挑战，他们简约地保留了原著的精华，并尽可能地拓展了它的境界。

不过，虽然原始素材那样有力量，但最终是导演、表演和制作一起塑造出了影片的形状，并赋予它灵魂。《断背山》并不是一部愤世嫉俗或讽刺人情世故的当代电影。虽然它以特定的历史时期和环境为背景，但你不能否认它那种世界性的诉求。某种意义上，这是关于两个人（只不过碰巧是牛仔和同性恋而已）为了爱情而向巨大的阻碍做抗争的一个古老传奇。

—*Emanuel Levy* 个人网站

While the notion of gay cowboys may induce some sniggering in the back row, *Brokeback Mountain* is a masterclass in subtle directing. That's not to say Ang Lee shies away from sex; indeed the passion between the lovers is shockingly brutal. But it's a testament to his sensitive handling, and fearlessly vulnerable performances by Jake Gyllenhaal and Heath Ledger, that this love story between two ranch hands stands for something essentially human. It is both raw and exquisite.

Ennis' ambiguity bleeds through the story with quiet foreboding. Each time he rebuffs Jack, he slips deeper within himself and Ledger plays it in every physical gesture—literally hunched in the shadow of his Stetson*. In some ways Gyllenhaal is more sympathetic as the incorrigible optimist, but there is always an aching claustrophobia about their predicament, poignantly offset by sweeping mountain vistas. The images reflect the heartbreak and beauty of a tortured love affair and, without resorting to pat sentimentality, Lee builds to a stirring and soulful finale. *Brokeback Mountain* is a truly epic romance story from a director at the peak of his powers.

——*Stella Papamichael*, *BBC*


　　牛仔同性恋这个概念可能会让某些观众在座位上窃笑，不过《断背山》确实是一部功夫细腻的大师之作。这并不是说李安避开了性这一主题，事实上影片中两个爱人之间的激情原始得让人震惊。话说回来，这也是对导演敏锐的处理能力，以及希斯·莱吉尔和杰克·吉伦哈尔无畏忘我的表演能力的一种证明，这让发生在两个农场工人之间的爱情显现出一种深刻的人性。它既是粗犷的，又是纤细的。

　　艾尼斯的被动中有一种冥冥的预感贯穿在故事中。他拒绝杰克一次，也就陷入得更深一寸，这一点被莱吉尔通过每个细微的动作传达出来——他在牛仔帽的阴影下弯下腰去。而在很多方面吉伦哈尔把一个不可救药的乐天派演绎得更富于同情心，不过他常常要忍耐和压抑住他们的困境和痛苦，然后去山里释放掉。影片映照出一段饱受折磨的爱情的那种心碎和美好，它并不让你一味感伤，相反地，李安赋予了它一个令人欣慰的升华的结局。总之，《断背山》是一个导演在他颠峰时期创作的一部确信无疑的浪漫史诗。

——*Stella Papamichael*, *BBC*


It isn't easy to make a first-rate tearjerker, but it can be done:

one need think only of David Lean's classic "Brief Encounter" (1945), and more recently Clint Eastwood's surprisingly effective "The Bridges of Madison County" (1995) as examples. Ang Lee's remarkable "Brokeback Mountain" joins the select group.

In its basic outline the story couldn't be much simpler—or more familiar. Two people have a short, spontaneous and hopeless sexual encounter and then separate, each marrying someone else and building a family. Yet their attraction to one another is irresistible, and they meet periodically over the years for brief, intense moments together. Ultimately, though, tragedy intervenes.

The twist in this telling of the tale, of course, is that the doomed lovers are both male. Not that such a circumstance is totally unheard of on film. This is, however, the first time it's been done in a major picture by an A-list director and with well-known stars; it doesn't come from one of the major studios, but isn't far from one. And the fact that the men are young cowboys—iconic figures of virility and strength—adds to the sense of provocation some will feel about it.

But ultimately this story of suppressed passion is, irrespective of gender considerations, a deeply moving, indeed lacerating, film. Though many commentators, and more importantly, viewers, may concentrate on the fact that the lovers are both men, that's really a secondary consideration in a narrative that succeeds beautifully merely because it's deeply human and profoundly real—and, of course, because in this incarnation it's also insightfully written, sensitively (some would say too sensitively) directed, and superbly acted. Within the "gay" genre, "Brokeback Mountain" is a triumph; but the fact that it extends that genre's boundaries only adds to its power.

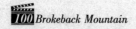

*—Frank Swietek, One Guy's Opinion*

拍出一部能够催人泪下的一流电影并非易事，但仍有可能：你只要想想大卫·里恩的《相见恨晚》（1945），以及更近一点的克林特·伊斯特伍德感人至深的《廊桥遗梦》（1995）等例子就知道了。李安的非凡之作《断背山》就可以和它们相媲美。

故事的基本轮廓再简单，再熟悉不过了。两个人迸发有了一段短暂、自然而又无望的爱欲后各奔东西，各自与他人结婚并组建家庭。但他们不可抗拒地彼此吸引，此后经年，他们定期相会，共渡苦短而幸福的时刻。然而悲剧最终降临了。

这个故事中特拧的一点，当然是这对宿命的爱人都是男性。这种情形以前的影片也不是没涉及过，然而，这却是头一次进入主流电影，并集合了一线导演和著名影星。虽然它并不是大制片厂出品的，不过相去不远。还有这两个年轻牛仔形象，他们身上的那种男子气概和力量，某些人可能会从中感到一种刺激和冒犯的东西。

然而最终，这个关于压抑的激情的故事是可以不顾性别禁忌的。它感人肺腑，深深地刺痛了我们。一些批评家和权威影评人对其中两个男人的同性之谊颇有顾忌，不过这对一部叙事完美的作品实在不足虑——因为它深刻的人性和伟大的真实，因为它富有洞见的剧本、敏感细腻（有人甚至觉得太敏感了）的导演、叹为观止的表演。在"同性恋"类型中，《断背山》是一次胜利，而事实上它用力量超越了这种类型的界限。

*—Frank Swietek*，个人观点

> **Note**
>
> Stetson：Stetson 本来是一种具有高顶阔边毡帽的商标，后来这个词泛指牛仔戴的宽边帽。

# Match Point

# 赛末点

**导演：** 伍迪·艾伦（Woody Allen）

**主演：** 斯嘉丽·约翰逊（Scarlett Johansson）

乔纳森·莱斯·迈耶斯（Jonathan Rhys-Mey）

艾米莉·莫泰默尔（Emily Mortimer）

马修·古德（Matthew Goode）

**片长：** 95 分钟

**发行：** 梦工厂（DreamWorks Pictures），2006 年

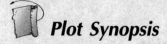

# Plot Synopsis

Tennis pro Chris Wilton takes a job as a tennis instructor and hits it off immediately with one of his students, wealthy young Tom Hewitt. Tom introduces Chris to his family and Chris falls quickly into a romance with Tom's sister Chloe. But despite the growing certainty that Chris and Chloe will marry, and the enormous professional and financial advantages that come Chris's way through his relationship with the family, Chris becomes increasingly intrigued and eventually romantically involved with Tom's fiancée, Nola Rice, a struggling American actress. Their passionate trysts leave Chris in danger of losing the wealth and position he has now come to enjoy. The only solution to the dilemma seems unthinkable.

## 剧情简介

网球手克里斯·威尔顿找到一份教练工作,并很快与他的学生汤姆·海威特,一个富有的年轻人成了好朋友。克里斯被汤姆介绍给家人,又迅速地和汤姆的妹妹克罗伊坠入爱河。然而,虽然克里斯和克罗伊的婚姻正在逐渐敲定,联姻也给他的职业和经济上带来莫大的好处,但是克里斯却一发不可收拾地迷上了汤姆的未婚妻诺拉·莱丝,一个孤军奋斗的美国女演员。他们频频激情幽会,这使克里斯面临着失去他贪恋已久的财富和地位的危险。解决这个困境的唯一方案似乎是不敢想象的。

## *Critique*

*Match Point* is a cool, classically elegant and concise film that addresses all of the big questions—love, morality, death, fate, chance—without ever seeming heavy or self-conscious. I've never seen a Woody Allen film to match it. As a matter of fact, I can't remember another film of late that I thought was quite this good. From the opening shot, the film draws you in and doesn't let up, moving from shot to shot with a fine sense of rhythm and a narrative drive that builds the viewer's curiosity through a series of unexpected switchbacks. Rhys-Meyers is superb as an ex-professional tennis player from a poor Irish background who has turned social climber. Too proud to accept a favor from his upper class friends without immediately offering to pay it back, he affects an interest in opera and Strindberg*. The viewer at once sympathizes with him and winces as he strains to seem refined and self-assured. Allen has put together a superb cast of young actors who bring his near flawless script to life so convincingly that one almost immediately suspends disbelief and becomes absorbed in the story. The shots of London are luxuriant and spacious, never self-indulgent. Few films, novels, or plays manage to form such rich dramatic material out of characters' inner obstacles. A classic piece of drama that reaches toward the likes of Shakespeare and Dostoevksy, every facet—from structure to dialog to editing to sound—is brought off with panache. This is not only Allen at his best but an example of what the cinematic medium is capable of when properly exploited.

—*Trevor Merrill, Imbd. com*

《赛末点》是一部冷静、古典而简约的电影，它覆盖了人生所有的大问题——爱情、道德、死亡、命运、偶然，但是在态度上并没有刻意地沉重起来或端起架子。我从没见过伍迪·艾伦有哪部片子可以比得上这一部。事实上，我都想不起最近还有哪部影片和《赛末点》一样好。影片从第一个镜头开始就紧抓住你不放，其镜头切换具有良好的节奏感，叙事动力充满出人意料的曲折，能不断激发你的好奇心。莱斯·迈耶斯极好地刻画出了一个爱尔兰穷人出身的职业网球手在社会中往上爬的形象。他大方地接受上流社会朋友的恩惠并不急于回报，还学会了热爱歌剧和斯特林堡。观众很快为他装优雅、装自信的努力感到同情和难过。艾伦用一批出色的年轻演员让人信服地实现了他完美的剧本构思，从而让观众立刻有了悬念，并全神贯注地投入故事之中。镜头里的伦敦看起来奢华而开阔，但又疏离而不自我沉溺。很少有电影、小说或戏剧会有意识地在人物的内在冲突之外创造出如此意蕴丰富的戏剧性环境。《赛末点》是一出在结构、对话、剪辑、声音等方方面面都精致华美的戏剧经典，比较接近莎士比亚和陀斯妥耶夫斯基的作品。这不只是艾伦最好的作品，它还恰到好处地拓展了电影媒介的表达可能性。

—*Trevor Merrill*，*Imbd* 网站

You could say that Woody Allen, by shifting his milieu from New York's Upper East Side to London's elegant Belgravia*, has not so much re-invented himself* (as some have suggested) as gone back to the motherland of the Wasp* good taste he's always aspired to. But there's no need to be rude. Whatever Allen's needs or motives, a change of light and scenery was obviously good for him. His new movie, "Match Point", devoted to lust, adultery, and murder, is the most vigorous thing he's done in years.

The way Chris "solves" his problem—by murdering one of the women—seems to have struck a number of the movie's early viewers as unbelievable. After all, they say, this is modern life, and these things can be worked out. But intelligent people do occasionally commit murder, and not just in fictions concocted by Patricia

Highsmith or P. D. James. If "Match Point" gives offense, the real reason, I suspect, is not that it's implausible but that it forces us into complicity with a killer. Filmmakers understand the laws of narrative all too well: an audience, properly hooked by point-of-view shooting, will root for a bank robber or a murderer to get away with whatever he's doing. Chris Wilton lies to everyone, grows more and more desperate, and, as he plans and pulls off a terrible crime, we are with him at every step. In the end, Allen returns to the role of luck and to an old obsession from "Crimes and Misdemeanors" —the question of whether there is any justice in the universe. But the abstract talk is just window dressing. "Match Point" is, at its core, the latest version of a story that has served as a bedrock of fiction for almost two hundred years: a young man from the provinces storms the big city with boldness and sexual charm and then gets in trouble. And we're left, as always, identifying with his desire and regretting its consequences—which means, willy-nilly, chastening our own desire, too.

—*David Denby*, *The New Yorker*

你可能要说，虽然伍迪·艾伦把他的居住环境从纽约的上东区换成了伦敦优雅的贝尔格莱维亚——他一直向往的"Wasp"上流品味的发源地，但他的本性并没有随之改变多少（如某些人曾指出）。不过不要太武断，不管艾伦的需要和动机如何，换换环境显然对他有好处。他的新片《赛末点》围绕着对欲望、通奸和谋杀的叙事，是他近年来最有活力的作品。

影片中克里斯解决问题的方式——杀掉那个女人，似乎让很多人在突然间难以置信。毕竟他们认为，这是现代社会，事情终究会解决的。不过智商高的人偶尔是会去杀人的，不只在帕特里西亚·海史密斯或 P·D·詹姆斯的小说里。如果《赛末点》引起我们的反感，我想真正的原因并不是它不可信，而是它让我们卷入了对一个凶手的认同中。电影制作人对叙事规律是了如指掌的：当观众恰如其分地投入主观镜头时，他们会站在银行抢劫犯或杀人犯这一边，而对其所作所为视而不见。克里斯·威尔顿对每个人撒谎，越来越变本加厉，而且当他计划并施行那桩可怕的谋杀时，每一步行动我们都和他在一起。结尾时，艾伦回到他对运气的思考和"爱与罪"的老问题上——正义是否真的存在？不过那深奥的谈话不过是哗众取宠而已。在本质上，《赛末点》是一个老故事的最新版本，这个故事的内核已经在小说中演绎了将近两百年：一个从外地到大城市来的年轻人靠大胆和性感征服了这座城市，然后惹上了麻烦。我们总是在旁观中认同于他的欲望，并惋惜他的结果——而这实际上也使我们在犹豫迟疑中磨炼了自己的欲望。

—*David Denby*,《纽约客》

Woody Allen returns to one of his favorite themes—infidelity—in "Match Point" (do you suppose it might carry some personal significance for him?), but with a change of accent. The picture is set not in his usual upper-crust New York City haunts, but in those of London instead. The dialogue is thus spoken not in Americanese but in crisp British tones. And that's not all. One of the plot devices has to do with the characters' devotion to opera, and the tale of lust and longing is accompanied musically by snippets of Italian arias rather than the jazzy stuff he ordinarily prefers. (He is true to form, however, in preferring scratchy old recordings—mostly those of Caruso—to more modern ones.)

As usual with Allen's movies, the purely physical aspects of "Match Point" are fine without being outstanding. One peculiar element, however, involves the periodic scenes in which characters attend operatic performances: the singers seem always to be accompanied by solo piano rather than the expected full orchestra. Is there any particular dramatic point to this, or is it merely a sign of budgetary constraints? Whatever the reason, it's an appropriate musical metaphor for the fact that as a whole the movie comes across as a bit thin, too. To adopt the terminology the script uses in its opening explanation of luck on the court, while not as awful as some of Allen's flubs, this film is one of those instances in which the cinematic ball doesn't quite make it over the net.

—*Frank Swietek*, *One Guy's Opinion*

伍迪·艾伦在《赛末点》中又回到了他热衷的主题——失贞（你认为这对他个人有些什么重要意义吗?）上，不过这次改了口音。影片的背景不再是他电影中常见的纽约上流社会，而是换成了伦敦的上流社会。因此人物的对话也相应地由美音变成了抑扬顿挫的英音。还不只如此。某些情节设置还要和人物对歌剧的热爱挂上钩，背景音乐要选择意大利咏叹调片断来搭配这个围绕着情欲和贪婪的叙事，而不是他一直喜欢的爵士乐（不过老实说，他更喜欢用那些粗糙的老唱片——大部分都是卡罗素的，而不是现代一点的）。

正如艾伦电影一贯的那样，《赛末点》在电影质地上也就是过得去，并不十分出色。不过有个地方值得注意，片中反复出现的人物常去欣赏歌剧演出的场景：歌唱演员的伴奏似乎总是钢琴独奏而不是理所应当的交响乐。这到底是出于某种戏剧表达的需要，还只是因为预算的限制？无论什么原因，这是一个恰当的音乐隐喻，表明影片在整体上有些单薄。借用剧本开头解释球场运气的术语来说，虽然《赛末点》并不像艾伦的某些败笔那么糟糕，但它是电影的"球"没有打过网的例子之一。

—*Frank Swietek*，个人观点

Despite four Golden Globe nominations, Woody's first flick shot entirely in Britain seems to be lacking something. Maybe it's because we never feel connected to any of his characters. Maybe it's because "Match Point" is a tale of romance, albeit dysfunctional, that's built on lust and convenience rather than true love. Maybe it's because even when the British are bad, they still come off nice.

"Match Point" isn't Allen's best project ("Take the Money and Run") and not his worst ("Soon-Yi Previn"). Instead, it's somewhere in the middle.

*—Mike Ward, Richmond. com*

　　虽然获得了四项金球奖提名，伍迪头一部完全以英国作背景的电影却好像少了点儿什么。可能是因为从来不觉得那些人物和我们有什么关系；可能是因为《赛末点》的浪漫故事有些畸形，它讲的是情欲和捷径，而不是真爱；可能是因为即便那些英国人品质恶劣，他们仍能体面收场。

　　《赛末点》既不是艾伦最好的作品（《傻瓜入狱记》，1969），也不是最糟的（宋宜·普里文，艾伦前妻的养女，后来嫁给艾伦）。它处在中不溜的位置上。

*—Mike Ward，Richmond* 网站

---

## *Note*

　　Strindberg：斯特林堡（Johan August strindberg 1849 - 1912），瑞典戏剧家、小说家。生于斯德哥尔摩。他的戏剧在世界文坛上享有盛誉，如有自然主义手法写的独幕剧《朱丽小姐》（1888）、用象征主义手法写的《通向大马士革之路》（1890 - 1904）、室内剧《鬼魂奏鸣曲》（1907）等。自传体长篇小说《在海边》（1890）也很著名。

　　Upper East Side：上东区，是纽约传统的富人区。

　　Belgravia：贝尔格莱维亚，伦敦的上流住宅区（位于伦敦海德公园附近）。

　　Wasp："白种安格鲁撒克逊新教徒"的英文缩写。

# Little Miss Sunshine

# 阳光小美女

**导演:** 乔纳森·戴顿 (Jonathan Dayton)
　　　维莱莉·法瑞斯 (Valerie Faris)
**编剧:** 迈克尔·安特 (Michael Arndt)
**主演:** 艾比盖尔·贝斯林 (Abigail Breslin)
　　　保罗·达诺 (Paul Dano)
　　　艾伦·阿金 (Alan Arkin)
　　　托妮·柯利特 (Toni Collette)
　　　格雷戈·金尼尔 (Greg Kinnear)
　　　史蒂夫·卡莱尔 (Steven Carell)
**片长:** 101 分钟
**发行:** 福克斯探照灯公司 (Fox Searchlight Pictures), 2006 年

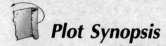

# *Plot Synopsis*

Dad Richard (Greg Kinnear) is a motivational speaker who can't win over his own kin. Working mom Sheryl (Toni Collette) is the juggler who tries to gratify everyone. Brother-in-law Frank (Steve Carell) is the nation's foremost authority on Marcel Proust, at least in his mind, and the dumpee in an affair that led to a suicide attempt.

The unnamed Grandpa (Alan Arkin) snorts heroin and peruses porn. Son Dwayne (Paul Dano) reads Nietzsche and has taken a vow of silence until he's admitted to the U. S. Air Force Academy, where he expects to become a jet pilot. And little daughter Olive (adorable Abigail Breslin) finds out at the last minute that she's qualified for the Little Miss Sunshine pageant in California; it seems the girl who beat her out at the regionals had an encounter with diet pills.

## 剧情简介

爸爸理查德（格雷戈·金尼尔）是一个连自己的家人都说服不了的职业演讲人。全职妈妈谢乐尔（托妮·柯利特）想方设法地让每个人高兴。妹夫弗兰克（史蒂夫·卡莱尔）是全国最权威的马赛尔·普鲁斯特专家，至少他自己认为是，而且因为在恋爱中被抛弃而试图自杀。

没有名字的爷爷（艾伦·阿金）吸食毒品，看色情杂志。儿子韦恩（保罗·达诺）阅读尼采，并发誓沉默到底，除非他能够如愿地进入美国空军学校做飞行员。还有小女儿奥莉芙（可爱的艾比盖尔·贝斯林）在最后一分钟发现她有资格参加加州"阳光小美女"的选美盛会，而在众人之面暴露无遗的她好像遇到了减肥问题。

## *Critique*

American dysfunction! Is there anything more comically inspiring than a hard, hilarious look at the reality behind this ruling cliché? For all the exaggerations in Michael Arndt's script (jauntily directed by the husband-wife team of Jonathan Dayton and Valerie Faris), it comes closer to the truth about the way people really live—on the edge of fantasy-driven desperation—than our sanctimonies permit us to think.

The whole Hoover bunch piles into a Volkswagen bus so that Olive can take her shot at the Miss Sunshine crown. The vehicle is a perfect symbol of the family's tenuous grip on reality: only the third and fourth gears are functioning. That metaphor is pitch-perfect, but the film works a little too hard at proving the vileness of beauty pageants. When the M. C. (Matt Winston) croons *God Bless America* into the contestants' innocent ears, he pretty much summarizes American awfulness. It is a broad and fertile field, and the Hoover family plows it desperately in a comedy that touches on blackness without surrendering to it.

—*Richard Schickel*, *Time Magazine*

多么畸形的美国人!还有什么比用犀利调笑的眼光来打量千篇一律的主流生活更滑稽更刺激呢?迈克尔·安特的剧本(很高兴地由乔纳森·戴顿和维莱莉·法瑞斯这个"夫妻档"执导)的种种夸张都接近于人们现实生活的某种真实——处在幻想和绝望的边缘上——比我们自欺欺人的判断要尖锐得多。

为了能让奥莉芙在"阳光小姐"中露脸,胡弗一家人跳进一辆面包车中开始了旅程。这个交通工具是对这个家庭现状的一种

绝妙的象征：只有第三个或第四个轮子能够正常工作。这个隐喻
已经很完美了，可惜影片在声讨选美活动的恶劣上有点用力过
多。当马特·温斯顿低声吟唱的《上帝保佑美国》传入了竞争者
无辜的耳朵时，他几乎提炼出了美国人的劣根性。这是一段幽深
地带，胡弗一家在一部喜剧中竭尽所能的挖掘它，他们碰到了黑
暗之处，但是没有屈服。

—*Richard Schickel*，《时代》杂志

"Little Miss Sunshine" is all about failure—personal failure,
public failure, professional failure, romantic failure, car failure, eye
failure, even heart failure. And yet the film, from newcomers Jonathan Dayton and Valerie Faris, is a winner.

This trippy, caustically funny road movie—a smash at last
winter's Sundance Film Festival—is one of the brightest (and dar-
kest) comedies to hit theaters in awhile.

Dysfunction is a river that runs through "Little Miss Sunshine", but so do the characters' unexpected moments of humanity, caring and understanding, which keep the film from being the
black comedy it otherwise might have been. The actors also serve
that end, with Carell, Dano and the marvelous Breslin striking a
comparatively calming balance against the manic heat provided by
Collette, Kinnear and Arkin.

In the end, "Sunshine" embraces an increasingly manufac-
tured, self-consciousness wackiness that strains believability, but
since believability seems beyond the point when the point is buried
in metaphor—much like their van, this clan continues to chug a-
long in spite of so many stripped gears—it doesn't harm the entertaining outcome, which is a free-wheeling blast.

—*Christopher Smith*, *Bangor Daily News*

　　《阳光小美女》讲述了一切的失败——个人的失败、公众的失败、职业的失败、爱情的失败、车的失败、眼睛的失败，甚至心脏的失败。但是出于新人乔纳森·戴顿和维莱莉·法瑞斯之手的影片本身，却是一名胜利者。

　　这部奇幻、尖刻、好笑的公路片（在去年冬天的圣丹斯电影节上大放异彩）是最明亮也最黑暗的喜剧之一，观众能被它一击即中。

　　畸形之河贯穿着《阳光小美女》，但是人物偶尔出人意料地闪耀着仁慈、同情和理解的光芒，这让影片脱掉了本来会加在头上的"黑色喜剧"的帽子。所有演员也都善始善终，相对冷静的卡莱尔、达诺、不可思议的贝斯林和狂躁不安的柯利特、金尼尔和阿金之间达成了一种平衡之感。

　　最后要说，《阳光小美女》那种程度渐深、刻意而自觉的疯癫古怪损伤了它的可信度，不过可信似乎不是问题，因为它有一种隐喻在其中——就像他们那辆破车，哪怕那么多轮子都坏了，这家人仍然会吱吱呀呀地前行。这一点都没有妨碍影片的娱乐性，它是一次随心所欲的宣泄。

　　　　　　　　　　　　——*Christopher Smith*，《班戈每日新闻》

　　A dysfunctional family, led by a workaholic patriarch, take a road trip, and the journey mends their wounds. This was the premise of one of 2006's most mirthless comedies, the formulaic "RV". As if to prove that God is in the details, along comes "Little Miss Sunshine". Same premise. Totally different results. This indie, a sweet, tart and smart satire about a family of losers in a world obsessed with winning, is an authentic crowd pleaser. There's been no more satisfying American comedy this year.

　　These are juicy roles, and the sterling cast makes the most of them, meshing into a wonderfully eccentric ensemble. Screenwriter Michael Arendt and the husband-and-wife directing team of Jonathan Dayton and Valerie Faris bring the Hoovers to life with swift, psychologically astute strokes and precise comic timing. Remarkably, this is his first screenplay and their first feature. "Little Miss Sunshine" won both the audience and critics awards at Sundance this year. That's usually the kiss of death: too feel-good Sundance phenoms fizzled in the real world. (Anybody remember "Happy, Texas"? "The Spitfire Grill"?) This one's the real deal.

—_David Ansen, News Week_

一个畸形的家庭在一位工作狂家长的带领下实践了一次公路之旅，而旅行则治疗了他们的创伤。它是 2006 年最忧郁的喜剧之一、公式化的房车之旅的预设。《阳光小美女》应运而生，好像是为了证明上帝存在于细节之中。不过虽然它和《房车之旅》的假设相同，结果却迥异。这部独立制作用一种温暖而尖酸机巧的讽刺刻画了我们世界中一个痴迷成功的失败者之家，它无疑会博得大众的好感。这是今年最令人满意的美国喜剧。

这些角色栩栩如生，而且那无可挑剔的演员阵容让大部分人物组成了令人惊叹的古怪合奏。编剧迈克尔·安特联合夫妻导演乔纳森·戴顿和维莱莉·法瑞斯用敏锐的心理触碰和精确的喜剧节奏生动地创造出了胡弗这家人。引人注目的是，这是他们的第一个剧本，也是第一个剧情片。在今年的圣丹斯电影节中，《阳光小美女》同时赢得了观众和评论界的好评。这通常是死神之吻：自我感觉过于良好的圣丹斯人才总是在现实世界中惨败。（还有谁记得《快乐德州》和《温馨真情》吗?）而这一部真的货真价实。

—_David Ansen_,《新闻周刊》

"Everyone just pretend to be normal", says a harassed father to his family, which is uniquely ill-equipped to do so in "Little Miss Sunshine." This indie favorite came out of the 2006 Sundance festival with its highest price tag ever ($10.5 million, paid by Fox Searchlight) and audience raves. Fox and the fans were right.

The typical Sundance movie usually seems fake-edgy, just strange enough to distinguish itself from big-studio product but smoothed over in the end to gratify a mass audience. "Sunshine" is a welcome corrective. The characters don't achieve epiphanies or objectives or self-awareness: They sail on in oblivious weirdness, glorying in the confusion they leave in their wake.

The satire of perverse beauty contests for pre-teens, in which oiled elementary schoolers strut in bathing suits for judges, hits hard. Yet the freshest part of the film is the journey toward this unsavory goal, as the six try to drive from Albuquerque, N. M. , to Redondo Beach without driving each other nuts.

Road trips with mismatched characters have been an American staple since "It Happened One Night" won the top five Oscars for 1934. The irony is, this family isn't mismatched: All six bickering characters are connected by empathy as well as blood, and we wait for them to figure that out.

Breslin, best remembered as Mel Gibson's child in "Signs", walks off with the acting laurels: She's funny with Dano, tender with Arkin, giddy or doubting when left alone. Olive is the hub that holds together the family, which acts in concert only on her behalf, and Breslin does the same for the picture.

Like most comedians with depth, Carell easily adjusts to a serious/sensitive role. The others deliver the goods, and former Charlottean Beth Grant—who'll never be out of work as long as there are roles for officious, big-haired women—spits venom as a beauty pageant coordinator. Of course, if you had to supervise pre-teen sexpots in sequins, you might turn into a bile fountain, too.

—*Lawrence Toppman*, *The Charlotte Observer*

"每个人只是假装自己很正常," 一个厌烦的父亲对他的家人如是说。这种假装在《阳光小美女》中显得格外病态。这部幸运的独立制作卖出了 2006 年圣丹斯电影节的最高价（1050 万美元，由福克斯探照灯公司支付）并收获了观众的狂热。福克斯和影迷没有错。

　　典型的圣丹斯影片好像总有点装另类，最初以足够奇怪来区别于大制片厂电影，而最终都会磨平棱角去迎合大众。《阳光小美女》让人高兴地矫正了这一点。影片中的人物保留着无辜和不自觉，不会跳出来对自己指手画脚：他们疯过之后就忘，清醒的时候也不会对自身的困惑而自责。

　　影片猛烈地讽刺和抨击了不正当的儿童选美比赛，比如让小学生穿着泳装搔手弄姿地接受评判。不过最新鲜有趣的段落却是那段奔向一个恶心目标的旅程，在从新墨西哥州中部的阿尔布开克市到丽浪多海滩的长途中，这六个人竟然没有把彼此逼疯。

　　从《一夜风流》（1934 年）获得五项奥斯卡奖开始，以搭配失谐的人物为主角的公路片就成了一种美国电影类型。不过反讽的是，这个家庭并非不合谐：感情和血缘维系着六个争吵不休的人，我们只是等待着他们发现这一点。

　　曾在《天兆》中让人印象深刻的扮演梅尔·吉布森女儿的贝斯林悄无声息地拿走了表演桂冠：她在达诺面前活泼俏皮，对阿金温柔呵护，独自一人的时候则疯疯癫癫、充满疑惑。是奥莉芙把全家紧密连接起来，一致听她调遣，而贝斯林在影片中也的确是这样表现的。

　　像多数有深度的喜剧演员一样，卡莱尔很容易就适应了这个时而严肃时而敏感的角色。其他演员表现亦佳，还有前夏洛特居民贝斯·格兰特扮演了一个说话恶毒的选美盛会的协调人——只要有爱管闲事、毛发粗重的女人那种角色，她就不会失业。当然，如果你也要照顾那么多衣着闪闪的性感小人儿，你不发狂才怪！

—*Lawrence Toppman*，《夏洛特观察家》

# The Da Vinci Code

# 达芬奇密码

**导演：**朗·霍华德（Ron Howard）

**原著：**丹·布朗（Dan Brown）

**主演：**汤姆·汉克斯（Tom Hanks）

　　　　让·雷诺（Jean Reno）

　　　　奥黛丽·塔图（Audrey Tautou）

　　　　伊恩·麦凯伦（Ian McKellen）

　　　　保罗·贝坦尼（Paul Bettany）

**片长：**147 分钟

**制作：**哥伦比亚（Columbia Pictures）

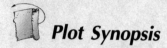

## Plot Synopsis

While in Paris on business, Harvard symbologist Robert Langdon is informed that the elderly curator of the Louvre has been murdered inside the museum. Near the body, police have found a baffling cipher. Solving the enigmatic riddle, Langdon is stunned to discover it leads to a trail of clues hidden in the works of Da Vinci—clues visible for all to see, and yet ingeniously disguised by the painter. Langdon joins forces with a gifted French cryptologist, Sophie Neveu, and learns the late curator was involved in the Priory of Sion—an actual secret society. In a breathless race through Paris, London and beyond, Langdon and Neveu match wits with a faceless power broker who appears to work for Opus Dei—a clandestine, Vatican-sanctioned Catholic organization believed to have long plotted to seize the Priory's secret. Unless Langdon and Neveu can decipher the labyrinthine puzzle in time, the Priory's secret and a stunning historical truth will be lost forever.

## 剧情简介

因公在巴黎逗留时，哈佛大学符号学家罗伯特·兰登被告知卢浮宫年迈的馆长在博物馆里被人谋杀。警察在尸体旁发现了一串难解的密码。在揭开这个深奥谜团的过程中，兰登震惊地发现了一条线索痕迹竟然隐藏在达芬奇的作品中——这条线索谁都能看见，但是被画家巧妙地掩饰住了。兰登和一名天资聪颖的法国女警索菲·奈芙一起合作，查找出原来已故的馆长是邙山隐修会成员，那是一个确实存在的秘密教会。兰登和奈芙马不停蹄地与一伙看不见的政治势力竞逐于巴黎、伦敦以及更远的地方，这伙势力似乎听命于天主事工会，一个经过罗马教会批准的天主教保密组织，该组织长期以来阴谋窃得隐修会的秘密。除非兰登和奈芙能够及时破译那迷宫般的谜团，否则隐修会的秘密连同一桩石破天惊的历史真相，都将永远地从历史中消失。

 *Critique*

There has been much debate over Dan Brown's novel ever since it was published, in 2003, but no question has been more contentious than this: if a person of sound mind begins reading the book at ten o'clock in the morning, at what time will he or she come to the realization that it is unmitigated junk? The answer, in my case, was 10: 00: 03, shortly after I read the opening sentence: "Renowned curator Jacques Sauni re staggered through the vaulted archway of the museum's Grand Gallery." With that one word, "renowned", Brown proves that he hails from the school of elbow-joggers-nervy, worrisome authors who can't stop shoving us along with jabs of information and opinion that we don't yet require. (Buried far below this tic is an author's fear that his command of basic, unadorned English will not do the job; in the case of Brown, he's right.) You could dismiss that first stumble as a blip, but consider this, discovered on a random skim through the book: "Prominent New York editor Jonas Faukman tugged nervously at his goatee." What is more, he does so over "a half-eaten power lunch", one of the saddest phrases I have ever heard.

Should we mind that forty million readers—or, to use the technical term "lemmings*"—have followed one another over the cliff of this long and laughable text? I am aware of the argument that, if a tale has enough grip, one can for a while forget, if not forgive, the crumbling coarseness of the style; otherwise, why would I still read "The Day of the Jackal" once a year? With "The Da Vinci Code", there can be no such excuse. Even as you clear away the rubble of the prose, what shows through is the folly of the central conceit, and, worse still, the pride that the author seems to take in his theological presumption. How timid—how undefended in their powers of reason—must people be in order to yield to such preening? Are they reading "The Da Vinci Code" because everybody on the subway is doing the same, and, if so, why, when they reach their stop, do they not realize their mistake and leave it on the seat, to be gathered up by the next sucker? Despite repeated attempts, I have never managed to crawl past page 100.

The film is directed by Ron Howard and written by Akiva Goldsman, the master wordsmith who brought us "Batman & Robin". I assumed that such an achievement would result in Goldsman's being legally banned from any of the verbal professions, but, no, here he is yet again. As far as I am qualified to judge, the film remains unswervingly loyal to the book, displaying an obedience that Silas could not hope to match. I welcome this fidelity, because it allows us to propose a syllogism. The movie is baloney; the movie is an accurate representation of the book; therefore, the book is also baloney, although it takes even longer to consume. Movie history is awash, of course, with fine pictures that have been made from daft or unreadable books; indeed, you are statistically more likely to squeeze a decent movie out of a potboiler than you are out of a novel of high repute. The trouble with Howard's film is that it is far too dense and talkative to function efficiently as a thriller, while also being too credulous and childish to bear more than a second's scrutiny as an exploration of religious history or spiritual strife. There is plenty going on here, from gunfights to masked orgiastic rituals and mini-scenes of knights besieging Jerusalem, yet the outcome feels at once ponderous and vacant, like a damp and deconsecrated Victorian church.

This is grim news for Tom Hanks, who has served Howard gamely in the past. How does the genial mermaid-lover of "Splash", or the jockish team player of "Apollo 13", feel about being stranded in this humorless grind? Apart from Paul Bettany, who finds a leached and pale-eyed terror in his avenging angel, the other players seem bereft. Molina, so violently vulnerable in "Spider-Man 2", is given no room to breathe, and, as for Audrey Tautou, it is surely no coincidence that Howard sought out and hired almost the only young French actress who emits not a hint of sexual radiation. "The Da Vinci Code" may ask us to believe that Jesus married Mary Magdalene, that she bore him a child, and that the Catholic Church has spent two thousand years not merely concealing this but enforcing its distaste for the feminine (and thus for all bodily delight), but did the movie have to be quite so pallid and prudish about breaking the news? Whose side is it on, anyway?

Behold, I bring you tidings of great joy, which shall be to all people, except at Columbia Pictures, where the power lunches won't even be half-started. The Catholic Church has nothing to fear from this film. It is not just tripe. It is self-evident, spirit-lowering tripe that could not conceivably cause a single member of the flock to turn aside from the faith. Meanwhile, art historians can sleep easy once more, while fans of the book, which has finally been exposed for the pompous fraud that it is, will be shaken from their trance. In fact, the sole beneficiaries of the entire fiasco will be members of Opus Dei, some of whom practice mortification of the flesh. From now on, such penance will be simple-no lashings, no spiked cuff around the thigh. Just the price of a movie ticket, and two and a half hours of pain.

— *Anthony Lane*, *The New Yorker*

丹·布朗的书自从2003年出版以来引发了无数的争论，但是没有哪个问题会比下面这个更尖锐：如果一个头脑理智的人在早晨10：00开始看此书，那么他或她会在几点意识到它不过是本彻头彻尾的垃圾呢？我的答案是10：00：03，也就是我刚看完头一句话："德高望重的馆长雅克·索尼埃跌跌撞撞地穿过博物馆大陈列室的拱廊。""德高望重"这个词证明了布朗是从那种神经过敏的惹人烦的作家学校里出来的，总是一惊一乍地扔给我们一些我们根本不需要的信息和观点。（这其实说明，在深层动机上，他们害怕基本的、朴实的语言不能招人喜欢；就布朗这一个案来说，这倒是对的。）你可以不去计较，跳过这头一块疙瘩，但你瞧，我随意翻翻就看到这个："杰出的纽约编辑 Jonas Faukman 紧张地扯着他的胡子。"要命的还有"一顿吃了一半的权力午餐"，这是我听过的最拙劣的表达。

我们不该想想有四千万读者——或者用术语"旅鼠"，在前赴后继地从这个冗长可笑的文本的悬崖上跳下去吗？我熟知，如果一个故事足够吸引人，那么对其文体上的粗劣，我们即使不能原谅，至少也可以暂时忘掉它，否则，我为什么每年都会重看一遍《豺狼的日子》呢？但这不能是《达芬奇密码》的借口。即便你清除了那些阅读障碍，你看到的也只是它核心表达的愚蠢之见，以及作者在神学假说上的狂妄自大。这理由是如此怯懦和漏洞百出，难道人们一定要屈从于这种自负吗？人们读《达芬奇密码》是因为看到地铁里每个人都在读吗？若是如此，他们干嘛不在看腻了的时候意识到这是个错误，然后把它甩了以便找别的乐趣？尽管努力过很多次，我读这本书还是难以超过 100 页。

影片由霍华德导演，戈德斯曼编剧。戈德斯曼是一个曾经写出了《蝙蝠侠与罗宾》的语言大师，因此我想他不会跟着小说的语言亦步亦趋，可是他偏就如此。影片百分之百地忠实于原著，那种顺从连赛拉斯（片中人物）都不希望。我赞成这种忠实，因为它能让我们提出这样一个三段论：电影是胡扯；电影精确地再现了小说；因此，小说也是胡扯，不过是更长的胡扯。电影史上充满了从三流小说改编出的一流电影；从概率上来说，从粗制滥造的小说改编出优秀电影的可能性确实要比名著大得多。霍华德的这部片子的问题是它的密度过大、废话过多，以至于背离了惊悚片的功能要求，而且在宗教史和信仰冲突的考察上过于轻信、幼稚、缺乏耐心。我们是看到了很多枪战、面具狂欢节、骑士围攻耶路撒冷的微缩场景，但是它们笨拙而空洞，就像一座被庸俗化了的维多利亚教堂。

对过去一直对霍华德不离不弃的汤姆·汉克斯来说，这是个打击人的消息。这个《美人鱼》中招人喜欢的情人和《阿波罗13号》的马术队员如今陷在这部了无生趣的烂片里是什么感觉？除了保罗·贝坦尼还能演一演复仇天使那恐怖黯淡的眼神，其他的演员好像没有可以施展的余地。曾在《蜘蛛侠2》中激动人心的莫利纳在此没有一点表演空间。至于奥黛丽·塔图，这简直是霍华德找出来的毫无性感魅力的法国年轻女演员的不二人选。《达芬奇密码》好像要我们相信妓女玛丽娅嫁给了耶稣并给他生了个孩子，相信天主教在两千年来不仅遮掩着这一事实并把恶名强加在这个女人身上（以及所有的肉体欢乐上），可是该片为什么非要苍白地假正经地透漏出这个消息呢？它到底是站在哪个立场上呢？

看哪，我告诉你们所有人（除了哥伦比亚公司，它的权力午餐连一半都不会开始）这个让人高兴的好消息：天主教对这部片子没有什么好害怕的。它不只是一堆废话，它还是一堆不言而喻的、精神低下的废话，它绝对不会让任何一个人皈依它的信仰。同时，艺术历史学家可以再次安然入睡了，而小说的狂热粉丝也最终会从华而不实的欺骗中回过神来。事实上，这场失败唯一的受益者将是天主事工会里的某些奉行禁欲主义的成员。从此他们的苦行将会变得简单——再也不用鞭笞自己，不用戴镣铐，只要花费一张电影票的钱，再忍受两个半小时的痛苦。

　　　　　　　　　　　　　　— *Anthony Lane*，《纽约客》

Just because a novel reads like a movie doesn't mean it should be one.

The Roman Catholic Church can rest easy. Ron Howard and screenwriter Akiva Goldsman struggle mightily to cram as much as possible of Dan Brown's labyrinthine thriller into a 2-hour-28-minute running time, resulting in a movie both overstuffed and underwhelming. This film is not likely to topple Christianity as we know it, though it could do serious damage to Audrey Tautou's hopes of a Hollywood career.

Brown's paragraphs alternate between pulpy cliffhangers and barely digested research, giving the reader a crash course in early Christian theology, pagan symbolism, religious-art history and the relationship between the Knights Templar and the papacy, with side essays on codebreaking and cryptology. The question about the movie was how could you fit all this exposition into a mile-a-minute thriller without bringing everything to a crashing, didactic halt?

The answer: awkwardly. One solution is the historical flashback. Periodically, Howard speeds us off to crowded, computer-generated visions of ancient Rome or the Holy Land or Ye Olde England for whirlwind history lessons that whip by so speedily you can barely take in the information, but not fast enough so that you don't notice how tacky they look. Then there are the desaturated-color flashbacks to traumatic moments in our characters' histories: little Robert falling down a well, the car crash that kills Sophie's parents or the back story of Silas, the albino hit man with a penchant for self-flagellation. Anyone who hasn't read the book will find this latter utterly confounding, as will anyone who has.

—*David Ansen*, *Newsweek*

　　就因为一部小说读起来像电影并不意味着就得把它拍成电影。

　　罗马天主教会这下可以高枕无忧了。霍华德和编剧戈德斯曼苦心经营，努力把丹·布朗迷宫般的惊悚小说填进2小时28分钟的片长里，结果拍出了一部臃肿而乏味的电影。如我们所知，该片不大可能颠覆基督教，倒是严重影响了奥黛丽·塔图跻身好莱坞的梦想。

　　布朗的小说穿插在扣人心弦的悬念和难以消化的研究之间，并让读者囫囵吞枣地了解了早期的基督教神学、异教徒的象征主义、宗教艺术史以及圣殿骑士团与罗马教皇的关系，还有附文中的密码学和密码破译研究。影片的问题就是你怎么才能把这么多的素材合理地放进一部篇幅有限的恐怖片里，而不显得支离破碎，没有说教腔？

答案是：笨办法。办法之一是历史闪回。霍华德频繁地闪回关于古罗马或圣地或古英格兰的电脑合成画面，像是刮了一场历史课旋风，速度快得使你什么信息也来不及吸收，但也没有快到让你觉得它俗不可耐。还有就是那些用颜色发旧的闪回表现的人物受害的瞬间：小罗伯特落井、索菲的父母车祸身亡、赛拉斯的黑色故事、白化病杀手自我鞭笞的趣味。不管有没有看过小说原著，都会觉得这部电影混乱得够呛。

— *David Ansen*，《新闻周刊》

For those who hate Dan Brown's best-selling symbology thriller "The Da Vinci Code", the eagerly awaited and much-hyped movie version beautifully exposes all its flaws and nightmares of logic. For those who love the book's page-turning intensity, the movie version heightens Brown's mischievous interweaving of genre action, historical facts and utter fictions. In other words, for those who bear witness to the film "The Da Vinci Code", what you see depends on what you believe. Kinda like religion itself.

—*Kirk Honeycutt*, *The Hollywood Reporter*

对于那些憎恨丹·布朗这部畅销的象征主义惊悚小说《达芬奇密码》的人来说，迫不及待和天花乱坠的电影改编把它所有的缺陷和逻辑漏洞暴露无疑。对于那些喜欢原著有极大悬念的人来说，电影则使故事在动作类型、历史史实和虚构想象几个方面得到了融合和强化。换句话说，对于见证了电影《达芬奇密码》的人，你相信什么你就能看到什么。这有点儿像宗教信仰本身。

—*Kirk Honeycutt*，《好莱坞报道》

~ **Note** ~

Lemming：旅鼠：一种体形短小但很健壮的啮齿目动物，尤指旅鼠属动物。它居住在北方地区，以其有时以淹死来结束生命的季节性群体迁徙而闻名。

# Howl's Moving Castle

# 哈尔的移动城堡

**导演/编剧：**宫崎骏（Hayao Miyazaki）

**原著：**戴安娜·韦恩·琼斯（Diana Wynne Jones）

**配音演员：**倍赏千惠子、木村拓哉
美轮明宏、我修院达也

**片长：**119 分钟

**制作：**东宝公司，2006 年

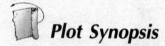

# *Plot Synopsis*

Young Sophie Hatter is cursed by the Witch of the Waste, and turns into an old hag. Ashamed of how she looks, she flees into the hills where a moving castle roams the hills. It is said to belong to the young and handsome wizard Howl, who has a bad reputation. Within the castle, Sophie befriends the fire demon Calcifer, who promises to help her become young again. One catch: she must help Calcifer to be free of Howl, and Calcifer cannot tell her how. However, Sophie agrees to stay and try to find out about the contract through other ways. Still, Howl can see that Sophie is under a spell like Calcifer can, and he falls in love with her for who she is and not for what she looks like. Sophie manages to bring life to the moving castle, and she helps Howl to face his former tutor, Madam Suliman.

## 剧情简介

做帽子的年轻姑娘索菲受到荒野女巫的诅咒后变成了一个老太太。索菲为自己的外表感到难为情，于是逃到山野中，遇到了一座可以移动的城堡在山野里游荡。传说城堡的主人是一个名叫哈尔的魔法师。他年轻英俊，但名声却不大好。在城堡里，索菲结识了火焰魔卡西法，二人相处得很友好。他承诺帮助她返老还童，但是有个条件：她也必须帮助卡西法逃脱哈尔的掌控——而卡西法不能告诉她如何做到这一点。索菲留在了城堡中，并想通过其它办法找出机关。哈尔像卡西法一样看出了索菲受了诅咒。他爱上了她，为了她的灵魂，而不是外表。索菲设法驱动移动城堡，并帮助哈尔对付他的前导师莎莉曼夫人。

# Critique

What I love so far about Miyazaki is how he never fails to take advantage of the fact that his entertainment medium of choice is animation. With animation, imagination flows unfettered—and the more you challenge reality with it, the more potent it becomes. *Howl's Moving Castle* may be hurt by not making much immediate sense, but so many things make up for it, not the least of which is its playful visual interpretation of a Western/European tale and setting. The scattered, unpredictable ideas infect its character interpretations, too— it's always delightfully surprising to see characters not acting like stock players. It shows great faith in the human being (and, yes, that goes for the many imaginary beings that populate this film) in showing there are no black-or-whites, just many shades of grey, or, more precisely, great varieties of color. The movie does feel a bit shackled by its source material, though—just trying to be even semi-faithful to it creates a subtle dynamic of Miyazaki's flights of fancy fighting to break free from someone else's story. The resulting mix of new ideas and already established elements contributes to the movie's confusion factor, but the wondrous weirdness of the animated world and the unique situations it presents are always worth sticking around for.

*—Jeffery Chen, Window to the Movies*

我至今喜欢宫崎骏的一点是他明白动画是最适合他的娱乐媒介，而且他在对这一事实的利用上从来没有失败过。在动画的世界里，想象力可以自由驰骋——你向现实挑战得越多，发掘出的潜力就越大。《哈尔的移动城堡》在直接的感观愉悦上可能略有遗憾，但是很多东西可以补偿它，至少它运用视觉有趣地再现了一个西方/欧洲的故事和场景。那天马行空、出人意料的念头也感染了对人物的演绎——我们总是很高兴地惊讶于那些人物看起来并不像炒股玩家。它显示了一种对人性的伟大信心（比如影片中充满了虚构的各色生命），那些人物并不是黑白分明，而是层次丰富的灰色，更确切地说，是丰富多彩的颜色。不过，影片确实受到了原著的一些束缚——宫崎骏试图忠实于原著，然而这在这个习惯奇思异想的人身上产生了一种微妙的驱动，这使他又不自觉地想要挣脱出别人的故事。新想法和旧元素掺杂起来，结果影片有些令人疑惑不解。但无论如何，那奇妙的动画世界和其呈现的独特的遭遇都会一直吸引着我们的目光。

—*Jeffery Chen*，《电影之窗》

*Howl's Moving Castle* is the latest enchantment from animation legend Hayao Miyazaki, whose *Spirited Away* won an Oscar and many fans in 2003. Transformed by a jealous witch into an aged crone, our young heroine Sophie leaves town to find employment in the wizard Howl's amazing castle—a wheezing, yomping monstrosity of the Terry Gilliam school—and is swept into a baffling and bizarre fable that enchants and amuses but never delivers on its magical promise.

Howl's aliases—Jenkins, Pendragon—are not the only survivors of Welsh author Dianne Wynne Jones' original novel, but enough liberties have been taken with plot and characterisation to create confusion. Youngsters and Miyazaki fans will coo at the world's depth and rich surreality, but opaque plotting, and a tendency to mope with Sophie whilst Howl is off affecting events let the momentum of the first act vanish into thin air. By the, shall we say, enigmatic ending, not even the relentlessly exuberant eye-candy can summon it back.

—*Jonathan Trout*, BBC

《哈尔的移动城堡》是动画大师宫崎骏最新的迷人之作，他曾在 2003 年以《千与千寻》赢得了奥斯卡和众多影迷。被一个忌妒的女巫变成丑老太婆后，我们年轻的女主人公离开村子，来到了魔法师哈尔那奇异的城堡中——那简直是一个超负荷的畸形的特里·吉列姆（一位热衷神话题材的导演）学校。紧接着，她就被卷入一个古怪的寓言世界中，这个世界魅惑而有趣，但是从不兑现它的魔法承诺。

哈尔的假名字詹金斯和潘德拉肯并不是威尔士作家戴安娜·韦恩·琼斯的小说原著中唯一保留下来的东西，不过影片在情节和人物塑造上过多的自由确实制造了一些困惑。年轻人和宫崎骏的影迷会为片中世界深厚的超现实性卖力叫好，但是晦涩的情节，以及当索菲在需要哈尔的关键时刻他却令人郁闷地缺席，这种处理几乎让我们淡忘了片头的叙事动力。那莫测高深（如果可以这么说）的结局即使是最厉害的视觉奇观都不能把它救回来。

—*Jonathan Trout*，*BBC*

Based on a novel by popular children's author Diana Wynne Jones, *Howl's Moving Castle* is the third Hayao Miyazaki feature to receive a theatrical release in the U. S. Displaying many of Miyazaki's signature themes and effects, the film tells a dense, complicated story in a challenging style. *Spirited Away*, his last picture, won an Oscar for Best Animated Feature, and as his reputation grows, Miyazaki draws more fans into his intricate, unpredictable works.

With its physical transformations and liberal, antiwar politics, *Howl's Moving Castle* would seem to fit in well with Miyazaki's other films. The director's grasp of animation techniques is as impressive as the depth and substance of his imaginary worlds. The changing weather, complex patterns of motion, lustrous color schemes and remarkable architecture envelop viewers, almost compensating for the thin plotting. The animator and his crew, many of whom have been working with him for 20 years, expertly juggle scenes of matter-of-fact magic, gentle humor and icy terror. Still, Miyazaki has trouble resolving some of the more prosaic elements of Jones' book. Fans may not mind the clich d plot turns, while others can lose themselves in Miyazaki's bravura action passages. It's wonderful watching Howl's castle crumble at one point, even if the reasons behind it are trite.

Along with the English version, which has been expertly cast and recorded, Disney is releasing a subtitled Japanese version in select markets. The inevitable differences between the films actually don't amount to much, perhaps the Japanese Calcifer (Tatsuya Gashuin) is a bit more spirited than Billy Crystal, but both are charming. The two versions simply confirm that Miyazaki is one of the world's master animators.

*—Daniel Eagan, Film Journal International*

改编自流行儿童文学作家戴安娜·韦恩·琼斯的《哈尔的移动城堡》是宫崎骏第三部在美国影院发行的动画长片。在很多贴着宫崎骏标签的主题和效果的衬托下，该片以一种颇具挑战性的风格讲述了一个情节紧凑的复杂故事。他的上一部影片《千与千寻》获得了奥斯卡最佳动画片奖，随着声名日盛，宫崎骏把越来越多的影迷吸引进了他错综复杂、难以预料的作品中。

物理变化和自由主义的反战政治学体现了《哈尔的移动城堡》与宫崎骏其它影片的一致之处。而他对动画技术的掌握与他的想象世界里那种深度和质感一样让人印象深刻。变化的天气、复杂的动作模型、和谐的配色以及非凡的建筑包围感几乎弥补了情节的不足。动画师和他的团队（其中有些人已经跟了他20多年）熟练地变幻着各种场景，时而是平常的魔法，时而是绅士幽默，时而是不寒而栗的恐怖。不过，宫崎骏在处理琼斯书中一些零散元素时还是有些问题。影迷可能不介意那些情节转折的俗套，而其他人却可能迷失在宫崎骏那炫技的动作段落中。人们很爱看哈尔的城堡曾经一度灰飞烟灭，即使背后的动机很老套。

除了英语版（配音录制得都不错），迪斯尼还在选定的市场中发行了带字幕的日语版。两个版本常见的差异并不太多，可能

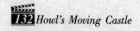

日版的卡西法（我修院达也）比比利·克里斯托更英勇一点，不过两个人都很迷人。两个版本都同样地证明了宫崎骏是世界动画界的大师之一。

——*Daniel Eagan*,《国际电影月刊》

Hayao Miyazaki's new film *Howl's Moving Castle* is so good that it shames virtually every animated film made since Miyazaki's last film, *Spirited Away*, graced movie screens in 2002.

If nothing else, it proves to Hollywood that its recent failure in the animated realm comes not from old-fashioned hand-drawn animation but from its severe lack of imagination and over-reliance on fart jokes and pop culture references.

The first of Miyazaki's films to be based on a book, *Howl's Moving Castle* quickly establishes itself with Miyazaki's personal signature, bursting with enough ideas and imagination to make up half a dozen summer movies.

Blessedly, Miyazaki doesn't bother to sort out the story using mere logic. He instead goes with his instincts, like a child inventing a playtime universe and making up the rules in the moment. The great filmmaker uses primal forces to tell his story, like wind and cold, feeling your age, or feeling hungry. It's a purely visceral ride.

The filmmaker's most unique attribute, his uncanny sense of space, time and weight, is still here. When Sophie and the witch climb the endless stairs to a royal palace, you feel every straining step.

Unlike most animated films, which feel the need to constantly move at a breakneck pace, Miyazaki loves to sit still from time to time, just listening or watching or waiting, as did the great Japanese director Yasujiro Ozu before him. It gives viewers a moment to rest and reflect, and it keeps the film from growing tedious.

But when Miyazaki starts moving, it's best to hold on. If the characters fly through the air, we can feel the height and the sensation of floating. Many movies use " roller coaster ride " to describe thrilling sensations, but Miyazaki takes that literally.

—Jeffrey M. Anderson, Combustible Celluloid

宫崎骏的新片《哈尔的移动城堡》以及 2002 年他的上一部《千与千寻》都是如此之好，以至于期间的每部动画电影都被对比得黯然失色。

要是没说错，这说明好莱坞近期在动画领域的失败并不是因为它那老式手工的动画制作跟不上时代，而是它严重缺乏想象力，过于依赖低俗的玩笑，过多地引入了流行文化。

虽然这是宫崎峻头一部从书改编来的电影，《哈尔的移动城堡》还是以宫崎骏鲜明的个人风格来确认了它自己，那层出不穷的念头和想象力使它抵得上数部暑期电影的份量。

值得高兴的是，宫崎骏并不仅仅依靠逻辑来找故事，他更多地是用直觉，像一个孩子自己发明了自己游戏的宇宙，并自己创造规则于瞬间。这个伟大的电影人用最原始本真的动力来讲故事，比如风、寒冷、你对年龄，或者对饥饿的感受。它是纯粹的内心之旅。

我们仍然能从该片中感受到这个导演最独特的地方，他对空间、时间和重量有一种奇异的感觉。当索菲和女巫沿着绵绵无尽的台阶走向一座王宫时，你感到每一步都在变形。

不像绝大多数动画总是以让人抽筋的速度动个不停，宫崎骏喜欢让人物偶尔静静地坐在那里，静静地听、看，或者等待，如同之前伟大的日本导演小津安二郎那样。观众由此得以喘息和回味，这也使影片远离了审美疲劳。

不过宫崎骏的人物一旦动起来，就不会停止。如果人物在天空中飞行，我们就能感受到那高度和漂浮的感觉。很多电影用"过山车"来形容心脏出壳的感觉，宫崎骏却能把它实实在在地表现出来。

—Jeffrey M. Anderson,   Combustible Celluloid

# Spring, Summer, Fall, Winter...
# And Spring

## 春去春又来

导演/编剧：金基德（Ki-duk Kim）

主演：金基德（Ki-duk Kim）

伍永秀（Young-soo Oh）

金英民（Young-min Kim）

片长：105 分钟

制作：韩国影业（Korea Pictures），2003 年

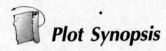 *Plot Synopsis*

The setting is a Buddhist monastery that floats in the middle of a lake set in a valley surrounded by mountains. As the seasons change, the story follows the life of one man:

Spring—Child Monk has a cruel streak when it comes to animals and his teacher, Old Monk, tries to makes him understand the consequences of his actions.

Summer—Young Monk is faced with the temptations of youth when a young woman is brought to the monastery to be healed. The young man opts for the freedom of the real world and leaves his mentor behind.

Fall—Young Adult Monk returns seeking refuge and the Old Monk teaches him about penitence. The Old Monk prepares to depart his life.

Winter—Adult Monk returns to the monastery alone. He trains on the frozen ice and prepares himself to take on the role of teacher when a baby is brought to the abbey.

Spring—the life cycle is renewed, as the student becomes the master.

## 剧情简介

群山环绕的山谷中是一片湖，湖中心漂浮着一座佛教寺院。在四季更替中，一个人的一生如此展开了：

春。小和尚做了一件虐待动物的事，老和尚努力让他明白这行为的后果。

夏。一个年轻女人来到寺院治病，小和尚感到了青春期的诱惑。他选择了红尘自由，离老师而去。

秋。小和尚回到寺院避难，老和尚教导他悔过自新。老和尚准备自行离世。

冬。成年后的小和尚独自一人回到寺院中。一个婴孩被送进寺院来，小和尚在冰上练功，并准备承担起老师的角色。

春。长大的婴孩宛如当年的小和尚，生命又轮回了一周。

## *Critique*

This is a beautiful, haunting Korean film about a Buddhist monk and his acolyte living on a small lake. The film could be watched with no sound or subtitles. There is very little dialogue in it. The story is conveyed quite well through images alone during most of the film. Most of those images are very beautiful ones.

Although the story has only a handful of characters and everything takes place in a small area, it encompasses a surprisingly large chunk of the human experience, including lust, love, jealousy, murder, suicide and redemption. It has important things to say about the difficulty of teaching and the elusiveness of wisdom.

A lot of films originating in Asia don't really show a world view that is all that different than that shown Western films. This is no doubt comforting to some, but not very instructive. This is one Eastern film that shows a world view that is very different than the Western view of the universe. In the west, we are all about assigning blame. We are all about retribution and punishment. Our response to the 9/11 attacks shows this clearly. This film has some punishment in it, but it is more about learning from one's mistakes and becoming a better person by seeking wisdom through mental and moral purification. The movie doesn't just give lip service to Buddhism, as so many films do, it demonstrates Buddhist principles clearly. One way the film demonstrates those principles is in a sequence that would never happen in a western film. It is the strangest, longest, most unlikely police arrest sequence that I can recall seeing in a film.

—*Robert Roten, Laramie Movie Scope*

这是一部美丽的、让人难忘的韩国影片，描写了一个佛教僧人和他的侍从生活在一个小湖上的故事。欣赏该片可以不要声音也不要字幕。它的对话很少。大部分的时候，故事通过画面独自地传达出来。多数画面美丽至极。

虽然片中人物只有寥寥几个，而且一切都发生在一个很小的地方，但它涵盖的人生经验却丰富得惊人，其中有欲望、爱、忌妒、谋杀、自杀，以及救赎。它郑重地表达了教育之难和智慧之深。

亚洲的很多电影在世界观上和西方电影并没有太大不同。这无疑会鼓舞某些人，但不见得就是好事。而《春去春又来》则是一部在宇宙人生观念上和西方迥异的东方电影。在我们的西方文化中，一直讲谴责有理，一切都有关报偿和惩罚。我们对9/11事件的反应就清楚地证明了这一点。这部影片中也有一些惩罚，但它更多地是表现一个人如何在精神和道德净化中寻求智慧，以此从教训中脱胎换骨，做个好人。该片也没有像很多影片一样仅在口头上宣扬佛教，而是清晰地呈现出了佛教的原则。方式之一是对一种形式程序的呈现，一种你在西方电影中决不可能看到的形式。比如警察逮捕归案的那些程序，那是我在电影中看过的最古怪，最冗长，最不可思议的繁文缛节。

—*Robert Roten*，   *Laramie Movie Scope*

Kim Ki-duk's *Spring*, *Summer*, *Fall*, *Winter* . . . *and Spring* is the official Korean entry for Best Foreign Language Film in next year's Academy Awards. It's already won prizes at the 2003 San Sebastián and Locarno International Film Festivals, but in America Mr. Kim is best known for the erotic absurdism of *The Isle* (1999). Since his 1996 debut, *Crocodile*, Mr. Kim has directed nine films, becoming a vital, if lesser-known, force in Asian cinema.

*Spring*, which the 43-year-old director also wrote and edited, probably represents the purest and most transcendent distillation of the Buddhist faith ever rendered on the screen. I say "probably" because I've seen not nearly enough Asian cinema to qualify as even an amateur authority. Still, it's hard to imagine another film of comparable visual splendor and spiritual intensity in the service of Buddhist contemplation and the quest for existence in eternity.

As the film's production notes tell us, the visual splendor of *Spring* begins with "the artificially constructed set of a small Buddhist monastery made to float atop Jusan Pond in North Kyungsang Province, Korea". Created about 200 years ago, Jusan Pond is an artificial lake in which the surrounding mountains are reflected. The lake retains its mystical aura by the ancient trees that emerge from within the water. After six months of negotiations with the Ministry of Environment, Mr. Kim's production company, LJ Film, was able to obtain permission to build the set.

The director's statement regarding his latest work is short and somewhat misleadingly simplistic: "I intended to portray the joy, anger, sorrow and pleasure of our lives through four seasons and through the life of a monk who lives in a temple on Jusan Pond surrounded only by Nature." To my strange European-American and Christian eyes, there is much, much more to this film than that.

The four seasons, for example, are spread over so many years that they gravitate from one generation to another with a grimly fatalistic circularity. One life ends and another begins, but the pond, the trees, the mountains remain seemingly ageless.

Bertrand Russell, an irascible atheist and a wittily skeptical disbeliever of all religions, undertook to grade them all on moral perspicacity. As I recall, he ranked Buddhism above Christianity on the basis of some unkind exclusionary dogma (i. e., the church's, not Christ's). Indeed, if I were to be given the option of choosing my religion for myself (instead of staying with the one I inherited from my parents), and all I had to go on were two films, Mr. Kim's *Spring* and Mel Gibson's *The Passion of the Christ*, I might well opt for Buddhism, as some of my friends have done.

There was a point in Mr. Kim's film when I found the Buddhist sutra carvings inordinately tedious. Perhaps there is some part of me that does not want to be part of a cycle that embraces nothingness as spiritual rebirth in the universe of which I'm an integral part. I prefer to fight on in the Alamo * of my ego even though I know I will eventually lose. The levels of acceptance and resignation that Buddhism demands are hopelessly above me. And I don't want eroticism to be subsumed as part of nature. I want a life bold, defiant and earth-shaking. But Mr. Kim's majestic narrative in the end does approach the sublime in its cumulative sense of sadness and renewal.

—*Andrew Sarris, The New York Observer*

金基德的《春去春又来》是由官方送审角逐下一年度奥斯卡最佳外语片奖的韩国电影。虽然该片已在圣塞巴斯蒂安和洛迦诺国际电影节上获奖，但金基德在美国最出名的还是表现性和荒诞的《漂流欲室》（1999 年）。从 1996 年第一部《鳄鱼》开始至今，金基德已经导演了 9 部影片（注：到 2007 年的《呼吸》已经 14 部），并日益在亚洲影坛中占有举足轻重（即使不够大众）的地位。

《春》是这位 43 岁导演自己编剧，自己剪辑的作品，也许是银幕上对佛教信仰最纯粹、最超越的提炼。说"也许"是因为我不够称职，没有看过足够的亚洲电影。而且很难想象还有电影能达到这样的视觉美感以及在佛意沉思和追求永恒上的精神深度。

从影片的制作笔记可以看到，《春》中的视觉奇观是"在韩国庆尚北道省的注小池湖上人工搭建一座小型佛教寺院"。注小池湖是一个有 200 年历史的人工湖，环绕的群山倒映在水面上，从水中伸出的古树渲染出一种神秘的氛围。在与环境部斡旋了六个月后，金基德的制作公司 LJ 影业终于得到了人工造景的许可。

导演本人认为自己的新作很简单，甚至容易被误解为太简单了："我试图将我们生活中的喜怒哀乐通过四季，通过一个僧人的一生传达出来。他住在湖中寺院里，环绕他的只有自然。"可是在我这个欧洲裔美国人和基督徒陌生的眼光中,该片比他说的要深奥得多得多。

比如说,片中的四季绵延数年,在无情的宿命轮回中见证了一代又一代人。旧人亡去,新生降临,但是那湖、那树、那山却似乎长存不老。

贝特兰·罗素,一个脾气暴躁的无神论者和一切信仰的怀疑论者,把各个宗教都按道德敏锐性划分了等级。我记得他把佛教置于基督教之上,因为基督教教义里存在着一些不好的排他性的教条(比如,教堂的教条,而非基督的)。说真的,如果给我机会让我选择自己的信仰(而不是像现在这样继承于父母),并且我能够接触的只有两部电影,金基德的《春去春又来》和梅尔·吉布森的《基督受难记》,我一定会选择佛教,就像我的一些朋友已经做的一样。

不过有一点,对我来说,影片中的佛经碑文不是一般地枯燥。或许是因为我身体的某部分不愿意以一种灵魂转世的方式进入虚空的宇宙轮回,因为我自己是一个整体。我更愿意让我的自我投入阿拉莫之战,即使我知道最终会失去它。佛教要求的忍和戒于我是无望的。而且我不希望把情欲看作是自然的一部分。我要过一个生猛无畏、惊天动地的一生。当然金基德片尾庄严的叙事通过悲哀和新生情绪的累积中也确实达到了一种崇高的境界。

—Andrew Sarris《纽约观察家》

*Spring Summer Fall Winter... and Spring* is a gorgeous motion picture. Using perfectly composed shots to amplify an emotionally resonant story, the film successfully argues that "artistic" films do not have to be boring. Although few in the audience are likely to identify intimately with the characters (Buddhist monks who live in virtual isolation), the movie's themes about the mutability of life and the desire for peace and atonement have universal implications. One can be a New York City Stockbroker or a Salt Lake City teacher and still understand the points being made by Kim Ki-duk's film.

The concept that existence is circular is much in evidence. The movie begins where it ends—with an aging man imparting wisdom to a young charge. We suspect that this has gone on for centuries and will continue to go on for centuries. The land around the monastery is untouched by time. The only clue that this is a contemporary story comes from the clothing and attitudes of the policemen who arrive in the third segment's autumn. The pace of *Spring Summer Fall Winter... and Spring* is deliberate, but there is too much richness in the movie's emotional tapestry for it to be considered dull or drawn-out. From a visual, thematic, and emotional standpoint, this represents rewarding cinema.

The film raises questions about how we live our lives and how actions, like ripples in the waters of time, can have unexpected consequences years later. By depicting the life of one unnamed individual in ten-year snapshots over the course of his development from boyhood to maturity, Kim provides us with insight and an uncommon perspective. Idealism is supplanted by a yearning for physical satisfaction. Romance turns to tragedy. Repentance leads to understanding. These things happen quickly on-screen, with the years elapsing in a heartbeat. We mourn for lost innocence and appreciate the accumulation of wisdom. By the end of the film, even though we do not know the main character's name, we feel that we have taken a long and rewarding journey at his side.

—*James Berardinelli*, *Reelviews*

《春去春又来》是一部绚烂的电影。它以构图完美的镜头表现了一个有情感共鸣的故事，这成功地证明了"艺术"电影不一定非得是沉闷的。虽然影院里的观众不大可能亲近地认同片中的人物（与世隔绝的佛教僧人），但是影片关于人生无常、追求宁静和赎罪的主题则是普遍性的。即使一个纽约的股票经纪人或某个盐湖城的教师也仍然能够明白金基德这部影片的内涵。

轮回的意味在片中很明显。影片自它的结尾处开始——都是一个老人在给一个年轻人传授智慧。我们猜这已经持续了数百年，并将永远延续下去。寺院周遭与世隔绝，我们只能从"秋天"部分警察的着装和态度上辨认出这是一个发生在当下的故事。《春》的节奏之慢是蓄意的，但其情感意蕴如此丰富，你不能认为它乏味或冗长。无论从视觉、主题还是情感的角度来说，《春》都值得你走进电影院。

该片使我们意识到，我们如何生活和如何行动，会像时间的水纹一样，在多年后得到不期然的果。在对一个无名氏从少年到成年十年光阴的速写中，金基德给了我们一种与众不同的洞察和眼光。理想主义被肉体欲望取代了。浪漫摇身变成了悲剧。忍受能够通向理解。种种因果在银幕上飞快掠过，而一年年的岁月以心跳的速度流逝着。我们哀悼纯真的失落，也欣喜于智慧的积累。当影片结束时，虽然我们都不知道主要人物的名字，但我们感觉和他们走过了一段漫长而充实的旅程。

—*James Berardinelli*，《旋风景》

> ## Note
>
> "Alamo"：指阿拉莫之战，德克萨斯争取独立的战争，是美国历史上最重大的战争之一。人数占劣势的阿拉莫保卫者以他们的智慧、激情以及独立自主的理想，奋起反抗强大的墨西哥政府军。

# Elephant

# 大　象

**导演**：格斯·范·桑特（Gus Van Sant）
**主演**：阿里克斯·弗瑞斯特（Alex Frost）
**片长**：81 分钟
**发行**：HBO 家庭影院影业（HBO Films），2003 年

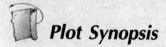

## Plot Synopsis

The movie starts as a car has a hard time driving straight down the road in a residential area. We think some kid has stolen this car. Nah. It's the dad driving his son to school, and he's drunk. The teenage son must take over. So, adults give up all responsibility towards their children and mayhem can take place. The film shows one day in the life of several teenage students as they go in and out of classes. They live their student lives and we follow their steps through the corridors and doors, taking them as guides one by one, like avatars in a giant video game.

### 剧情简介

影片开头是一辆车摇摇晃晃地驶过一片住宅区。我们还以为那车被几个小孩偷了呢，其实是父亲开车送儿子上学，他喝多了，一定是儿子接替他做了驾驶员。大人们就是这样对他们的孩子甩手不管，任凭坏事发生。影片展现了一些青少年学生进出课堂一天里的生活。我们跟随着他们的脚步穿过走廊和门，把他们当作一个又一个的向导，感觉他们就像是巨型电脑游戏中的动漫人物。

## Critique

Winner of the two top awards at the Cannes Festival, Van Sant's daring and inventive film is a fictionalised telling of the horrific events at Columbine High School. It plays out like a fly-on-the-wall documentary as the camera follows students through their day, circling back on each other as the students' paths cross in banal ways, adding to the ominous, foreboding tone. There's no explanation of the title (it refers to that huge thing in the corner we're afraid to talk about), and little actual plot to speak of. The film merely tracks a number of students up to the fateful moment when the first shot is fired. What follows is almost impossible to watch, and yet we can't turn away either, because it's far too important for us to at least try and understand.

Most actors use their own names. Frost and Deulen play the gun-obsessed teens, plotting their evil actions with almost clinical detachment as if it's a paintball game. Robinson is a friendly guy trying to cope with his drunken father and the perhaps-imagined attentions of the school hottie. McConnell is a photographer, casually documenting life in the school. Finklea and Tyson are the cool couple wandering the halls; Taylor, George and Mountain are a trio of chattering gossips who get the film's best joke. And we also meet Hicks, an unconfident girl terrorised by her gym coach, and Dixon, a muscly boy who doesn't run from the gunfire.

This is one of the most realistic depictions of an American high school ever put on screen. Mostly because these are real highschoolers, not 20-something Hollywood actors. They're shockingly real;

we can palpably feel their emotions——that complex mix of the ex-
citement of learning and the agony of adolescence. And Van Sant
films it with gorgeous cinematography in extremely long tracking
shots that snake through the hallways with an unstoppable momentum. This is complex, lyrical filmmaking that takes the breath away
and leaves us emotionally wrecked. There are profoundly important
points made along the way (including the frightening ease of buying
assault weapons online), but without heavy-handed moralising.
And the way the camera approaches scenes from differing points of
view is not only telling, but also builds the tension beautifully. In
the end it might be slightly self-indulgent, but it's also haunting and
devastating.

—*Rich Cline, Shadows on the Wall*

　　拿了两项戛纳电影节最高奖（最佳影片、最佳导演）的《大
象》是范·桑特的一部大胆的实验作品，以一种小说手法叙述了
发生在科伦拜恩高中的那场恐怖事件。它看起来像一部拍摄者隐
身的纪录片，摄影机一整天地跟着学生们，贴着他们的后背转，
记录着平常的擦肩而过，背景声音里隐隐传出一种不祥的兆头。
影片里没有解释片名（那是我们轻易不敢谈起的角落里的庞然大
物），也很少有什么实在的情节。它只是跟踪着数个学生一直到
第一声枪响的那个致命的时刻。接下来的我们几乎不能看，又不
能不看，因为它太让人震惊，以至于很难理解和接受。

　　大部分演员用的都是他们自己的名字。弗罗斯特和杜林扮演
迷恋枪的少年，他们冷静超然地制定着犯罪计划，好像那只是个
颜料球射击游戏。温和的鲁宾逊努力应付着喝醉酒的父亲以及学
校里辣妹的注意（也可能是敏感过头了）。迈克科奈尔是个摄影
师，偶尔会用相机记录下学校里的生活。芬克利和泰森是一对在
大厅里游荡的酷家伙。泰勒、乔治和大山是一个说长道短的三人
组合，也是片中最有趣的笑料。还有希克丝，一个被她的体育老

师和狄克逊吓唬的自卑的女孩，狄克逊是一个没有从枪口前跑开的肌肉男。

这是银幕上对美国高中生活最真实的反映之一。很大程度上是因为他们本身就是高中生，而不是20来岁的好莱坞演员。他们真实得惊人，我们很容易感受到他们的情绪，其中纠缠着学习的兴奋和青春期的烦恼。范·桑特把这些都收进了他精湛的摄影中，我们看到极长的镜头透迤地穿过重重走廊，气息从不间断。该片的摄制复杂而有激情，它让我们无比惊讶，让我们感情虚弱。它给了我们一些极其重要的警示（包括在网上可以购得杀人武器，容易得吓人），但一点没有笨拙的说教。而摄影机从不同视角观察同一场景的方式不仅有意义，而且漂亮地制造出一种紧张感。最后要说的是，它可能稍有些自我陶醉，但还是让人震惊和难忘。

—Rich Cline，《墙上影》

The peculiar story "structure" and pacing may test the patience of those expecting a more traditional cinematic story, but those who can understand what director Gus Van Sant is trying to do here won't be disappointed.

Van Sant uses the same approach he employed—though less effectively—in his previous film, 2000's patience-testing "Gerry". In "Elephant", he simply follows the students of a fictional Northwest high school during what appears to be a typical school day. As it begins, bleached-blond John is in trouble for being late, while aspiring photographer Eli has been more constructive, taking snapshots of some of the school's more colorful students.

Admittedly, after awhile, Van Sant's "fly-on-the-wall*" approach does become a bit tiresome (he really overdoes multiple perspectives on the same scene). However, he does know how to build tension, and there's plenty here.

—*Jeff Vice*, *Deseret News*

对那些更期待一个传统电影故事的观众来说，罕见的故事结构和节奏对他们的耐心是一次考验，而那些能够明白导演格斯·范·桑特意图的人则不会失望。

范·桑特再次使用了他上一部影片《盖瑞》（2000年）曾用过的手法，《盖瑞》同样需要耐心，不过要生硬一些。在《大象》中，他只是简单地跟踪虚构的西北部某高中的学生们，看起来就像是典型的中学里的一天。影片的开头，金发白肤的约翰惹上了迟到的麻烦，而精力旺盛的摄影爱好者艾里则积极得多，他正抓拍学校里比较有个性的学生。

不过毕竟要说，范·桑特的"零度观察"方法的确有点儿烦人（他用多重视角记录同一场景的做法用得实在太多了）。然而，他是真的知道如何制造张力，影片的紧张感十分突出。

—*Jeff Vice*，《德塞莱特新闻》

As for the shootings and possible motives, Van Sant says he didn't want to explain anything. That's his artistic choice, of course, and one can appreciate his unwillingness to offer up facile explanations for these episodes that have confounded the country. But the film lacks insight. We learn nothing that advances our understanding of these tragedies beyond the initial news reports.

Reactions will be mixed. The most interesting will be from those critics who slammed Michael Moore's "Bowling for Columbine" at last year's festival, finding it too didactic or too entertaining. Is "Elephant" what they prefer: a film that is maddeningly aloof and noncommittal? Controversy may help get "Elephant" theatrical distribution, but the boxoffice potential is modest.

As an exercise in technique, the film is not without merit as Harris Savides' camera and Leslie Shatz's sound design capture the mood and rhythms of campus life. But as a social document, its dispassionate demeanor and commitment to "pure" observation deprives the film of any real significance.

*—Kirk Honeycutt, The Hollywood Reporter*

对于那场校园枪击案和凶手可能的动机，范·桑特说自己不愿发表任何看法。这当然是他艺术性的选择，我们也可以欣赏他对这些曾经困扰全国的事件不轻慢不武断的态度。但是该片缺乏洞察力。我们对这些悲剧的理解没有任何促进，仍旧停留在那些最初的新闻报道上。

外界对此各种反应都有。最有趣的是在去年电影节上抨击了迈克尔·摩尔《科伦拜恩的保龄》的那些评论家，要么说《大象》太教条，要么说它太娱乐。《大象》不正是他们喜欢的那种沉闷晦涩得让人发狂的电影吗？争议或许对影院发行有好处，但是票房潜力一定是保守的。

影片在技术实验上的贡献颇多，摄影师哈里斯·萨维兹和音效师莱斯利·沙慈很好地捕捉了校园的气氛和节奏。然而作为一种社会纪录，它温吞吞的风格和"零度"观察原则剥夺了它任何的实际意义。

*—Kirk Honeycutt，《好莱坞报道》*

According to filmmaker Gus Van Sant, the title to his controversial *Elephant* is a reference to British director Alan Clarke's 1989 short film about the violence of Northern Ireland, which discussed the "metaphorical elephant in the room no one wanted to recognize". Given that Van Sant's movie is inspired (if that's the right word) by the Columbine Massacre, the conceit is provocative, but not easily addressed. The so-called elephant is provided by tension, portent, and haunted feelings that something bad is about to happen. But who ever knows if those feelings are really going to elicit such damage? Brilliantly, it's the absence of answers and, in many ways, that one uneasy elephant that makes the film so potent. Unlike Michael Moore's *Bowling For Columbine*, Van Sant isn't attempting to tell us why this happened; he just offers a portrait. The result is much more powerful and grievous.

—*Kim Morgan, Reel. com*

 

根据格斯·范·桑特自己所说，他的备受争议的影片《大象》这一片名参考了英国导演阿兰·克拉克 1989 年的那部反映北爱尔兰暴力的短片，其中讨论了"房间里谁也不愿去面对的一个隐喻意义上的大象"。范·桑特的创作灵感（如果这个说法合适）来源于科伦拜恩大屠杀，大象这个意象固然震撼，但并不容易理解。"大象"意味着紧张、凶兆，一种坏事来临前毛骨悚然的感觉。但是谁又知道这种不祥之感真的会兑现出这样的灾难？恰恰是这一答案的缺席，或者某种意义上一个不好对付的"大象"让该片有一种艺术力量。范·桑特不像迈克尔·摩尔的《科伦拜恩的保龄》那样试图告诉我们这件事为什么发生，他只是描述它，但是结果更有穿透力，更让人忧伤。

—*Kim Morgan, Reel. com*

## Note

Fly-on-the-wall documentary：fly on the wall 直译是"墙上的苍蝇"，常用来比喻"悄悄在旁观察的人"。在这里指一种纪录片美学观，主张不干预、不介入、不评价、不解说，犹如墙上的苍蝇一般，尽量隐蔽自身来旁观整个事件的自然进程。鼓励摄影师将自己隐藏起来，使被摄对象习惯他的存在，保持对事物的"零度情感"。

# City of God

# 上帝之城

**导演：**费尔南多·梅里尔斯（Fernando Meirelles）
　　　卡迪亚·兰德（Kátia Lund）
**原著：**保罗·林斯（Paulo Lins）
**主演：**亚历山大·罗德里格斯（Alexandre Rodrigues）
　　　马修斯·纳克加勒（Matheus Nachtergaele）
　　　道格拉斯·西尔瓦（Douglas Silva）
　　　艾丽丝·布拉加（Alice Braga）
**片长：**130 分钟
**发行：**米拉麦克斯影业公司（Miramax Films），2003 年

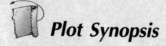

# Plot Synopsis

City of God is a housing project built in the 1960's that—in the early 80's—became one of the most dangerous places in Rio de Janeiro. The tale tells the stories of many characters whose lives sometimes intersect. However, all is seen through the eyes of a singular narrator: Buscap , a poor black youth too frail and scared to become an outlaw but also too smart to be content with underpaid, menial jobs. He grows up in a very violent environment. The odds are all against him. But Buscap soon discovers that he can see reality differently than others. His redemption is that he's been given an artist's point of view as a keen-eyed photographer. As Buscap is not the real protagonist of the film—only the narrator—he is not the one who makes the decisions that will determine the sequence of events. Nevertheless, not only his life is attached to what happens in the story, but it is also through Buscap 's perspective of life that one can understand the complicated layers and humanity of a world, apparently condemned to endless violence.

## 剧情简介

上帝之城是一个始于 60 年代的住房计划，到 80 年代早期，这里成了里约热内卢最危险的地方之一。本片叙述了不同时间横断面上许多人的故事。所有的故事都是通过阿炮的眼睛来看的，阿炮是一个可怜的年轻黑人，既因为胆小怯懦而做不了强盗，又因为太聪明而不满意低贱的工作。阿炮很快意识到他看到的现实与别人不同。这种艺术家的视角拯救了他，使他成了一个目光敏锐的摄影师。不过阿炮并不是影片的主角，他只是叙述者，并不是那个做决定并影响事件结果的人。然而，不只阿炮的个人生活是卷入其中的，而且只有通过阿炮的眼睛我们才能理解这个看起来无休止的暴力世界的那种复杂和人性。

# Critique

Consider it one of the signal ironies of world cinema: The A-
merican director Martin Scorsese pines for three decades to make a
great movie about urban gangs, and finally he gets a hundred million bucks from Miramax to turn his dream into reality.

And three years later, Miramax releases a great movie about urban gangs.

But that movie is not Scorsese's. It's not "Gangs of New
York", it's the gangs of Rio. It's Fernando Meirelles' astonishment
"City of God", about life and death—well, mostly death—in what
used to be called slums. In short, it's a trip to Hell and back, and
testimony for embittered cynics of all that a movie can be.

Do these pathologies sound familiar? Young men, no hope,
too many guns, too much testosterone, crushing impoverishment,
a macho mythology, a failed economy, municipal corruption everywhere, and rock music? Subtract the last, substitute knives for
guns, and you could have any slum cesspool in the world over the
last 4,000 years; restore the guns and the rock and you have . . .
well, you pick 'em just about anywhere in the good old U. S. of
A.; but you certainly have the City of God, the actual name of a
huge housing project built in the '60s outside Rio that oozes pus
and pestilence for the three generations that this movie tracks.

The movie is conceived as a kind of anecdotal history (it is de-
rived from a huge novel by a survivor, an escapee from the place)
of one of the world's previously impenetrable, blasphemed zones. It
rolls across the decades, charting the rise and fall of petty empires,
the brief supernova of gangster superstardom, the overturning of an
older order by a yet meaner, more ruthless younger one; these e-

vents are lit up, here and there, by little spurts of recognizable behavior, even love.

It is a young man's movie: It adores action, swagger, local color, eccentricity, machismo, stupidity. Meirelles just can't stop telling stories, and he can't stop reveling in the goopy mud of bad behavior as it plays out in the swamp of heart and city. He's like a mad anthropologist who's found an undiscovered tribe in the mountains of New Guinea and can't leave it alone. You feel his love of his subject, of his own infernally gifted filmmaking, of the freedom he suddenly feels in features (he'd directed commercials in San Paolo); you feel the quickening of energy and endless possibility in him. So the result is a contradiction: a joyous film about murder.

"City of God" never gives itself over to pure nihilism. In fact, under the bravado, it's tragic, and that shell of ironic bravado keeps it watchable, though even that may be a close call for many genteel moviegoers: It's not for the weak of heart or stomach. Its evocations of casual, almost numbingly regular violence just go on and on and on.

If one of the moral responsibilities of the movies is to put you in places where you'd never go and live lives you'd never live, then "City of God" is great moviemaking. This one admits no other moral responsibilities. It merely gazes pitilessly at the real, and maybe that reality is too hard to take. It offers scant optimism to policymakers of any stripe. It advises liberals that social programs are pointless when applied to the violent vitality of the streets, and it advises conservatives that stern bromides about responsibility are as ineffective against the will to violence as a fistful of feathers. It says man is dark and doomed and stupid. But it also says he's alive and kicking and magnificent.

—*Stephen Hunter, Washington Post*

　　这简直是世界电影的一大笑话：美国导演马丁·斯科赛斯渴望了30年要拍一部关于城市黑帮的伟大作品，最终他从米拉麦克斯拿到了可以把梦想变为现实的一亿美金。

　　三年以后，米拉麦克斯发行了一部关于城市黑帮的伟大电影。

　　但该片并不是斯科赛斯的作品，并不是"纽约黑帮"，而是里约热内卢的黑帮，是费尔南多·梅里尔斯让人惊讶的《上帝之城》，关于所谓的贫民窟的生活和死亡——尤其是死亡。简而言之，这是一趟地狱之旅，是苦难和愤怒的明证，是一部电影所能承载的极致。

　　这些症状听起来不熟悉吗？年轻人，渺茫的希望，泛滥的枪支，过剩的荷尔蒙，致命的贫穷，雄性的神话，崩溃的经济，遍地的政治腐败，还有摇滚乐？减去最后这条，并把枪替换成刀，这些特征就可以概括过去4000年来所有的贫民窟；加上枪和摇滚乐，它就是过去那可爱美国的任何地方。但你看到的确实是上帝之城，这是60年代建在里约热内卢外面的住房计划的真实名字，而这个住房计划则用脓疮和瘟疫足足淹没了影片所追踪的三代人。

　　该片被看作是世界上一个曾经被隔绝、被诅咒的地带的野史（它取材于一个从中逃离出来的幸存者写下的大部头的小说）。它跨越了数十年，描绘了一个微型王国的起起伏伏，一个横空出世的超级强盗短暂的一生，一种旧秩序被更卑鄙、更残忍的年轻一代所替代的过程。这样的事情此起彼伏着，而导火索都是一些我们熟悉的行为，甚至是爱。

　　这是一部年轻人的电影：它崇尚行动、狂妄、乡土色、怪癖、雄性、还有愚蠢。梅里尔斯克制不住地要讲故事，他在这个人性和城市的沼泽里筋疲力尽，同时也忘情于那种暴行的粗俗野蛮中。他像一个发疯的人类学家，在新几内亚岛的山上发现了一个不为人知的部落，不忍离去。你感到了他热爱他的研究，热爱他自己魔鬼般的电影才华，热爱他在剧情片中突然找到的自由（他过去在圣保罗做商业广告的导演）。你感到了他迸发的活力和无穷的可能性。因此，这是一个悖论性的结果：一部欢乐的凶杀片。

《上帝之城》从来没有向虚无主义投降。事实上，它那虚张声势的喧哗之下是不折不扣的悲剧。这个反讽性的外壳保证了它的可看性，尽管这甚至在很多趣味高雅的电影观众那儿冒了风险：它的目的不是要刺激你的心脏或胃。它把我们从对暴力的习以为常和麻木不仁中不断地唤醒又唤醒。

如果电影的道德责任之一是把你放在你从不会去的地方，让你过你从不会过的生活，那么《上帝之城》绝对是一部伟大的电影。它不用再承担其它的道德责任。它无情地凝视着现实，哪怕这现实严酷得让人难以接受。它把侥幸的乐观主义坦陈给各种决策者。它告诉自由派们，在暴力生长的地方，社会项目毫无意义。它告诉保守派们，道德的陈腐教条在暴力意志面前轻如鸿毛。它陈述人是黑暗的、宿命的、愚蠢的。它也陈述人是活泼的、好斗的、壮阔的。

—Stephen Hunter，《华盛顿邮报》

Even further from left field* came the Miramax film, *City of God*. I have to tell you, I had zero awareness of what I was walking into when I got to the screening room. And all it turned out to be was one of the most impressive directorial debuts in what has been an exceptional few years for directorial debuts. This film is better than *Amores Perros*. This film will be more influential than movies like *Chungking Express*. This film suggests that director Fernando Meirelles has even more upside than Christopher Nolan. This film is the most original synthesis of pop storytelling into a new form since *The Matrix*. And this film offers Meirelles managing to top the work of a highly talented and experienced director, Barbet Schroeder, in a similar look at violence, *Our Lady of the Assassins*.

I don't know whether Brazil will off the film up as their Best Foreign Language Academy Award nominee. But if they do, it's pretty hard to imagine that any other film will be any better. It is possible that Oscar voters will turn away from the violence of the story and find something "nicer". But that would be a shame. You never know quite whom you have after just one film, but Fernando

Meirelles looks like he could be up on the very, very highest level of directors.

This is movie of extreme violence, which will certainly put off much of the audience. But, like *Our Lady of the Assassins*, the violence is directly attached to the moral ambiguities of its characters lives. One of Meirelles strong influences, visually and on the soundtrack, is blaxploitation*. This makes enormous sense, since this is, in its way, a ghetto exploitation film. Another film it reminded me of was last year's Toronto attention-getter, *Malunde*, which told the story of a black street kid in South Africa who hooks up with an older white man. In what was a pretty soft-hearted film there were shocks, like kids sniffing glue in brown paper bags. Here, there are entire mini-gangs of kids 10 and under. But their motivations and the growth of their anarchic attitudes is a key part of the storytelling.

I was taken, time after time, by the way Merielles wove this story, with a skill that made *Pulp Fiction* seem simplistic, *Memento* confusing and Guy Ritchie as shallow as he obviously is. Meirelles uses time and space and movement with wild abandon and absolute authority.

—*David Poland*, *The Hot Button*

　　《上帝之城》是由非主流的米拉麦克斯发行的。说实话，当我走进放映室时我对该片几乎一无所知。不料这竟是少见的让人印象最深刻的导演首映场之一。它好过《爱情是狗娘》。它的影响将比《重庆森林》还要深远。它证明费尔南多·梅里尔斯的优势甚至比克里斯托弗·诺兰还要大。它是《黑客帝国》之后把流行的叙事元素综合得最新颖的影片。它让梅里尔斯可以超越才华横溢、经验丰富的导演巴贝特·施罗德，后者的《杀手的童贞》是一部同样关照了暴力的影片。

　　不知道巴西是否会将该片送审奥斯卡最佳外语片提名，如果被送审，则很难想象还会有哪部电影比《上帝之城》更优秀。不过奥斯卡的投票人很可能因为反感该片的暴力转而去找"更好"

的东西。但这将会是一种耻辱。你根本不确定除了该片还有谁有资格，然而费尔南多·梅里尔斯看起来可以跻身于水准最最高的导演之列。

这是一部极端暴力的影片，它必定会引起很多观众的厌恶。但就像《杀手的童贞》一样，其中的暴力是直接反映了人物在道德上的含糊性。不论是在视觉还是在声音的处理上，梅里尔斯都深受黑人电影风格的影响。这种风格的意义是巨大的，因为这是一部探索少数民族聚居区的影片。该片还能让我联想到的另外一部影片是去年在多伦多颇有影响的《马伦地》，讲的是一个南非黑人街区的男孩与一个年长的白人相勾结的故事。震惊总要出现在一部慈悲为怀的影片中，就像小孩嗅到了褐色牛皮纸袋里浆糊的味道。我们在该片中看到了一些不折不扣的小土匪，他们连十岁都不到。然而他们的动机，他们无政府态度的形成是影片叙事中关键的一部分。

我一再地折服于梅里尔斯叙述故事的技巧，相形之下，《低俗小说》太简单，《记忆碎片》太混乱，盖·里奇太浅薄。无论在时间、空间还是运动上，梅里尔斯都疯狂放肆又把握十足。

——David Poland，《热按钮》

## Note

Left field：棒球术语，指左外场，从本垒板处看起来左边外场的第三个。引申为一个远离中心或主流的位置、观点或原因。

Blaxploitation：英文原意为"对黑人兴趣的利用"，专指在美国70年代兴起的一种黑人电影风格，该类型的电影主要倾向于满足黑人观众的电影欣赏品位，以黑人英雄题材为主，电影全篇很少会出现白人演员，主题大多为惩恶扬善以暴制暴的主题。Blaxploitation电影由于题材、制作人员、欣赏观众的多方面原因，使得电影音乐偏重使用当时黑人流行风格，节奏明快、贯穿流畅。

# 2046

**导演/编剧**：王家卫（**Kar Wai Wong**）

　　**主演**：梁朝伟（**Tony Leung**）

　　　　　巩俐（**Li Gong**）

　　　　　章子怡（**Ziyi Zhang**）

　　　　　木村拓哉（**Takuya Kimura**）

　　　　　王菲（**Faye Wong**）

　　　　　刘嘉玲（**Carina Lau**）

　　　　　张　震（**Zhen Zhang**）

　　　　　董　洁（**Jie Dong**）

　　　　　张曼玉（**Maggie Cheung**）

　　**片长**：129 分钟

　　**制作**：春光映画（**Block 2 Pictures Inc.**），2004 年

2046

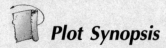

## *Plot Synopsis*

Director Wong Kar-Wai moves back and forth in time as he reexamines and amplifies the themes from his film In the Mood for Love in this offbeat romantic drama. Opening in the year 2046, in which a man named Tak (Takuya Kimura) attempts to persuades wjw 1967 (Faye Wong) to travel back in time with him, the film soon shifts to the year 1966, in which Chow Mo-wan (Tony Leung Chiu-wai), a struggling author, asks the woman he loves, Su Lizhen (Gong Li) to sail with him from Singapore to Hong Kong on Christmas Eve. She declines, and over the next three years, we return to Chow Mo-wan on December 24 as he finds himself with another woman each year—lighthearted Lulu (Carina Lau) in 1967, eccentric hotel heiress Wang Jingwen (Faye Wong) in 1968, and Bai Ling (Zhang Ziyi), a high-class prostitute, in 1969. In time, Chow Mo-wan and Wang Jingwen become reacquainted, and a love affair blooms, but the fates are not on their side.

## 剧情简介

在这部风格化的浪漫剧中，导演王家卫在时间中来回穿梭，回味和放大着《花样年华》中的主题。影片开头，2046年的Tak（木村拓哉）试图说服1967年的王静雯（王菲）和他一起回到时间的过去。时间刹那间回到1966年，挣扎中的作家周慕云（梁朝伟）请求他爱的女人苏丽珍（巩俐）在圣诞夜和他一起从新加坡坐船回香港。她拒绝了他，在接下来的三年中，我们看到他和不同的女人一起度过12月24日这个晚上——1967年和快乐的Lulu（刘嘉玲），1968年和孤僻的酒店女继承人王静雯，1969年和高级妓女白玲（章子怡）。最终，周慕云和王静雯重新相知，爱火重燃，但是命运不由他们自己做主。

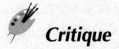
## Critique

It is always too early or too late for love in a Wong Kar Wai film, and his characters spend their days in yearnings and regrets. "In the Mood for Love" (2001) brought that erotic sadness to a kind of perfection in its story of a man and a woman who live in hotel rooms next to each other, and want to become lovers but never do, because his wife and her husband are lovers, and "for us to do the same thing would mean we are no better than they are". Yes, but no worse, and perhaps happier. Isn't it strange, that most of the truths about love are banal?

"2046" is an indirect, oblique continuation of the earlier one. It stars Tony Leung as Chow Mo Wan, also the name of his character in "In the Mood for Love", and there is a brief role for Maggie Cheung, his co-star in that film; they are not necessarily playing the same characters. There was also a room 2046 in the other film, so there are subterranean connections between the two, but they operate something like the express train to the year 2046 in this one: All memories are there in the future, we are told, but no one has ever returned.

We gather that "2046" is the name of a science fiction novel being written by Chow. It is also the room next to his in the hotel where much of this movie takes place—a room lived in by a series of women he loves. Not coincidentally, 2046 is also the year set by China for the expiration of Hong Kong's quasi-independence from the mainland. Does that make the movie "2046" a parable about

Hong Kong? You could find parallels, I'm sure, but that doesn't seem to be the point. Chow observes that if he hadn't seen the number 2046 on a room, he wouldn't have started his futuristic novel, and it is just barely possible that Wong is telling us this movie was inspired when he asked himself what happened in Room 2046 after "In the Mood for Love" was over. Or before it began. Whatever.

These speculations are probably of no help in understanding the movie, which exists primarily as a visual style imposed upon beautiful faces; Josef von Sternberg's obsession with Marlene Dietrich is mirrored here by Wong Kar Wai's fascination with the beauty of Ziyi Zhang, Gong Li, Faye Wong, Carina Lau and Maggie Cheung, and in the careworn eyes and tired smile of Tony Leung, his Bogart. Like von Sternberg, he films his actors mostly in close-up and medium shot, with baroque architectural details in the background, with cigarette smoke constantly coiling through the air. There are a lot of foreground screens (doorjambs, draperies, walls, furniture) to add texture and detail while concealing parts of those faces. The film is in lurid colors, a pulp counterpoint to the elegance of the action.

Since it is by Wong Kar Wai, "2046" is visually stunning. He uses three cinematographers but one style, that tries to evoke mood more than meaning. The movie as a whole, unfortunately, never seems sure of itself. It's like a sketchbook. These are images, tones, dialogue and characters that Wong is sure of, and he practices them, but he does not seem very sure why he is making the movie, or where it should end.

"2046" arrived at the last minute at Cannes 2003, after missing its earlier screenings; the final reel reportedly arrived at the airport almost as the first was being shown. It was said to be unfinished, and indeed there were skeletal special effects that now appear in final form, but perhaps it was never really finished in his mind. Perhaps he would have appreciated the luxury that Woody Allen had with "Crimes and Misdemeanors"; he looked at the first cut of the film, threw out the first act, called the actors back and reshot, focusing on what turned out to be the central story. Watching "2046", I wonder what it could possibly mean to anyone not familiar with Wong's work and style. Unlike "In the Mood for Love", it is not a self-contained film, although it's certainly a lovely meander.

—*Roger Ebert, Chicago Sun-Times*

　　置身于王家卫电影中的感觉不是太早，就是太晚，他的人物不是活在憧憬中。就是活在悔恨中。《花样年华》将爱欲之伤托付于一种完美。故事中的男人和女人相住一墙之隔，相爱而不得相亲，因为他的妻子和她的丈夫有染，因为"我们要是也这么做，就不比他们好多少"。没错，不过这样不一定更难过，说不定还会有一种欢喜。这难道不奇怪吗？爱的真谛原来如此平凡。

　　《2046》是对以往影片的一种别样继续。梁朝伟以《花样年华》中周慕云的身份再度出场，他在那部影片中的搭档张曼玉亦有一个简短的角色，不过他们不一定仍然饰演当年的人物。《花样年华》中也有一个2046号的房间，因此两部影片之间有一种隐晦的联系，这大约体现为那列开往2046年的特别快车：据说所有的记忆都存在于未来中，但是没有一个人返回来。

　　我们归纳出"2046"是周慕云所写的一部科幻小说的名字，也是酒店中周慕云隔壁房间的号码，影片中有很多故事都发生于此——这个房间曾经入住了一系列他爱过的女人。无独有偶，2046年也是香港回归50年期满的日子。《2046》因此成了一个关于香港的寓言吗？我相信你能找到这种类比，但这似乎不是题中之义。周慕云说如果他没有看见门上的这个2046号，他不会动手写这部未来主义的小说。而这似乎也不可能是王家卫想告诉我们，该片的灵感来源于他自己问自己，2046号在《花样年华》之后还有什么故事发生；或者之前，无论哪一种。

或许这些猜测对帮助理解影片毫无用处，影片看起来就是一堆讲究视觉风格的美丽面孔。就像约瑟夫·冯·史登堡迷恋玛琳·黛德莉，王家卫沉迷于章子怡、巩俐、王菲、刘嘉玲和张曼玉的美丽，以及梁朝伟忧郁的眼神和疲倦的笑容里，梁朝伟就是他的鲍嘉。和冯·史登堡一样，王家卫总将他的演员置于特写和中景镜头中，背景是巴洛克建筑的细节，烟雾一直在空气中缠绕。前景中各种屏障（门框、帏帐、墙壁、家具）增加着肌理和细节，并半遮半露出那些面孔。影片的色彩浓得逼人，森森鬼气呼应着优雅的动作。

不愧是王家卫的作品，《2046》在视觉上绚烂夺目。他起用了三个摄影师而统一于一种风格中，一种唤起情绪而不是意义的风格。然而，该片似乎并不确信自身是一个整体，看起来就像一个写生集。对于形象、色调、对话、人物，王家卫足以把握它们，实践它们，但他似乎并不确定为什么拍这个片子，也不知道该在哪里结束。

错过了早先的放映后，《2046》在最后一分钟抵达2003年的戛纳电影节，传说第一卷胶片放映时，最后一卷才刚到机场。听说这一版并未完成，而事实上在最终版中仍然能看到特效的痕迹，说不定在导演的脑子里它永远都没有真正地完成。说不定他喜欢像伍迪·艾伦拍摄《爱与罪》那样奢侈，在看过粗剪后决定放弃第一版演出，召回演员重新拍摄，集中打磨出那个核心故事。看《2046》时，我好奇那些不熟悉王家卫作品和风格的人对该片会怎样看。它不像《花样年华》那样独立完整，虽然它的确是一场愉快的漫游。

——*Roger Ebert*，《芝加哥太阳时报》

This is really Zhang's movie far more than Gong's or Cheung's.

And that's what makes it so wondrous: It's so nice to see this fiery young actress in a more or less modern-day role ( her turn in the ridiculous Jackie Chan comedy "Rush Hour 2" doesn't count ). She's got spunk; I love spunk. She's not just beautiful, she's so athrob with life that the movie almost makes you feel her physical presence. Moreover, she's the only person in the film whom Wong seems to care about, and her identity is so strong that it seems to hold the story together most of the time; it really should have been only about her.

——*Stephen Hunter*, *Washington Post*

这绝对是一部章子怡的电影，而不是巩俐或张曼玉的。

是她让影片惊艳照人：不知有多高兴地能看到这个激情丰沛的年轻女演员终于演了一个多少现代点儿的角色（她在成龙那部可笑的喜剧《尖峰时刻2》的转型可不算数）。她非常有爆发力；我喜欢爆发力。她不只是漂亮，她能为生活而悸动，影片几乎能让你感受到她的生命气息。此外，她似乎是王家卫在影片中唯一关心的人，而且她的气场太强大，似乎多数时候故事都被她紧紧地抓在一起。这部电影本来就应该是只关于她的。

——*Stephen Hunter*，《华盛顿邮报》

Wong is less abashed by the insanely beautiful than any other current director. Every shot is colored and composed to within an inch of[*] its life, which may be another way of saying that "2046" is a near-death experience. So many pearls gleaming in the half-dark; so much creaseless ravishment in the high silk collar of a Chinese dress; so much smoke, and so much rain, though never enough to leave the characters cross or damp-merely enough to patter around them, like applause. When even the munching of a sandwich is glossed by slow motion, as if it were a sacred rite, should we kneel in awe, or could we be forgiven for suppressing a yawn?

—*Anthony Lane*, *The New Yorker*

和其他当代导演相比，王家卫很少为过度的美感到不安。每一个镜头的色彩和结构都无限的生动，用另一种表达来说，《2046》是一场濒死体验。太多的珍珠在黯淡处微光隐隐；太浓的销魂气息从中国旗袍的高领下幽幽泛出；太多的烟，太多的雨，但从来没有多到能夺去人物的风度——只是多到能够在他们的周围轻轻拍打着，仿佛掌声。甚至连咀嚼三明治也要在镜头升格中变得意味深长，如同神圣的仪式——我们是该肃然起敬呢，还是原谅自己刚刚压下去一个呵欠？

—*Anthony Lane*,《纽约客》

> **Note**
>
> Within an inch of：临近，几乎达到某一点。比如 came within an inch of death, 意为临近死亡的边缘。

# The Sun

# 太 阳

**导演:** 亚历山大·索科洛夫 (Aleksandr Sokurov)

**编剧:** 尤里·阿拉波夫 (Yuri Arabov)

**主演:** 尾形一成 (Issei Ogata)

　　　　罗伯特·唐森 (Robert Dawson)

**片长:** 115 分钟

**制作:** Downtown Pictures, 2005 年

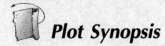

# *Plot Synopsis*

As Japan nears defeat at the end of World War II, Emperor Hirohito starts his day in a bunker underneath the Imperial Palace in Toyko. A servant reads to him a list of activities for the day, including a meeting with his ministers, marine biology research, and writing his son. Hirohito muses about the impact on such schedules when the Americans arrive but is told that as long as there is a solitary Japanese person living, the Americans will not reach The Emperor. Hirohito replies that he at times feels like he himself will be the last Japanese person left alive. The servant reminds him that he is a deity, not a person, but Hirohito points out that he has a body just like any other man. He later reflects on the causes of the war when dictating observations about a hermit crab, and then about the peace to come when composing a letter to his son. Soon enough General Douglas MacArthur's personal car is sent to bring him through the ruins of Tokyo for a meeting with the supreme commander of the victorious occupying forces. Underlying all the conversation that follows is the question of Hirohito's future, either as Emperor or a war criminal. The two very different men strangely bond after sharing dinner and Havana cigars, and Hirohito leaves, renounces his divine nature, and is re-united with his family in the palace to face a new life to help re-build his war-ravaged country as a constitutional monarch.

## 剧情简介

二战即将结束日本临近战败时,在东京皇宫的地下堡垒中,昭和天皇裕仁开始了他的一天。一个仆人念给他当天的日程安排,包括和大臣的会议、海洋生物学研究、给儿子写信。裕仁正在考虑对日程的影响,美国人来了,并对他说,只要住在这里的只是一个孤独的日本人,美国人便不会对皇帝动手。裕仁回答,他常常感到自己将是最后一个存活的日本人。仆人提醒他,他是神,不是人,而裕仁指出他觉得自己的身体和其他人没有什么不同。稍后,他一边反省战争的原因,一边指示对寄生蟹做观察,之后他的心情随着给儿子写信而平静下来。不一会儿,麦克阿瑟将军的私人车接他赴会,汽车穿过东京的废墟,把他带到获胜方占领军的最高指挥官面前。所有谈话的言下之意都指向裕仁的前途,是继续做皇帝还是做战犯。两个十分不同的人在共享一餐和哈瓦那雪茄后产生了一种微妙的联系,裕仁离开,宣布放弃他天赋的神的身份,回到宫中和家人团聚。从此他要面对新的生活,把这个被战争摧毁的国家重建成一个君主立宪制的日本。

## *Critique*

The Sun is an extremely quiet film—often quite difficult to e-ven hear—but notably present on the film's soundtrack is the persis-tent sounds of recording. Often the scratching of pen on paper—as Emperor Hirohito composes a haiku in his diary, or as a secretary records meetings between the emperor and his advisors—are the loudest sounds to be heard, and the whir and crackle of a detuned radio floats occasionally in the background. This is particularly nota-ble as so little is known about Hirohito, and his diaries and the re-cords of his meetings remain hidden from the public.

The third of Aleksandr Sokurov's films of conjectural biogra-phy, The Sun is an idiosyncratic portrait of Emperor Hirohito, nar-rowly focused on the days leading up to and following Japan's sur-render to Allied forces at the end of World War II. Like his previ-ous films, Moloch and Taurus (which respectively portrayed Hitler and Lenin), The Sun depicts its central figure as a rarefied and slightly buffoonish person who is physically and mentally cut off from the world. Like Hitler in his Alpine Eagle's Nest, and Lenin in his convalescence, the emperor exists in complete isolation in his palace, his personal and political life inextricably bound by a rigor-ously organized schedule of work and leisure.

Contrary to many contemporary histories, Sokurov's film de-picts Hirohito as a complete na f with little or no concept of the military expansion and operations of his country's regime. Late in the film, Hirohito tells General MacArthur that, following the bombing of Hiroshima and Nagasaki, he feared his country was be-ing invaded by wild beasts. Such a fear finds no sympathy in Mac-Arthur, who instantly invokes Pearl Harbor, much to the emperor's bemusement.

What the film portrays is a Hirohito who is wholly imprisoned in his deification and cloistered by tradition and politics. Decades of obsequiousness and a boundless indulgence of his eccentricity have given Hirohito the aspect of a sheltered manchild, puttering around the dim confines of his palace, occasionally poking into his laboratory to immerse himself in the study of marine biology. As inhabited by Issey Ogata, in a very strange performance, Hirohito mutters to himself, makes peculiar fish-mouth faces, and inquisitively pores over photographs of Marlene Dietrich, Hitler, and Charlie Chaplin. Oddest of all, with his furtive movements and childlike charm, Ogata even exploits the emperor's resemblance to Chaplin's Tramp, hammily sniffing flowers for U. S. Army photographers and leaving General MacArthur with the feeling that, "he reminds me of someone, but I can't think whom".

Historically factual or no, Sokurov's film serves as an interesting exercise in the shattering of myths. Just as the emperor eventually renounces his status as a god—to the shame of his country, and to the seeming relief of him and his wife—*The Sun* divests the image of Hirohito of any remaining vestiges of mystery or imperial prestige. The only mystery that remains is a sense of the confusion that awaits Japan in the wake of its surrender, a confusion reinforced by the characteristically muddy grayness of Sokurov's images.

In presenting this eccentric, historically dubious biography, Sokurov seems to have a certain faith in his audience, trusting their perceptiveness about the ways in which history is portrayed onscreen. To make a film about Hirohito (as a film about Hitler or Lenin) is to tread a dangerous path, one likely to incite controversy about the relative truth of its portrayal and to leave bewildered those who want a neat and comprehensive historical primer. Throughout the film, Sokurov playfully adopts historiographic ideas, only to drop them quickly. Familiar analogies and explanations are tried on and discarded at random—like the "emperor : state :: brain : body" syllogism. In many ways, *The Sun* accomplishes the greatest feat that any historical film can: to leave the viewer more confused and uncertain about his or her knowledge than he or she was before the film began.

—Leo Goldsmith, *Not Coming to a Theater Near You*

《太阳》是一部极端安静的影片，甚至常常静得使你听不见，但是你又能很明显地听到音轨上持续录音的声音。有时那种笔划在纸上的声音（当裕仁天皇在日记中记下一首俳句，或者当书记员记录天皇和顾问间的会议时）响亮得刺耳，还有一架失真的收音机偶尔在背景里呼哧呼哧哔哔剥剥地发出声响。这种引人注意的独特的处理方式似乎意味着我们对裕仁所知甚少，他的日记和会议记录一直存在于公众的视野之外。

《太阳》是亚历山大·索科洛夫的第三部猜测型传记片。它以一种极特殊的风格描绘着天皇裕仁，篇幅全部集中在二战结束后日本向盟军宣告投降前后的日子里。像前两部《莫洛赫》和《金牛座》（分别描绘了希特勒和列宁）一样，《太阳》把主人公刻画成一个无辜的，略微有些像小丑的，无论身体还是心灵都与外界断绝的形象。像希特勒呆在他的鹰巢里，列宁在他的疗养处，日本天皇则完全隔绝在皇宫中，他的私人生活和政治生活都被一种严密计划的工作和休闲日程所束缚，无法解脱。

与许多当代史相反，在索科洛夫的电影里，裕仁一派天真，对帝国的军事扩张和政权运行全无概念。在影片后面，裕仁告诉麦克阿瑟将军，当原子弹炸了广岛和长崎后，他惊恐地感到他的国家正遭到野兽的侵袭。这种恐惧并没有引起麦克阿瑟的同情，对方立刻提起珍珠港，让裕仁困惑不已。

该片所刻画的裕仁是一个完全被传统、政治和神的身份所监禁、疏离的人。几十年的奉承以及孤僻性格的放纵养成了裕仁惯于被呵护、像个孩子一样长不大的一面，他喜欢在皇宫的幽深处闲逛，偶尔逛进他的实验室，沉浸在海洋生物学研究中。在演员尾形一成十分陌生化的诠释中，裕仁自言自语着什么，脸孔绷成奇特的鱼嘴形，好奇地凝视着玛琳·黛德莉、希特勒和查理·卓别林的照片。最奇特的要属他那种鬼鬼祟祟的姿势和儿童般的快乐，尾形一成甚至让裕仁像卓别林那样走路，或者为了给美国军队的摄影师摆造型而凑近花朵使劲儿闻，这让麦克阿瑟感觉"他让我想起一个人，可又想不起来是谁"。

不论历史真实性如何，索科洛夫的电影都是一次为神话去魅的有趣尝试。就像天皇最终抛弃他神的身份，让他的国家放下耻辱，让他和他的妻子也如释重负一样，《太阳》将裕仁作为一个人的形象从一切残存的神秘和天皇的声望中剥离出来。而仅存的神秘是等待着日本的那种投降后的困惑，一种被索科洛夫有意晦暗不明的影像所加强的困惑。

在呈现这部古怪的、历史含糊的传记片时，索科洛夫似乎对观众充满信心，相信他们能够理解这种在银幕上描绘历史的方式。拍摄这种关于裕仁（还有希特勒或列宁）的电影等于踏上了一条险途，它既可能引起在历史真实性上的争议，又可能让那些喜欢顺畅的、易于理解的历史普及读物的人不知所措。索科洛夫在影片中随时玩笑般地引用着史学观点，然后随时抛弃。一些司空见惯的类比和阐释被随拿随扔，比如"天皇相对于国家 = 大脑相对于身体"的荒谬逻辑。某种意义上，《太阳》具有一种任何历史片都难以达到的罕见的品质，即让观众在看过影片之后对自己旧有的认识更加困惑，更加怀疑。

—*Leo Goldsmith*，《*Not Coming to a Theater Near You*》

After examining Hitler in "Moloch" and a stroke-addled Lenin in "Taurus", Alexander Sokurov's "The Sun" completes the helmer's dictator trilogy on an up note with Emperor Hirohito surrendering at the end of World War II. Although not as crowd-pleasing as Sokurov's 2002 hit "Russian Ark", at least "The Sun" isn't as rebarbative as his last, "Father and Son". It even packs in a few stylized special effects and has some outright funny moments, a pleasant surprise from a helmer hardly known for laffs. Still, box office forecast predicts heavy weather for "The Sun", with warmer climes in sell-through.

—*Leslie Felperin*，*Variety*

继《莫洛赫》中审视了希特勒和《金牛座》中刻画了一个毁于中风的列宁后，亚历山大·索科洛夫的《太阳》这次将镜头对准了二战结束后日本天皇裕仁投降的前前后后，从而给他的独裁者三部曲划上了句号。虽然该片没有像他 2002 年的《俄罗斯方舟》那样轰动一时，但也不像他的上一部《父与子》那样惹人讨厌。它甚至有很多逗人的特效和直率的滑稽，让人惊讶而愉快地看到领袖那难得一见的滑稽可笑的一面。此外，《太阳》的票房预计不会太好，DVD 的销售则相对要好一点。

—*Leslie Felperin*，《综艺》

The film moves with a very deliberate and slow pace, much like a film by Andrei Tarkovsky. The difference is that there is a lot of history to think about in these pauses. This film seems to show the man as a prisoner of his status. It is claimed that he knew little of that his generals were doing in his name and would not have condoned a lot of what was happening.

Issey Ogata plays the emperor as a quiet contemplative man. His expressions with its mouth suggest that of a carp, a fish revered in Japan for its tenacity. Above all he is a man who desperately is searching for his responsibilities to do not what he wants but what is right.

—*Mark R. Leeper*, *rec. arts. movies. reviews*

影片的运动节奏异常地缓慢而意味深长，就像安德烈·塔可夫斯基的作品一样。不同之处是这种踟蹰给历史思考留下了空间。该片似乎是要证明这个人是他的身份的囚徒。他对将军们以他的名义所做的一切一无所知，而且对所发生之事发自内心地难以原谅。

尾形一成将天皇塑造成了一个安静的，喜欢沉思的人。他的表情和嘴型看起来像鲤鱼一样。日本人尊敬鲤鱼，因为觉得它坚韧。总而言之，他是一个拼命地从责任出发，做应做（而不是想做）之事的人。

—*Mark R. Leeper*, *rec. arts. mouies. reviews* 网站

# The Blind Swordsman：Zatoichi

# 座头市

**导演/编剧**：北野武（Kitano Takeshi）

**主演**：北野武（Kitano Takeshi）

浅野忠信（Tadanobu Asano）

夏川结衣（Yui Natsukawa）

**片长**：116 分钟

**制作**：北野武工作室（Office Kitano），2003 年

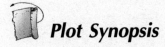

# *Plot Synopsis*

Zatoichi is a 19th century blind nomad who makes his living as a gambler and masseur. However, behind this humble facade, he is a master swordsman gifted with a lightning-fast draw and breathtaking precision. While wandering, Zatoichi discovers a remote mountain village at the mercy of Ginzo, a ruthless gang-leader. Ginzo disposes of anyone who gets in his way, especially after hiring the mighty samurai ronin, Hattori, as a bodyguard. After a raucous night of gambling in town, Zatoichi encoutners a pair of geishas—as dangerous as they are beautiful—who've come to avenge their parents' murder. As the paths of these and other colorful characters intertwine, Ginzo's henchmen are soon after Zatoichi. With his legendary cane sword at his side, the stage is set for a riveting showdown.

## 剧情简介

座头市是一位双目失明的流浪者，他生活在19世纪，以赌博和给人按摩为生。然而在这一卑贱的身份背后，他实际是一个名震江湖的剑客，其剑法快如闪电，而且准确得让人窒息。在流浪中，座头市来到一个偏远的山村，把持山头的是残忍的黑社会老大银藏。银藏要铲除一切拦路之人，尤其是雇用了本领高强的武士服部后就更加肆无忌惮。在一个无声的夜晚，座头市在镇里的赌场上遇到一对美丽而危险的艺妓，她们的使命是向杀害父母的凶手复仇。这些故事相互交织起来，还有其他一些形形色色的人物卷入其中，银藏的党羽很快开始追捕座头市。座头市握起传说中的武士刀，令人激动的摊牌时刻来临了。

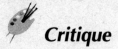

## *Critique*

Zatoichi, the hero of 26 feature films and a long-running television series in his native Japan, was a wandering masseur, gambler, and warrior (played by Shintaro Katsu from 1962 to 1989) who fought for the rights of the downtrodden working-class man against villainous crime lords and land barons. In this reinterpretation of the Japanese icon, director Kitano plays Zatoichi with blond hair and a red cane (which houses his ferocious blade), and reimagines the friendly samurai as a dour, remote hero prone to isolate himself in meditative silences. While Kitano retains the character's impish chuckle and sympathy for the countryside's maligned outcasts, his Zatoichi substitutes Katsu's balletic gracefulness with a swift physicality. This new Zatoichi is a viper coiled to strike with tornado-like ferocity at any moment, and in his silent-but-deadly manner, the character more than slightly resembles the gun-toting yakuza madmen of Kitano's Sonatine and Brother.

Kitano shoots with a steady efficiency that favors slow, graceful dolly shots and, in the film's signature visual flourish, 360-degree rotating pans around characters. His unadorned direction provides logical visual coherence to the frenetic, bloodstained action sequences, which include a duel on the beach and a stunning rain-soaked skirmish that pays tribute to Kurosawa. The furious sword-fights, replete with geysers of spurting blood and blades puncturing torsos courtesy of comic book—esque CGI, benefit from an anime-influenced hyper—realism. An aerial shot of Hattori dispatching an army of foolhardy samurais has a Gauntlet videogame aesthetic, while Zatoichi's moonlit massacre at the gambling house is exhilaratingly elegant. And when Zatoichi and Hattori cross blades, the din of the swords' hurricane-force clash is akin to the clanking of locomotive wheels grinding and springing to life.

Kitano choreographs scenes of farmers tilling the land or workers building a house to the beat of Keiichi Suzuki's score, which utilizes strings, organs, and synthesizers to create a fusion of modern and classic Japanese melodies. This aural and visual synchronicity mirrors the film's harmonious themes of inclusion, tolerance and rebirth. Yet Kitano's premiere triumph is his deft directorial blending of action and comedy. Whether it's the terrified looks of Zat ichi's enemies after he's displayed his daunting swordsmanship, or the blind samurai nonchalantly tossing newly cut logs over his shoulder into a perfectly arranged pile, humorous vignettes provide the blood-soaked battles with a wry levity. Things culminate in an energetic tap-dance routine that perfectly encapsulates the film's humane spirit, as well as displays the director's heretofore unexploited gift for song-and-dance set pieces. Action-adventure, comedy, and musical any way you slice it, Takeshi Kitano's Zatoichi rocks.

—*Nicholas Schager, Filmcritic. com*

在日本国内，座头市是 26 部剧情长片和长篇电视剧中经久不衰的主人公，是一个为维护下层人民的权利而向地主阶层和恶势力挑战的按摩师、赌徒和武士（从 1962 年到 1989 年一直由胜新太郎饰演）。在此次对这一民间偶像的重新阐释中，导演北野武让座头市金发红杖（里面藏着他削铁如泥的刀锋），把人们印象中和蔼的武士形象改造成了一个孤僻寡言，喜欢离开人群沉思默想的英雄。北野武保留了座头市的经典特征，比如那顽童般的吃吃的笑声和他对乡下被遗弃之人的同情，同时用一种敏捷的肢体语言替代了胜新太郎芭蕾舞式的优雅姿态。这个新版的座头市就像一条盘旋着的随时置人于死地的毒蛇，他那种沉默而致命的方式像极了北野武的《奏鸣曲》和《大佬》中那些持枪发狂的土匪。

影片的摄影可圈可点，以缓慢、优雅的移动镜头见长，最具标志性的视觉奇观是绕人物旋转的 360 度摇镜头。北野武的调度朴实无华，他让一种视觉的连贯性逻辑贯穿于那些狂热、血腥的动作场景——包括一场海边的对决，一场向黑泽明致敬的让人目眩神迷的暴雨中的打斗。片中激烈的击剑场景常常伴随着血如泉涌和剑锋刺穿身体等那种漫画式的电脑特效，其灵感显然来源于动漫中的超现实主义。表现服部派遣一队有勇无谋的武士的那个航拍镜头则带有电脑枪战游戏的美学特征。而座头市身披月光在赌场上大开杀戒实在美不胜收。当座头市和服部剑锋相交时，那裹胁着飓风般力量的巨响就像是火车从人身体上碾过一样。

　　在北野武的舞蹈场景中，农人耕田、工人盖房都踩在铃木庆一的作曲节拍上，弦乐、管乐与合成器被混合起来，创造出一曲古典与现代相融合的日本旋律。这种视听的浑然一体反映了该片一种关于接纳、容忍和新生的主张和谐的主题。不过北野武最受尊崇的却是他在动作和喜剧的巧妙结合上。不论是敌人们见识了座头市剑术后那惊恐的表情，还是这个失明的武士劈柴过肩又码放整齐的景象，都以一种轻盈的幽默平衡了战斗场面的血腥刺激。影片的高潮是那段热情澎湃的踢踏舞，它不仅完美地张扬了影片的人道精神，还显示了导演在歌舞片上尚未开发的才华。动作冒险、喜剧、音乐——不论你要哪个，北野武的《座头市》都能震撼你。

——*Nicholas Schager*，*Filmcritic* 网站

The great Bruce Lee twirled his limbs around with such fearsome speed and control that he seemed to be slicing through time itself. His whirling, precision chop kills weren't just fast—they were instantaneous, and thus beautiful. I was reminded of the gratifying shock-force of Lee's fleet savagery when I saw The Blind Swordsman: Zatoichi, in which the director and star, Takeshi Kitano, revives the venerable hero of Japanese action cinema. Drawing on that mystique, Kitano, his hair dyed a startling blond, plays him as the ultimate pop myth of a samurai—a blind and wandering 19th-century masseur who eases down country roads with an old man's cautious shuffle, leaning on what appears to be an ornate red cane. Actually, it's a sheathed sword, and whenever he draws its gleaming blade, the movie enters what I can only describe as slasher heaven.

Poised before a foe, Zatoichi keeps his eyes calmly closed, yet his other senses are pure, his strokes thrilling in their razory suddenness. He stands in perfect serenity, and then—rip! rip! — he has sliced, with cathartic finality, through someone's chest, or neck, or eyes. His sword becomes a magic wand of death. This is well beyond fury—it's Zen annihilation. You'd think that filmmakers would have exhausted the possibilities of how to depict a blade slicing through someone's torso, but Kitano had an inspired idea: He uses digital technology to create profoundly physical meetings of steel and flesh and blood. Though you can occasionally tell that you're watching a synthetic image, the effect is to give swordplay a smooth, brutal lethality it has never had on screen before.

The odd thing is, as much as I adored the action in "Zatoichi", everything else about the movie is awful. Takeshi Kitano is a brazen stylist who indulges in happy flights of delirium, such as the group tap dance at the end. He is also, however, a hopelessly convoluted and inept storyteller. His maddeningly fragmentary gangster films, like Fireworks and Sonatine, have made him the darling of critics, yet I have never been able to sit through them. I would gladly summarize what happens in "Zatoichi" —it has something to do with a criminal gang trying to take over a village, as well as a pair of geisha out to avenge their family's death—except that I could scarcely make heads or tails of it. The movie, quite simply, goes to sleep whenever Zatoichi isn't fighting. When he is, it's a pulp dazzler.

—*Owen Gleiberman*, *Entertainment Weekly*

让人景仰的李小龙以惊人的速度和控制感挥舞着他的胳膊，像是切割着时间本身。他的挥舞、精确的砍杀不只是快，那是真正的瞬间，因此有一种美。当看到这个由北野武亦导亦演的盲剑客座头市时，我便不禁想起了李小龙那让人心悦诚服的力量、速度和野性。北野武复活了日本动作电影中这位令人尊敬的英雄。在传统光环的映照下，北野武将头发染成惊艳的金色，书写最后一部关于武士的广为流传的神话——一个19世纪失明的按摩师、流浪者在田间游荡，凝重的步伐中有一种老人的谨慎，手中挂着一根装饰华丽的红色拐杖。而事实上，它是一把内藏良剑的剑鞘，只要寒光出鞘，影片就立刻到了风驰电掣的天上（我只能如此形容）。

大敌当前稳如泰山，座头市一直冷静地闭起双眼，同时其它感观丝缕分明，只一击便让敌人瞬间丧胆。他立于纯粹的平静中，然后突然间砍向某人的胸、颈、目，状如瀑布飞泻，眨眼间已成定局。他的剑成为一支死亡的魔棒。这绝不是发狂发怒——它是一种禅宗的断灭。你或许认为电影制作者已经穷尽了表现剑锋如何刺穿身体的种种可能性，但是北野武却有这样一个灵动的想法：用数字技术毫发毕现地创造出金属接触到肌肉和血液的景象。虽然你偶尔能够意识到你看到的是合成画面，但你在银幕上从来没有见过击剑场面的这种流畅、残忍、致命的效果。

奇怪的是，虽然我对《座头市》中的动作场景喜爱有加，影片的其它一切却实在糟糕。北野武顽固不化、自以为是地放纵于狂欢中，比如片尾那段集体踢踏舞。此外，他讲故事的能力也颇让人怀疑，总是无望地自己绕晕了自己。虽然他让人发狂的碎片化的强盗片（比如《花火》和《奏鸣曲》）颇得评论界好评，我却从没耐心彻底看完过。我乐于这样总结《座头市》中的故事，大致关于一个强盗企图接管一个村庄，还有一对艺妓谋划着为家族复仇——但是我很难搞清楚其中奥妙。毫无疑问，座头市一旦停止战斗，影片就让人昏昏欲睡。只有他打起来，才让人精神为之一振。

—*Owen Gleiberman*，《娱乐周刊》

# The Child

# 孩 子

**导演：**让·皮埃尔·达尔代涅（Jean-Pierre Dardenne）
吕克·达尔代涅（Luc Dardenne）
**主演：**黛博拉·弗朗索瓦（Déborah FranGois）
奥利弗·古尔迈（Olivier Gourmet）
**片长：**100 分钟
**发行：**索尼经典（Sony Pictures Classics），2005 年

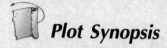

# *Plot Synopsis*

Bruno and Sonia are boy friend and girl friend, playful, immature. She's still in her teens; they chase each other, share cigarettes, spray sodas and wrestle. The thing is, they also have a new baby. Just out of hospital, Sonia seeks out Bruno to bring him his son. Bruno's indifferent. In the grimy Belgian city of Seraing, he's a petty thief with no interest in work, no plan, spending money as fast as he can fence cameras and jewelry. He sells the baby. Sonia's reaction and Bruno's surprise at her response inform his subsequent actions. The camera follows and observes him: has he a nascent conscience or any chance at redemption? Can he help himself?

## 剧情简介

布鲁诺和索尼娅是一对贪玩的不够成熟的男女朋友。索尼娅还是个未成年少女,他们互相追逐嬉戏,一起抽烟,互喷汽水和摔跤。问题是,他们生下了一个小孩。刚刚出院的索尼娅要布鲁诺把儿子带来见她,而布鲁诺的反应是冷漠的。在比利时肮脏的瑟兰市,布鲁诺是一个得过且过的小偷,对工作毫无兴趣,对生活没有计划,刚刚做完赃物交易,转手就会把钱花光。他把儿子卖掉了。但他对索尼娅因之而起的反应很意外,于是又有了接下来的行动。摄像机一直跟踪并观察着他:他良心发现了吗?有救赎的机会吗?他能够自救吗?

## Critique

Ever since it premiered at last year's Cannes Film Festival, where it won the Palme d'Or, "L'Enfant", the latest film from Belgian filmmaking brothers Jean-Pierre and Luc Dardenne, has been collecting rave reviews from around the world praising its spare storytelling, realistic performances and a finale that shows a seemingly irredeemable scoundrel groping for forgiveness, redemption and salvation at the hands of a pure and angelic young woman. Inevitably, these reviews make reference to the works of the late French director Robert Bresson, whose legendarily austere works (especially "Pickpocket") have been a chief source of inspiration for the Dardennes throughout their films. If I wanted to, I could easily knock out a review that would include all of these elements and simply call it a night*, especially considering the fact that the majority of those reading this will probably never actually get around to seeing it in the first place. And yet, I cannot write such a thing because to do so would mean that I would have to overlook the fact that it is a grim and glum slog that is so hell-bent on being a profound emotional experience that it winds up suffocating itself. In other words, this is one of those films that turns out to be good for you without ever being especially good.

Walking out of "L'Enfant", I found myself grudgingly admiring the film on a technical level while being slightly annoyed with it on an emotional level. What I still can't grasp is how this film won the top prize at Cannes over such clearly worthier titles as "A History of Violence", "Cache", "Broken Flowers", "Last Days" and "Don't Come Knocking". All of those titles told complicated stories that inspired deep emotions without resorting to the hard sell tactics that the Dardennes have done here. There are moments of value in "L'Enfant" and I suppose that those interested in the world cinema scene should probably check it out but if you haven't seen any of the other movies cited earlier in this paragraph yet, you should make catching up with them a higher priority.

—*Peter Sobczynski*, *Filmcritic. com*

　　《孩子》作为比利时达尔代涅兄弟导演的最新作品，从去年在戛纳电影节上首映并夺得金棕榈奖以来，世界各地的赞誉和追捧纷至沓来，一致肯定它节制的叙事、写实的表演，以及一个不可思议的向善的结局（让一个无药可救的无赖在一个纯洁如天使的女孩的帮助下寻求救赎）。几乎无法避免的是，这些评论都提到了已故的法国导演罗伯特·布烈松，认为他那些传奇性的严苛之作（尤其是《扒手》）是达尔代涅兄弟所有电影最主要的灵感源泉。如果我愿意，我能够轻而易举地用一句简单的"不辨道德是非"来驳倒这样一篇典型的评论，尤其是考虑到多数读到我这篇文章的人实际上没有时间真的去看一下电影。而我不能这样做，因为这种简单化会使我忽略掉它的严酷和阴郁，它过分地执着于情感经验的深度甚至到了自我窒息的程度。换句话说，《孩子》就是那种你会觉得不错，但绝不会好得不得了的影片。

　　看完《孩子》后，我发现自己有点分裂：我在技巧的层面上勉强向它致意，而在情感层面上却有点被它触怒了。我仍然不能理解的是它怎么会在这样一批毫无疑问的杰作中脱颖而出摘走了最高奖：《暴力史》、《隐藏摄影机》、《破碎之花》、《最后的日子》、《别来敲门》等等。所有这些影片都是用复杂的故事激发起深刻的情感，而不是像达尔代涅兄弟这样诉诸于强买硬卖的手段。《孩子》中有一些比较有价值的片断，我想那些对世界电影现状了如指掌的人能够判断它；而如果你还没有看过我上面列举到的这些影片，你应该把它们放到更优先观看的位置上。

—*Peter Sobczynski*, *Filmcritic* 网站

To that small but intense percentage of moviegoers for whom all Belgian realism is a cause for joy, the arrival of "L'Enfant" will be no less exciting than the birth of their own offspring. The movie, which won the Palme d'Or at the Cannes Film Festival last year, was directed by Jean-Pierre and Luc Dardenne, who are not to be confused with the Coen brothers, the Wachowski brothers, or, in a major way, the Farrelly brothers. The Dardennes' finest hour was "Rosetta" (1999), set mainly in a trailer park. This time, they have shifted to a defiantly unbeautiful town, with a rat-colored river running through it. The flow of traffic is no less relentless, and the grimmest motif, in a dispiriting tale, is the sight of characters pacing the shoulders of busy roads, or crossing a swollen stream of cars as if it were the Styx. Few of us risk that at the best of times, so what kind of person would try it with a babe in arms?

Sonia and Bruno, whom you would struggle to describe as a couple, have just had a son, named Jimmy. We first see Sonia, fresh out of the hospital, looking for Bruno and finding him begging at a stoplight. He has sublet their tiny apartment, so the choice of abode is either a hovel down by the water's edge or the local homeless shelter. (If you wish to hear echoes of an earlier family, who also found nowhere to lodge with their firstborn, go right ahead.) In the recklessness stakes, Bruno is the clear winner. "Only fuckers work", he says, and, if money flutters his way, either as alms or through fencing stolen goods, he blows it instantly, as if to prove that preserving or treasuring anything is the act of a dull soul. Even by Bruno's standards, however, his next move sets a new low: he wheels Jimmy off for a walk and returns without him. "I sold him", he tells Sonia, who promptly faints. The rest of the story follows Bruno's efforts to retrieve first his son and then, more haltingly, his girlfriend's good will. You stare at this parade of folly and tell yourself, It will end in tears. And so it proves.

Viewers in Europe have swooned, it is said, at this movie's painful inching toward redemption. Against that, I have to report a slow drip of disappointment. There is much to admire here, not least the speed with which the Dardennes delve into Sonia's plight, and I was suitably spooked by the terrible twilight-the interiors of locked-up garages and vacant, curtained apartments-in which the baby-selling trade unfolds. One should always be wary, however, of being gulled by the rough, harsh-grained manner of a film into assuming that its authenticity must, by definition, run deep. In fact, there is something willed and implausible at the heart of "L'Enfant", beginning with the child himself—the first non-crying, non-hungry infant in human history, let alone in cinema. Could the budget really not extend to a single diaper scene? I have met toy dolls who required more attention to their hygiene needs than young Jimmy.

—Anthony Lane, The New Yorker

对那些钟爱比利时现实主义的，人数虽不多，热情却很大的电影观众来说，《孩子》的问世所激起的兴奋度不亚于他们自家孩子的出生。这部摘得去年戛纳金棕榈奖的影片，导演是一对兄弟：让·皮埃尔·达尔代涅和吕克·达尔代涅，他们不会被混淆为科恩兄弟、沃卓斯基兄弟，或者最有可能的法拉利兄弟。他们最出色的作品要算《罗赛塔》，那部影片以一座拖车停车场为主要拍摄背景。这一次，他们干脆把场景换到一个颇有挑衅意味的丑陋的镇子上，一条灰秃秃的河流从中穿过。滚滚车流还是那么无情，而这个让人灰心丧气的故事最冷酷的主题，是让人物在忙乱的路上踱步，或者穿越这宛如冥河一般拥挤的车流。我们很少有运气冒这样的风险，那么到底是什么人可以这样穿来穿去，而且手中还抱着一个婴孩？

索尼娅和布鲁诺，一对你很难形容他们是夫妻的夫妻，刚刚生下一个儿子，取名吉米。我们先看到索尼娅，她身体恢复后出院，寻找布鲁诺，看见他正在路边乞讨。他们的公寓被他转租出去了，剩下能去的地方要么是河边一所简陋的小屋，要么进当地的收容所。（如果你在此看到了刚建立家庭的年轻人的影子，他们的第一个孩子出生时就像这样没有立足之地，那么继续往下看）布鲁诺鲁莽得理直气壮，他说"蠢蛋才工作呢"，如果手里有钱（不论是施舍来的，或是洗赃物得来的），他一定会立刻挥霍掉，好像好证明储存或珍藏什么东西是笨蛋才做的事情。然而，即便依照这样低的标准，布鲁诺接下来的举动还是每况愈下：他推着吉米去散步，回来时却独自一人。"我把它卖了。"他对索尼娅说，索尼娅立刻昏了过去。于是后面的故事就是关于布鲁诺如何寻回儿子以及女朋友的心意了。如果你盯着这一段蠢事并暗示自己说，结尾一定催人泪下——那么到片尾你真就哭了。

据说欧洲的观众为这个朝向救赎的痛苦之旅交口称赞。恰恰相反，我要表达一下我的一点失望情绪。影片中让人佩服的地方的确不少，不只是导演切入索尼娅状态的速度，我还适时地被那可怕的景象吓住了，那大门紧锁的汽车间和空荡荡的窗帘拉上的公寓内部正是婴儿交易的现场。然而，我们恰恰需要提醒自己不要被影片那种粗糙的质感所欺骗，要坚信它的真实性必须是深刻的。事实上，《孩子》的关键之处是刻意而失真的，问题就从"孩子"本身开始，它好像是人类历史上第一个不哭也不饿的婴儿似的，更不要说在电影史上。而且影片预算就不能多拍一个有尿片的场景吗？就是玩具我也见过比小吉米更有卫生需要的。

——*Anthony Lane*，《纽约客》

We talk about the "point of view" of a film. "L'Enfant" sees with the eye of God. The film has granted free will to its central character, Bruno, and now it watches, intense but detached, to see how he will use it. Bruno is so amoral, he doesn't register the meaning of his actions. At first, his behavior is evil. He attempts repairs. Whether he is redeemed is a good question. At the end, he is weeping, but he cannot weep forever, and he has a limited idea of how to survive and make a living.

The Dardennes achieve their effects through an intense visual focus. They follow their characters as if their camera can look nowhere else. In "L'Enfant", their gaze is upon Bruno. They deliberately do not establish the newborn child as a character. Unlike the equally powerful "Tsotsi", their film doesn't show Bruno caring for the child. The child is simply something he carries, like loot or a video game. The movie also avoids the opportunity to develop Sonia, except as her behavior responds to Bruno's. When she lets out a cry of grief and faints, this is not so much what she does as what Bruno sees her do.

There is a theological belief that God gives us free will and waits to see how we will use it. If he were to interfere, it would not be free will at all. If we choose well, we will spend eternity in the sight of God; if badly, banished from his presence. If God were to issue instructions, what would be the point of his creation? If we are not free to choose evil, where is the virtue in choosing good?

It's with that in mind that the visual strategy of the Dardennes reflects the eye of God. Having made a universe that has set this creature Bruno into motion, God (and we) look to see what he will do. Bruno has little intellectual capital and a limited imagination. He has been so damaged that he lacks ordinary feelings; when he visits his mother to arrange for an alibi, we get some insights into his childhood. After Sonia faints, he sets about trying to get the baby back. Does he do this because he knows that selling the baby was wrong? Or because Sonia is a companion and convenience for him, and he must try to restore her to working order?

The greatness of the Dardennes is that they allow us to realize that these are questions and leave us free to try to answer them. What happens at the end of the film perhaps suggests grief and a desire to repent. I hope it does. But "L'Enfant" is not so simple as to believe that for Bruno there can be a happy ending. Here is a film where God does not intervene and the directors do not mistake themselves for God. It makes the solutions at the ends of other pictures seem like child's play.

—*Roger Ebert*, *Chicago Sun-times*

我们谈谈电影中的"视点"。《孩子》是用上帝的目光来打量世界的。影片把自由意志赋予了核心人物布鲁诺,然后既热切又超然地看着他如何运用这意志。布鲁诺这个人物完全没有道德感,他对自己的行动从不作价值判断。最初他的行为是罪恶的,然后他尝试进行补偿。他是否获得拯救的确是个好问题。最终他还是落泪了,但他不能永远哭,而且他不大懂得如何生存和经营生活。

达尔代涅兄弟喜欢用一种专注的镜头感实现他们所希望的效

果。摄影机紧密地凝视着它的人物，好像它别无选择。《孩子》中被凝视的焦点是布鲁诺，导演有意地不把那个新生的婴儿当作人物来处理。和同样震撼人的《黑帮暴徒》不同，该片不表现布鲁诺对孩子的在意。孩子简单得如同他携带的一件物品，就像战利品或电脑游戏。影片也尽量避免去刻画索尼娅，除了她对布鲁诺的反应。当她悲痛得大哭或昏倒时，影片不是表现她到底怎么样，而是布鲁诺看见她怎么样。

神学认为上帝给了我们自由意志，然后等待我们如何使用它，如果他予以介入，我们便不再自由。如果我们的选择是正确的，上帝将永远庇护我们；如果是错误的，他会离我们而去。如果是非对错由上帝说了算，那么他造人的意义在哪里？如果我们可以自由作恶，那么又为什么要选择善？

心怀这样的困惑，达尔代涅兄弟的视觉策略反映出了上帝的目光。上帝创造出一个孕育了布鲁诺的宇宙，然后（和我们一起）看着他会做什么。布鲁诺的智力和想象力都十分有限，他的条件太差以至于使他缺乏正常人应有的感觉。当他去找母亲做不在场证明时，我们依稀看到了他的童年。索尼娅昏倒后，他开始试图找回孩子。他这么做是因为知道了贩卖婴儿是不对的吗？还是因为他需要索尼娅这个伴侣和方便，因此必须让她恢复正常工作？

达尔代涅兄弟的伟大之处就在于他让我们意识到这些问题，并让我们自己去努力回答它。影片的结局或许是在表达忧伤和悔改的愿望。希望如此。不过《孩子》不是简单地认为布鲁诺会有一个不错的结局。这是一部上帝没有介入，导演也没有把自己当成上帝的影片。相形之下，很多电影结尾的解决办法简直是小儿科。

——Roger Ebert，《芝加哥太阳时报》

**Note**

Night：night 有一层含义指道德伦理沦丧时刻，缺乏道德观念或伦理价值的时期或状况。

# Perfume：The Story of a Murderer

# 香 水

**导演**：汤姆·提克威（Tom Tykwer）

**原著**：帕特里克·聚斯金德（Patrick Süskind）

**主演**：本·威士肖（Ben Whishaw）

阿伦·瑞克曼（Alan Rickman）

蕾切尔·哈伍德（Rachel Hurd-Wood）

达斯汀·霍夫曼（Dustin Hoffman）

**片长**：140 分钟

**制作**：康斯坦丁影业公司（Constantin Film），2006 年

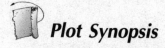

# *Plot Synopsis*

Jean-Baptiste Grenouille, orphaned as a newborn in the streets of Paris, is alone in the world. A peculiar child who rarely speaks, Grenouille is alienated from others but blessed with a remarkable gift. His sense of smell is so refined. There comes a day when Grenouille does an errand in town and discovers the object that will transform his life: perfume. Eager to learn the art of creating sophisticated fragrance, he apprentices himself to a once-renowned perfumer, and proves to be a savant whose almost mystical knowledge of scent surpasses anything that can be taught to him by masters of the craft. Ironically, he was born with no scent of his own, a distinction which colors his undistinguished life. But Grenouille is fearless when it comes to the pursuit of a perfect perfume. When he discovers the most intoxicating scent he has ever experienced—the natural fragrance of a beautiful young girl—he learns that the only method to preserve her innocence and fresh beauty will require murder.

## 剧情简介

主人公葛奴乙是一个出生在巴黎街上的婴儿，在世上孤苦无依。他生性孤僻、沉默寡言，但是天赋异秉——他有独一无二的灵敏的嗅觉。某天葛奴乙在镇上办差时邂逅了改变他一生命运的东西：香水。为了学习发明香味的艺术，他向一个曾负盛名的香水师拜师学艺，并很快证明了他对香水拥有的近乎神秘的了解超越了师傅的任何传授。讽刺的是，葛奴乙生来没有自己的味道，这让平凡的他因为缺陷而与众不同。不过每当葛奴乙在捕捉一种非凡的香味时便无所畏惧。当他发现了他捕捉到世界中最美妙的香味——美貌少女的体香时，他同时也意识到保留这种纯洁之美的唯一途径就是谋杀。

# *Critique*

Long regarded as unfilmable, Patrick Suskind's 1985 novel "Perfume" has finally reached the screen in a blockbuster production that succeeds reasonably well in achieving what many said was beyond the scope of cinema: conveying the world of scent and smell.

Reportedly budgeted at more than $60 million, "Perfume" has proved a runaway hit in Tykwer's native Germany, where it opened Sept. 14, but being highly culture-specific it may receive a mixed reception in other countries. In France, where people know a thing or two about fragrances, audiences so far have been distinctly sniffy.

Tykwer is merely following the novel's story line. His adaptation, scripted with Andrew Birkin and producer Bernd Eichinger, is arguably too faithful to the original, as well as being occasionally over-literal and laborious. At nearly 21/2 hours, it is certainly too long.

But Tykwer has a sure sense of spectacle, and despite its faults the movie maintains its queasy grip. The director makes minimal use of computer effects, preferring to use extras (more than 5,000 in all) in the many crowd scenes.

Rather than trickery, he relies on the power of images to evoke smells, whether rotting fish and oysters or roses and fields of lavender. The production design by Uli Hanisch (at Munich's Bavaria Studios and in Provence) brings 18th century France vividly to life. The narration, voiced by John Hurt, was presumably seen as

necessary for exposition in the early scenes but is maintained super-
fluously to the end. The mainly English cast serves the film well,
and Hoffman's neat turn as the fading star in the perfumers' firma-
ment provides some lighter moments.

—*Bernard Besserglik*, *The Hollywood Reporter*

多年来被认为不可拍摄的帕特里克·聚斯金德的小说《香水》(1985 年) 终于以大制作的面貌出现在银幕上,而且成功地拓展了电影表达的可能性:用声画来表现味道和嗅觉的世界。

9 月 14 日首映以来,这部传说成本超过 6000 万美元的巨制在提克威的祖国德国反响空前,但是考虑到高度的文化特殊性,该片在本土之外的国家可能会毁誉参半。比如法国观众对它就颇不以为然,因为法国是香水的国度。

提克威跟随着小说的叙事亦步亦趋。他的改编(编剧安德鲁·伯金,制片人伯纳德·艾辛格)太忠实于原著了,甚至有时过于被文字所束缚。而且两小时又二十一分钟的片长也的确太长了。

尽管有种种不足,提克威还是以对奇观的非凡把握维持住了影片的吸引力。他对电脑特效的使用相当节制,他更喜欢在大场面中使用临时演员(总共比 5000 人还要多)。

提克威没有玩魔术,而是用影像的力量来激发我们对味道的感知,不论这些味道来自臭鱼、牡蛎、玫瑰,还是熏衣草草场。影片的美术设计尤里·汉尼许(摄影棚选在慕尼黑的巴伐利亚制片厂以及普罗旺斯)在银幕上栩栩如生地复活了 18 世纪的法国。影片的旁白约翰·赫特似乎在片头起着交代来龙去脉的作用,在片尾则略显多余。以英国人为主的演员阵容表现可嘉,而霍夫曼的漂亮转型——香水师天空中一颗正褪色的星星,则赋予了影片一些闪耀的瞬间。

—*Bernard Besserglik*,《好莱坞报道》

Not only does "Perfume" seem impossible to film, it must have been amost impossible for Patrick Suskind to write. How do you describe the ineffable enigma of a scent in words? The audio-book, read by Sean Barrett, is the best audio performance I have ever heard; he snuffles and sniffles his way to greatness and you almost believe he is inhaling bliss, or the essence of a stone. I once almost destroyed a dinner party by putting it on for "five minutes", after which nobody wanted to stop listening.

Patrick Suskind's famous novel involves a twisted little found-ling whose fishwife mother casually births him while chopping off cod heads. He falls neglected into the stinking charnel house that was Paris 300 years ago, and is nearly thrown out with the refuse. But Grenouille grows into a grim, taciturn survivor, who possesses two extraordinary qualities: he has the most acute sense of smell in the world, and has absolutely no scent of his own.

It is in the nature of creatures like Grenouille (I suppose) that they have no friends. Indeed he has few conversations, and they are rudimentary. His life, as it must be, is almost entirely interior, so Twyker provides a narrator to establish certain events and facts. Even then, the film is essentially visual, not spoken, and does a remarkable job of establishing Grenouille and his world. We can never really understand him, but we and cannot tear our eyes away.

"Perfume" begins in the stink of the gutter and remains dark and brooding. To rob a person of his scent is cruel enough, but the way it is done in this story is truly macabre. Still it can be said that Grenouille is driven by the conditions of his life and the nature of his spirit. Also, of course, that he may indeed be the devil's spawn.

This is a dark, dark, dark film, focused on an obsession so complete and lonely it shuts out all other human experience. You may not savor it, but you will not stop watching it, in horror and fascination. Whishaw succeeds in giving us no hint of his character save a deep savage need. And Dustin Hoffman produces a quirky old master whose life is also governed by perfume, if more positively. Hoffman reminds us here again, as in "Stranger than Fiction", what a detailed and fascinating character actor he is, able to bring to the story of Grenouille precisely what humor and humanity it needs, and then tactfully leaving it at that. Even his exit is nicely timed.

Why I love this story, I do not know. Why I have read the book twice and given away a dozen copies of the audiobook, I cannot explain. There is nothing fun about the story, except the way it ventures so fearlessly down one limited, terrifying, seductive dead end, and finds there a solution both sublime and horrifying. It took imagination to tell it, courage to film it, thought to act it, and from the audience it requires a brave curiosity about the peculiarity of obsession.

—*Roger Ebert*, *Chicago Sun-times*

　　不只把《香水》拍成电影是不可能之事，甚至连帕特里克·聚斯金德写出《香水》这样的小说都是不可能的。你如何能将那妙不可言的味道诉诸笔端？由肖恩·贝瑞特配音的语音书是我听过的最出色的声音表演，他用他特有的方式把鼻音发挥到了极致，听起来你几乎觉得他吸入的是幸福本身，或者是一块石头的本质。我曾经忍不住在一个宴会上放了"5分钟"，结果谁的耳朵都不愿意停下来。

　　帕特里克·聚斯金德的这部著名的小说以一个扭曲的弃儿为主人公，他的母亲是一个卖鱼妇，在鱼市上随随便便地生下了他。他和垃圾一起被抛弃在300年前巴黎最脏最臭的藏尸所。葛奴乙逐渐长成了一个阴郁、沉默的幸存者，并有两个与众不同的特点：他有世界上最敏锐的嗅觉，却完全没有自己的味道。

　　天性如葛奴乙这样的人（我猜测）是没什么朋友的，事实上他很少与人交谈，偶尔说话也极其生涩。他的生活必然是完全向内的。因此，提克威用旁白来交代一些必要的事件和事实。即便如此，从根本上讲，该片是用视觉传达出来的（而不是说出来），它出色地完成了对葛奴乙形象的塑造和对其精神世界的表现。我们一直没能真正地理解他，但也不能把目光从他身上移开。

　　《香水》的镜头始于腐臭的阴沟，此后影片一直保持着阴暗、深沉的基调。剥取一个人的气味已经够残忍的了，而该故事中那种特殊的方式更让人毛骨悚然。虽然仍然可以说葛奴乙是受他的生活条件和自然天性的驱使，而当然我们也可以理解为他就是魔鬼之子。

　　这是一部黑暗至极的影片，它彻底孤僻地专注在一种特殊爱好上，阻隔了所有其它的人性经验。你可能并不欣赏它，但你在既恐惧又着迷中不会停止观看。威士肖成功地表演出了那种与生俱来的残忍，而达斯汀·霍夫曼则塑造出了一个连生命都被香水统治的诡诈的老师傅，不过要比葛奴乙人性得多。霍夫曼让我们再次想起他的《奇幻人生》，再次确认了他是一个细节充实、魅力四射的性格演员，他将必要的幽默和仁慈恰到好处地注入葛奴乙的故事中，又适时巧妙地抽身离去。虽然他的戏分并不算多。

　　我不知道我为什么喜欢这个故事，也不能解释为什么能把小说读两遍，还四处分发它的语音书。这故事没什么有趣的，它只是一往无前地向一个狭窄的、可怕的、诱惑的死亡终点迈进，并找到了一个既庄严又骇人的解决之道。它需要想象力来讲述它，需要勇气来拍摄它，需要动脑筋来表演它，并需要观众付出勇敢的好奇心来对待这种不同寻常的激情。

　　　　　　　　　　　　　　—*Roger Ebert*，《芝加哥太阳时报》


　　This film is an uneven experience. Fans of the book will appreciate its earnest attempts to capture much of the novel's details,

· spirit and texture. But most will see director Tom Tykwer's failure to find the tonal balance that reprises the novel's arch irony and that makes us appreciate Jean-Baptiste's olfactory sensibilities despite his heartless serial killing. And few will applaud Dustin Hoffman's annoying performance as an Italian perfumer. There's also the matter of evoking Jean-Baptiste's sense of smell in a medium made for sight and sound. Tykwer, best known for his fabulously kinetic "Run, Lola, Run", has no choice but to convey it visually. Thus, we are forever shooting in and out of nostrils, then cutting to extreme close-ups of whatever's being smelled: a luscious virginal girl or the writhing maggots inside a dead rat. After a while, good readers, we got nose-cammed out.

—*Desson Thomson*, *Washington Post*

　　人们对这部电影的反应是不一致的。小说的爱好者会欣赏影片对书中的细节、精神和质地的努力还原。但在多数人眼中，导演汤姆·提克威没有能够在重复小说的戏谑反讽与表现葛奴乙的敏感嗅觉（且不论他做了一系列无情的谋杀）之间达到适度的平衡。还有些人会交口称赞达斯汀·霍夫曼对意大利香水师那惹人烦的表演。而在一个视听媒介中如何表现出主人公的嗅觉感受也是影片遇到的一个麻烦。以动感十足的惊人之作《罗拉快跑》扬名影坛的提克威只能通过视觉来传达嗅觉，他别无选择。于是，我们看着镜头没完没了地在鼻孔中进进出出，然后切到任何所闻之物的大特写上：要么是一个赏心悦目的处女，要么是在一只死猫的尸体内翻腾的蛆。天哪，要不了多会儿，我们的鼻子就可以退休了。

—*Desson Thomson*，《华盛顿邮报》

# Pride and Prejudice

# 傲慢与偏见

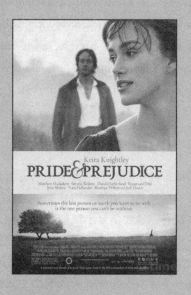

**导演：**乔·怀特（Joe Wright）

**原著：**简·奥斯汀（Jane Austen）

**主演：**马修·麦克费登（Matthew Macfadyen）

　　　　凯拉·奈特莉（Keira Knightley）

**片长：**127 分钟

**发行：**焦点电影公司（Focus Features）

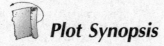 *Plot Synopsis*

The story is based on Jane Austen's novel about five sisters—Jane, Elizabeth, Mary, Kitty and Lydia Bennet—in Georgian England. Their lives are turned upside down when a wealthy young man (Mr. Bingley) and his best friend (Mr. Darcy) arrive in their neighborhood.

## 剧情简介

故事基于简·奥斯汀的小说，关于英格兰乔治亚的一家五姐妹：简、伊丽莎白、玛丽、基蒂和丽蒂亚·班耐特。当一个富有的年轻人（宾利先生）和他最好的朋友（达西先生）来到村庄与她们成为近邻时，她们的生活发生了天翻地覆的变化。

# *Critique*

Austen's novel, written in 1797 but not published until 1813, is one of the most fiercely beloved books in the English language, and those of us who love it are ferociously protective of the characters at the center of it: Twenty-year-old Elizabeth Bennet (here played by Keira Knightley), whose intelligence is her greatest gift and whose cleverness is her greatest burden, and Darcy (Matthew Macfadyen), a young man of privilege and breeding who unconsciously hides his sensitive, fine-grained character behind a scrim of snobbery. The casting here is more perfect than in any "Pride & Prejudice" adaptation I've seen (I confess I'm not a fan of the popular 1995 British miniseries, which I found so slow, proper and reverent that it seemed a direct inversion of the spirit of the book), and Wright is fearless in his handling of the characters, refusing to bow to their iconic stature. It's as if he's unraveled every golden thread we've spun around Elizabeth and Darcy over the years to reveal living, breathing people underneath. He's saved them from the mummification of our love.

—*Stephanie Zacharek*, *Salon. com*

奥斯汀这部写于 1797 年但直到 1813 年才出版的小说是英语文学中最具有杀伤力的言情小说之一。那些喜欢这部书的人狂热地钟爱它的主人公：21 岁的伊丽莎白·班耐特（这一版由凯拉·奈特莉扮演），她的智慧是她最大的财富，同时她的聪明也是她最大的负担；还有达西（马修·麦克费登），一个优越而有教养的年轻人，在他势利而傲慢的外表下藏着一颗敏感细腻的心灵。

在所有根据《傲慢与偏见》改编的影视作品中，这一部的演员阵容堪称最佳（我得承认我不是1995年英国电视剧那一版的影迷，那部剧的慢节奏、节制和虔诚在我看来与原著的精神恰恰背道而驰），导演怀特在处理人物时非常大胆，能够不为刻板形象所限。他仿佛解开了我们多年来束缚在伊丽莎白和达西身上的金丝线，解放了他们，复活了他们，把他们从我们的爱情僵壳中解救了出来。

—*Stephanie Zacharek*，《沙龙》

Anyone working up a good derisive snort at this movie's tagline—"Sometimes the last person on earth you want to be with is the one person you can't be without"—would do well to snort-suppress: The 1940 Laurence Olivier Greer Garson version of Jane Austen's most famous novel was promoted with the slogan "When pretty girls t-e-a-s-e-d men into marriage." There's always been a Cosmo-girl approach to peddling Austen's wares; the movie industry is perpetually jittery around the author's razor-edged comedies of manners* (All those words! All those crucial things left unsaid in the silences between those words!) and invariably tries to promote them as silly fun for the popcorn chewer. (The one terrific success that merited such treatment, of course, was Amy Heckerling's Clueless adaptation of Emma.)

In condensing to a mere two hours Austen's elaborately arrayed tale, this P&P will probably not pass muster with those viewers who still tremble happily at the memory of the BBC's five-hour-plus 1995 production, which starred Colin Firth as the most hotsy Darcy ever, give or take your imagination the first time you read the book. Still, there are pleasures to be had here. The boobish Mr. Bingley (Simon Woods, sporting bright red hair styled to resemble

Archie Andrews) makes a rare intelligent remark when he observes (in the novel; the movie has no time for such felicities) that Elizabeth is an astute "studier of character." Thanks to the vivacious and brainy Knightley, the new P&P renders this quality exceedingly well, and when you combine her with Donald Sutherland, portraying Elizabeth's father as a man who knows which daughter to adore while merely loving the others, the movie has moments of true Austen shrewdness.

If only Knightley had a co-star equal to her here: The 1995 edition of Colin Firth, come to think of it, would have been perfect. As it is, we get something appropriate—an earthbound *Pride & Prejudice*, as befits the sins and errors of its title—when what we want is what we always want from a romantic period piece*: something transcendent. Maybe in the techno-future, when we'll all sit around creating our own films on sub-iPod-size gizmos, we'll be able to splice together Knightley and Firth and achieve a mash-up made in movie heaven.

—*Ken Tucker*, *New York Magazine*

"有时候世界上你最讨厌的人恰恰就是你离不开的那个人"，如果你看见该片这句宣传语时哑然失笑，那么当你看到1940年劳伦斯·奥立弗和葛丽·亚嘉逊那一版在推销简·奥斯汀这部最著名的小说时说："当漂亮女人把男人玩弄进婚姻中……"，你大概会哑口无言。我们总在用都市女孩的办法来兜售奥斯汀，而电影工业永远盯紧作者刻薄的喜剧风格不放（总是那些话！总是把最关键的话留着偏不说出来！），然后当成愚蠢的噱头推销给那些吃着爆米花的人。（艾米·哈克琳对《爱玛》的无能改编就算得上是这样一部"求仁得仁"的成功之作。）

在把奥斯汀精心布局的故事压缩成2个小时后，这一版的

《傲慢与偏见》大概无法引起某些观众的热情——他们还沉醉在1995 年 BBC 五小时制作的美好记忆中，科林·费尔斯饰演的达西颠倒众生，他唤起了你看小说时的最初印象。不过从新版中还是能找到一些乐子的。傻呵呵的宾利（西蒙·伍兹饰演，一头扎眼的鲜红的头发像极了动画人物阿奇·安德鲁斯）在观察伊丽莎白时（小说中，影片没功夫这么细腻）说出了一句难得的聪明话：伊丽莎白是个狡黠的"研究人性格的专家"。多谢活泼机智的奈特莉，新版的《傲慢与偏见》将这一特点表现得尤其好，奈特莉与唐纳·萨瑟兰配合得相得益彰，后者演出了伊丽莎白父亲那种明白地知道心里偏爱哪个女儿，对其他女儿也不差的微妙态度，这使影片时不时飘出地道的奥斯汀式的睿智和洞察力。

要是奈特莉有一个能和她配得上的男主角就好了：想想如果能把1995 年科林·费尔斯版的达西借过来，该多么完美。我们这种想法其实挺适合世俗的《傲慢与偏见》，挺适合这一名称中的过失和错误——我们想要的就是我们想从浪漫的老套中得到的东西：一种具有超越性的永恒的完美。说不定到科技发达的未来，当我们大家都无聊地在比 iPod 还小的设备上创作自己的电影时，我们或许能把奈特莉和费尔斯拼起来，搞一出电影天堂里的大杂烩。

—Ken Tucker，《纽约》杂志

Sniff all you like at the Bridget Jones franchise, *Pride & Prejudice* and all other past and future rip-offs of Jane Austen's most dog-eared novel. They're all testaments to the enduring power of *Pride and Prejudice* as one of the most potently wishful fantasies in the female dream-book. Barring an end to the war between the sexes, we'll never see a shortfall in female demand for this particular high concept: Brainy girl—pretty, but no bombshell—meets filthy-rich, granite-jawed hunk reeking of unavailability, ignores him, sasses him, tames him, marries him. Pride and Prejudice's Elizabeth Bennet is the most serviceable of role models, a feminist icon who's well able to take care of herself, but who also gets to live happily ever after with a moneyed honey straight out of a Harlequin romance. Which may be why, in years of literary dish with well-read friends, I've yet to meet a woman who doesn't drool over her.

So why, in no less than five miniseries and two official film adaptations of *Pride and Prejudice*, have we yet to encounter a satisfying screen Lizzie? From the giddy 1940 movie featuring a disastrously miscast Greer Garson (opposite Laurence Olivier) to Andrew Davies' bushy-tailed 1995 BBC crowd-pleaser (with a talented but too rosy and demure Jennifer Ehle opposite Colin Firth, who seemed to be constantly on the verge of cracking up), there hasn't been a single Elizabeth Bennet that has hit the spot. In part, that's because they've all skewed too young. Though not yet one-and-twenty (an age when, in her rural corner of Regency England, unmarried damsels start rummaging through the governess want ads), Lizzie Bennet, unlike her flighty sisters, is wise, sophisticated and intellectual beyond her years. When I cast her in my head, actresses in their 30s or 40s keep popping up: ideally Emma Thompson or Juliet Stevenson; Emily Mortimer maybe; Madeleine Stowe at a pinch; even Julia Roberts, who has dry wit aplenty if only she got more opportunities to flaunt it.

If you're going to go with youth, as director Joe Wright does in his new adaptation of *Pride and Prejudice*, the sublimely understated Zooey Deschanel springs to mind, or cocky, mouthy Reese Witherspoon. But Keira Knightley? Elizabeth Bennet is a watcher, not a doer, a subtle observer and coolly analytical commentator on the parochial society in which she's trapped. She's nothing if not low-key, and not even the male critics who have rushed to anoint

Knightley the next big thing would call this endearing colt subtle, cool or analytical. I haven't seen Knightley in *Domino*, but she was a risibly ill-conceived, karate-chopping Guinevere in the very odd *King Arthur* and a charisma-free Lara in the British miniseries of *Dr. Zhivago*, though good, broad fun in *Bend It Like Beckham* and *Pirates of the Caribbean*. But for all her creamy beauty and enthusiastic vitality, Knightley has yet to do anything I'd call acting. She's an open book who charges through every role with the same undiscriminating gusto.

—*Ella Taylor*, *L. A. Weekly*

实在不能理解为什么你们都像布里吉特·琼斯（《BJ 单身日记》的女主人公）一样那么钟爱《傲慢与偏见》，或者所有其它那些与这本简·奥斯汀最泛滥的小说大同小异的读物。这些都证明了《傲慢与偏见》是女性幻想小说中最让人心动的一个白日梦。除非两性战争结束，否则我们永远不会看到女性对这一特殊"高概念"的需求出现下滑趋势：一个有头脑的女孩，漂亮但不惊人，遇上一个一身铜臭、顽固不化、毫无可能的人，忽视他，顶撞他，驯服他，最后嫁给他。《傲慢与偏见》里的伊丽莎白是角色模型中最经久耐用的那一款，一个女权主义的偶像，她既能把自己照顾周全，又能干净利落地从绯闻中攀上枝头，一劳永逸。这大概能解释为什么多年来我和博览群书的朋友们一起享用文学大餐时，很少看见哪个女人不为她流口水。

可又是为什么，在对《傲慢与偏见》多达五部电视剧和两部电影的改编后，我们仍然没有在屏幕上看到一个令人满意的伊丽莎白？从 1940 年那部让人眼花的影片严重不当地使用葛丽·亚嘉逊（对手戏是劳伦斯·奥立弗），到 1995 年由安德鲁·戴维斯操刀的风格细腻的 BBC 热剧（由虽有才华但是太红润、太端庄的珍妮弗·埃勒和科林·费尔斯搭档，而后者似乎一直处于精神崩溃的边缘），从来没有一个恰到好处的伊丽莎白·班耐特。部分的原因是她们都偏于年轻了。虽然还不到 21 岁（在大英帝国时期的乡下，到这个年龄还没有结婚的闺中女子已经开始被愁嫁弄得焦头烂额了），伊丽莎白并不像她那些轻浮的妹妹，她的聪明、复杂和智慧超过了她的年龄。在我的想象中，适合出演这一角色的三四十岁的女演员层出不穷：最理想的是埃玛·汤普森或茱丽叶·史蒂文森，艾米莉·莫迪默也不错，关键时可用玛德琳·斯托，甚至可以是朱莉娅·罗伯茨，她身上有一种冷峻的机智，只要你给她展示的机会。

如果你要用年轻演员，就像怀特导演对《傲慢与偏见》的这个新改编，我马上想起非常有分寸感的佐伊·丹斯切尔或者自信饶舌的瑞茜·威瑟斯彭。怎么能用凯拉·奈特莉呢？伊丽莎白并不是个实干家，她是一个旁观者，一个精明的观察家，一个能够对自己所置身的狭隘社会冷静分析的评论员。她应该相当地低调克制，并不是这种让男性批评家趋之若鹜的可爱的毛头小姑娘。我没看过奈特莉在《多米诺》中的表现，在古怪的《亚瑟王》中，她把格温娜维尔演得拙劣可笑，孔武好斗；在英国电视剧《日瓦格医生》中她塑造了一个性格奔放的娜娜，当然在《我爱贝克汉姆》和《加勒比海盗》中带给我们不少乐趣。虽然奈特莉年轻美丽热情活泼，但她所做的一切都与表演无关。奈特莉就是那种让人一眼看穿的"本色"演员，她的每个角色都演得没有分别，大同小异。

—*Ella Taylor*，《洛杉矶周刊》

> **Note**
>
> Comedy of manners：风尚喜剧，一种喜剧风格，以讽刺特殊社会群体为乐，常常针对上流社会。
>
> Period piece：本身并没什么价值，但却能代表某一时代特征的小说、画、家具等物品。

# The Painted Veil

# 面 纱

**导演:**约翰·卡兰(John Curran)

**编剧:**罗恩·内斯万尼尔(Ron Nyswaner)

**原著:**索默斯特·毛姆(W. Somerset Maugham)

**主演:**娜奥米·沃茨(Naomi Watts)

爱德华·诺顿(Edward Norton)

**片长:**124 分钟

**发行:**华纳独立影业(Warner Independent Pictures), 2006 年

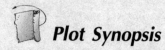 ***Plot Synopsis***

Based on the novel by W. Somerset Maugham, The Painted Veil is a love story set in the 1920s that tells the story of a young English couple, Walter (Edward Norton), a middle class doctor and Kitty (Naomi Watts), an upper-class woman, who get married for the wrong reasons and relocate to Shanghai, where she falls in love with someone else. When he uncovers her infidelity, in an act of vengeance, he accepts a job in a remote village in China ravaged by a deadly epidemic, and takes her along. Their journey brings meaning to their relationship and gives them purpose in one of the most remote and beautiful places on earth.

## 剧情简介

在毛姆小说的基础上改编的《面纱》讲的是一个发生在上世纪 20 年代的爱情故事。主角是一对年轻的英国夫妇——中产阶级医生沃特（爱德华·诺顿饰）和出身上流社会的吉蒂（娜奥米·沃茨饰），吉蒂出于与爱情无关的原因嫁给沃特，她在他们搬迁到上海后爱上了别人。当沃特发现妻子出轨后，出于报复的目的，他接受了一份传染病正肆虐的中国边远山村地区的工作，并带吉蒂同行。旅程对他们的关系产生了影响，并使他们在这个世界上最偏僻也最美丽的地方发现了真谛。

# *Critique*

Intelligent scripting, solid thesping and eye-catching location shooting aren't enough to make a compelling modern film of "The Painted Veil," W. Somerset Maugham's yarn about Brits run amok in 1920s China. Well appointed in all respects, this story of a shallow adulteress's gradual discovery of her starchy husband's worth while battling a cholera epidemic in a backwater village feels remote and old-school despite a frankness the two previous film versions lacked. Cast and some mainstream critical support could launch the Warner Independent release to a respectable commercial life.

Maugham's novel, one of his numerous works about Westerners come to grief in the Far East, was published in 1925. MGM's dim 1934 adaptation, starring Greta Garbo and directed by Richard Boleslavsky, deviated madly from the book, while the studio's 1957 remake, "The Seventh Sin" with Eleanor Parker under Ronald Neame's direction, steered closer to its source but still couldn't engage certain core issues.

Maugham focused exclusively on the vicissitudes of the colonials, who presumed they were bringing help, enlightenment and civilization to the citizens of an unruly land he portrayed strictly as a backdrop. Nyswaner, director John Curran and Norton, also aboard as one of the producers and prime movers of the project, have made a point of turning China into more of a character in the piece. This they do in part by bringing to the fore the nationalist, anti-English politics of the time, a movement spurred by a real-life

British military massacre of Chinese demonstrators in 1925. Angry peasants combined with the cholera make for a volatile cocktail.

All the same, the film is still dominated by the stuffy, repressed personality of Fane, whose emotional stonewalling of his wife produces a stifling of Kitty's naturally more vivacious, if common, personality. Despite the extremes of human experience on view, there is a certain blandness to them as they play out, a sensation matched by the eye-catching but picture-postcard-like presentation of the settings (rural scenes were shot in Guangxi province in southern China).

Even the ultra-capable Norton and Watts aren't fully able to galvanize viewer interest in their narrowly self-absorbed characters. Norton puts on a thin, reedy voice to help express Walter's insecurity and sexual unassertiveness, all the better to contrast with his resolve once faced with dramatic decisions down the line. Watts holds down the story's emotional center, but still finds herself more limited in expression than usual, perhaps from the character's own limitations.

—*Todd Mccarthy*, *Variety. com*

聪明的编剧、扎实的表演、夺目的风光并不足以拍出一部让人信服的现代电影版的《面纱》（索默斯特·毛姆的作品，写英国人在上个世纪 20 年代的中国狼奔豕突的逸闻）。影片描述一个生活出轨的肤浅女人在穷乡僻壤的村子里和霍乱厮捱时重新认识她木讷丈夫的过程，影片拍得四平八稳，一副久远的老派气，不过有一种前两版影片所没有的率真。演员阵容和一些主流评论的支持会让华纳独立影业的取得可观的发行放益。

《面纱》首度出版于 1925 年，是毛姆写的关于西方人在遥远的东方遭受不幸的众多作品中的一部。米高梅公司在 1934 年晦暗的改编（理查德·波列拉夫斯基导演，葛丽泰·嘉宝主演）几乎完全偏离了小说原作。1957 年，该制片厂重拍了它（片名改为《第七罪恶》，罗纳德·尼姆导演，依莲娜·派克主演），该片虽然与原作较为接近，但仍然没有抓住小说的要义。

毛姆的本意在于描述殖民地的兴衰史，其叙事背景严格限制在那些自以为自己正在帮助、启蒙和教化蛮荒地城居民的殖民者身上。内斯万尼尔、导演约翰·卡兰和同样也是制片人和项目策划人之一的诺顿达成一致，要把中国也变成影片的一张牌。其做法之一是把当时一件反英爱国政治运动（由 1925 年英国军队屠杀中国游行者的真实事件所引发）推到前台来。于是愤怒的农民加上霍乱流行，矛盾一触即发。

和前几部一样，这一版电影还是把重心放在了费恩沉闷克制的性格上，他了无生趣的感情生活让天性活泼（这种性格更普遍）的吉蒂不能忍受。除了对极端的人性经验的呈现，影片中确实还有一种温柔的情绪，它源于那些动人的风景（田园风光取景于中国南部的广西省），虽然被展示得像明信片一样。

然而，就是诺顿和沃茨再有魅力也不能激发起观众对这两个狭隘的、自我沉迷的人物产生兴趣。诺顿用尖细的嗓音来表达沃特的不安全感和缺乏性感，这反倒更好地衬托出了他义无反顾的戏剧性的决心。沃茨虽然始终置身于故事情感漩涡的中心，但她的表达远不如以往自由，或许这是因为角色自身的限制。

　　　　　　　　　　　　　　　　　—*Todd Mccarthy*，综艺网站

Nyswaner's expert hand is visible in the film's intriguing shape: The action opens in the middle, as the despairing Kitty gets schlepped by litter through the heat and green rice paddies of rural China, while Walter, powered by hatred, leads the way. Then, after quick flashbacks to their dubious courtship, followed by Kitty's affair, the film tackles its main theme: a couple finding each other out of the wreckage of their past. Director John Curran (*We Don't Live Here Anymore*) favors giant, pore-revealing close-ups, as he peers into his characters' hearts. Watts, in her '20s coif and shifts, has lovely pores, yet she relies too much, until the end, on a single expression of outraged petulance, and Schreiber is underused in an underwritten role.

But as an innately cold, repressed scientist, Edward Norton adds yet another layered portrait to his gallery of unlikely and inscrutable heroes. Not only is it rare to watch an actor's intelligence beam through his features, it's a godsend to find a story, in the epoch of *Saw III*, with such humanistic resonance. The score of the doomed romantic adventure sort is spot-on, and the orphans' song at the end ("Jamais je ne t'oublierai") rends the heart. As an added bonus, this Chinese co-production shot in Guangxi Province in Southern China displays towering, dreamy tableaux seldom viewed by Westerners.

—*Erica Abeel*, *Film Journal International*

编剧内斯万尼尔用专业手艺无形地编织着魅惑人的结构：影片从故事的中间展开，绝望的吉蒂坐在轿子里穿过中国乡村热气逼人的绿色稻田，前面带路的是满腹怨恨的沃特。接着，影片快速闪回了他们可疑的姻缘以及吉蒂的出轨，然后进入真正的主题：一对夫妻从过往的伤害中走出来，重新发现彼此。导演约翰·卡兰（导过《爱不再回来》）钟爱深入毛孔的特写镜头，似乎这样便能窥探到人物的内心世界。身着20年代装束的沃茨有着可爱的毛孔，但是她的表达方式过于单一，始终一副闹腾腾的怒气。而施瑞博尔的表演在一个单薄的角色中完全没有施展开。

不过在出演费恩这个生性冷淡压抑的科学家后，爱德华·诺顿对众多莫测高深的主人公的演绎又多了一个丰富的层面。不只是因为他很少把一个演员的才华暴露在外部特征上，更幸运的是我们能在《电锯惊魂3》的时代发现这样一个具有人性共鸣的故事。它那种充满宿命和浪漫历险意味的配乐恰如其分地感动着我们，而片尾孤儿的歌声（《永不能忘》）则让人心碎。此外与中国的合拍镜头则锦上添花地呈现了一幅西方人从未见过的神仙幻境。

—Erica Abeel，《国际电影月刊》

The third time, directed by John Curran, may be as close to a charm as a Maugham tale can hope for, although the story is still crazily overdetermined: To punish his straying wife for her affair with a slick English bureaucrat in Shanghai, the doc insists on dragging her to the disease-plagued countryside, where he volunteers to do good for the dying populace in a kind of mutually assured destruction by epidemic. The evocative scenery, captured by cinematographer Stuart Dryburgh (*The Piano*), trembles with an appreciation for China's hard beauty. Indeed, the scale of the geography itself seems to awe the cast and unite them, intensifying the easy performance chemistry between stars Norton and Naomi Watts as middle-class Dr. Walter Fane and his restless upper-class wife, Kitty. Whenever the story gets a bit too blurry (there were bureaucratic wrangles over just how much actual political unrest and illness the filmmakers were allowed to show), one can always enjoy the interesting dynamic of Walter and Kitty damp with sweat in the humid Chinese air and quite loathing each other.

The always surprising Watts creates a woman at once contemporary and retro. And Norton, as a producer as well as star, concedes enough space for Schreiber and the effortlessly fascinating Jones to earn their own spotlights—indeed for China herself to assume a starring role, assisted by a thoughtful script from Philadelphia's Ron Nyswaner and an enchanting score by Alexandre Desplat (*Girl With a Pearl Earring*). Kitty's slow-cooking recognition of Walter's lovable goodness may flatter the kind of misunderstood character Norton likes to play. But the real Norton here warrants the flattery.

—*Lisa Schwarzbaum, Entertainment Weekly*

由约翰·卡兰导演的第三次改编或许比较接近于毛姆原作的气质，然而这个故事仍然太过偏执了：医生为了惩罚妻子与一个滑头的英国驻上海官僚通奸，坚持把她拖到瘟疫流行的乡下，在那里他加入了救助垂死居民的志愿行动。摄影师斯图亚特·瑞伯（《钢琴课》）捕捉到了那动人的风景，一种中国山乡的让人难过的美。事实上，这种寥廓的地理风貌似乎震慑住了演员们，加强了诺顿作为中产阶级医生沃特·费恩与沃茨作为他的不安分的上流社会妻子之间的表演氛围。虽然故事有时候展开得模糊不清（因为官方能够准许影片在多大程度上暴露政治动荡和瘟疫还存有争议），我们还是可以饶有兴致地看着沃特和吉蒂浸泡在中国的湿气里相互怄气。

总是让人惊讶的沃茨为我们塑造了一个既现代又怀旧的女人。身兼主演和制片人的诺顿则慷慨地为施瑞博尔和悠游迷人的琼斯留下了足够的施展空间——当然"中国"在片中也是一个永恒的角色。可圈可点的还有心思细密的编剧、来自费城的罗恩·内斯万尼尔，以及拨动心弦的作曲亚历山大·蒂斯普莱德（《戴珍珠耳环的少女》）。吉蒂在慢热中爱上沃特的可爱和善良或许会让诺顿乐于扮演的这个角色喜不自禁，而真正的诺顿本人在此也确实有资格喜不自禁。

——丽莎·施瓦茨勃姆《娱乐周刊》

# Paris, I Love You

# 巴黎，我爱你.

**导演:** 诹访敦彦 Suwa Nobuhiro

奥利维耶·阿萨亚斯 Olivier Assayas

顾伦德·查达哈 Gurinder Chadha

西维亚·乔迈 Sylvain Chomet

伊桑·科恩 Ethan Coen

乔尔·科恩 Joel Coen

伊莎贝尔·科赛特 Isabel Coixet

格斯·范·桑特 Gus Van Sant

汤姆·提克威 Tom Tykwer

丹妮拉·托马斯 Daniela Thomas

沃尔特·塞勒斯 Walter Salles

布鲁诺·波达里德斯 Bruno Podalydès

亚历山大·佩恩 Alexander Payne

杜可风 Christopher Doyle

杰拉尔·德帕迪约 Gérard Depardieu

阿方索·卡隆 Alfonso Cuarón

韦斯·克雷文 Wes Craven

弗里德里克·奥伯汀 Frédéric Auburtin

埃曼纽·本比 Emmanuel Benbihy

文森佐·纳塔利 Vincenzo Natali

奥利弗·舒密兹 Oliver Schmitz

理查德·拉·格拉文斯 Richard LaGravenese

片长：116 分钟

制作：Canal + , 2006 年

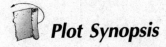 *Plot Synopsis*

This is about the plurality of cinema in one mythic location: Paris, the City of Love. Twenty filmmakers will bring their own personal touch, underlining the wide variety of styles, genres, encounters and the various atmospheres and lifestyles that prevail in the neighborhoods of Paris. Each director has been given five minutes of freedom, and we, as producers, carry the responsibility of weaving a single narrative unit out of those twenty moments. The 20 films will not appear in the order of the arrondissements, from one to twenty, but rather, in a pertinent narrative order, initially unknown to the audience.

## 剧情简介

这是一部短片集粹型电影，背景围绕着传说中的地方：拥有"爱之城"之誉的巴黎。20个导演通过他们的个人感受来呈现巴黎各个街区的风格、类型，多种多样的邂逅、氛围和生活方式。每个导演有5分钟的时间自由表达，我们这些制片人则负责把这20个独立片断用一致的叙事线索穿起来。换句话说，20个短片并不是像按照行政区的编号一样从1排到20，而是遵照一种观众起初并不清楚的内在相关的叙事顺序。

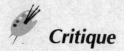

## *Critique*

How wonderful to be a filmmaker in Paris! Every morning you step out the door into the greatest standing set in the world. It's not just the places all of us tourists know—the Tuileries, the Eiffel Tower, the Latin Quarter—it's the anonymous streets where the food in the humblest bistro makes your mouth water, the women are always pert and smartly dressed, the men rueful and wise. Everything and everyone merely awaits further transformation by the cinematographer's glamorizing light. Even a sad story does not seem quite so doleful in this context.

*Paris, Je T'Aime* offers the pleasures of a Paris shoot to an international gang of directors and a bunch of good actors—some well-known, some less so—who have contributed 18 short films, some no more than inconsequential vignettes, other rather nicely worked out short stories, to this largely festive enterprise. All of them are handsomely mounted—Air France should work out a promotional deal with the producers—and they are variable in quality. But even when one of the pieces stutters, stammers or just lies deathly still, we are consoled by our knowledge that it will not trifle with us for very long. And by the fact that there is an excellent likelihood that it will soon be replaced by something more engaging.

I particularly liked the Coen Brothers piece about an American tourist (Steve Buscemi), waiting for a Metro train, who does not heed his guidebook's advice (don't make eye contact with strangers) with comic-violent results, Wes Craven's work about a pair of bickering British tourists visiting Oscar Wilde's grave site in the *Pre-Lachaise* cemetery with romantically restorative results, and Tom Twyker's take on a faltering love affair between a pair of young people, one of whom is blind, yet is also a brave and wily navigator of the sighted world. There's even a piece by Sylvain Chomet, about a mime—yes, I know, but set your prejudices aside—finding true love that has a sort of wayward charm.

Finally, a little masterpiece lurks here. It is called *14eme Arrondissement* by Alexander Payne (Election, Sideways). It consists of no more than a middle-aged Denver woman (Margo Martindale) wandering around the city and reflecting on its sights and her life in her awkward, self-taught French. There's innocence, honesty, sadness and resolve. There's also a wonderful lack of irony or patronization in Payne's treatment of this story, an artlessness in Martindale's performance that is exemplary. It's the last work in *Paris, Je T'Aime* and its worth waiting for. It's worth the price of admission, too.

There seems to be something in Paris air or water that encourages compendium filmmaking—multiple characters and multiple stories. *Paris, Je T'Aime* may be the grandest such work currently on view, but it is not the only one. You may recall the recent *Avenue Montaigne*, in which a young waitress finds herself mixed up with an insecure actress, a great pianist withdrawing from performing and an art collector selling his collection. It has a chipper spirit, and, in the end, things work out all right for all concerned, yet it also carries with it an air of regret, a sense that life is harder, less rewarding than its many characters would like it to be. It's a movie the regretful spirit of which is somewhat at odds with its blithe manner.

—*Richard Schickel*, *Time Magazine*

在巴黎拍电影是多么爽的一件事！每天清晨一出门你便站在了世界上最受瞩目的地方。不仅仅是我们所有旅行者所熟知的那些名胜——杜乐丽花园、艾菲尔铁塔、拉丁区，即便是那不知名的街上最普通的小餐馆都会让你垂涎三尺。女人们活泼奔放、衣着考究，男人们忧郁多情、智慧博学。每个人、每件事物都时刻准备着承接摄影师灯光的照耀。在这样的环境中，即使一个忧伤的故事都显得不再那样忧伤。

《巴黎，我爱你》把拍摄巴黎的乐趣赠送给了一批国际导演和优秀演员（有声名显赫的，也有名气不太大的），共同创作出了18个短片集锦，其中有的只是随意的小品，有的则构思出了完整的微型故事。每个短片外观上都有板有眼（法国航空公司实在应该把制片人好好奖励一番），内在质量则有所出入。不过就算是其中有一两个让人感到乏味无聊，我们也会倍感安慰地凭经验知道它不会烦人太久，还可以想想美妙的事实上的可能性——会有更吸引人的片断来取代它。

我尤其喜欢科恩兄弟的那一段，一个美国旅行者（斯蒂夫·巴斯米饰）在地铁里等车，他把头埋在他的旅行指南里以便省去与陌生人打招呼的麻烦，结果他等来一个喜剧性的暴力结果；韦斯·克雷文的故事是关于一对争吵不休的英国恋人造访拉雪兹公墓，他们瞻仰了奥斯卡·王尔德之墓后关系得到了浪漫的修复；汤姆·提克威讲两个年轻恋人之间的起起伏伏，其中一人虽然双目失明，却可以勇敢无畏、游刃有余地行走于光明的世界；还有西维亚·乔迈的关于一个滑稽小丑寻找真爱的故事——是的，你要放下你的偏见，然后感受它那种不可名状的魅力。

在最后，一段杰作现身了，它是亚历山大·佩恩（曾执导过

《选举》、《杯酒人生》）导演的《第14街区》。故事再简单不过了，它描述一个来自美国丹佛州的中年女人（玛格·马丁戴尔饰）在巴黎市里闲逛，她用自学的笨拙的法语喃喃自语地诉说着自己的感受和生活。这个故事中流淌着天真、坦诚、悲伤和决心。佩恩对故事的处理中难得地没有任何讽刺或谦卑的成分，而马丁戴尔则树立出了一种质朴的典范。这是《巴黎，我爱你》的最后一个片断，它值得期待与肯定。

巴黎的空气和水中似乎浮动着一种异样的东西，在这里拍出的电影总是集粹式的，拥有多人物和多故事。《巴黎，我爱你》大概是目前我们见到的这一类型电影中规模最大的一部，但并不唯一。你或许还会想起《蒙田大道》，一个年轻女服务生发现她被人误认成了一个不靠谱的女演员，一个伟大的钢琴家离开了演出舞台，一个艺术品收藏家出卖他的藏品。影片风格轻松愉悦，最终事情的方方面面都尘埃落定，尽管也有遗憾，也令人觉得生活艰难，回报不如期待的多。这就是那种在怅惘和欢乐之间左冲右突的电影。

——*Richard Schickel*，《时代》杂志

The French capital is also at its most lush and inviting in *Paris, je t'aime*, which signals its celebration of the Gallic romantic spirit right there in the title, which translates in English to Paris, I love you. Consisting of 18 roughly-five-minute-long short films, each one helmed by a different acclaimed director (or directing team, as the case may be), Paris, je t'aime is the rare omnibus film that attains a real cumulative power as it goes on.

Themes of loneliness, loss and giddy love connections made and rekindled reverberate throughout the anthology, granting a pleasing emotional coherence upon the proceedings. The result is that you feel that the assorted characters in each of the shorts, though they never interconnect until a joyous coda, really are co-existing in the same city at the same time, going through their individual triumphs and setbacks in the one place in the world that un-ambiguously demands you let your feelings all hang out.

Besides consistency of theme and setting, another factor that helps to create this sense of gestalt is that of the 18 shorts, there's only one genuine dud—a bit of indulgent fetishism from Wong Kar-Wai's favored cinematographer Christopher Doyle about a Chinese hair salon—and a couple other minor disappointments, including a farcical entry from deadpan masters Joel and Ethan Coen that unfor-tunately recalls the strained slapstick of their weakest feature to date, *The Ladykillers* (though Steve Buscemi, as an unlucky American tourist is, as always, a bonus).

—*Brett Buckalew*, *Film Stew*

法国的首都在《Paris, je t'aime》中得到最奢华最动人的展现，高卢人的蚀骨浪漫都恰如其分地体现在这个名字中，翻译成英文便成了"巴黎，我爱你"。它由 18 个 5 分钟的短片连缀而成，每个短片均由风格迥异的导演（也可能是摄制组）完成，这部集合式的电影因此拥有一种累积起来的力量。

孤独、失落和热情似火的爱的主题在这个集合中此起彼伏，使影片的情绪走向有一种动人的连贯性。其结果，虽然各个短片中各种各样的人物从未相互接触过（除了片尾有一个喜悦的联欢），但你确实感到他们在同一个时间同一个城市里存在着，各自经历着自己的胜利和挫折，而这个地方在世界上如此特殊，它毫不含糊地召唤着你表达出你所有的感受。

这 18 部短片不仅仅是主题和场景一致，它们还有一种浑然一体的效果——可惜的确有一个不折不扣的败笔，导演是王家卫的御用摄影师杜可风，镜头围绕一家中国发廊，该片有一种放纵过度的恋物癖。除此之外还有些小失望，比如说冷酷主义大师科恩兄弟的那一段闹剧，那种矫情和滑稽不幸地让人想起了他们迄今最差劲的剧情片《老妇杀手》（不过值得一提的是斯蒂夫·巴斯米把一个运气不好的美国游客演得活灵活现，他总是那个加分项）。

—— *Brett Buckalew*，*Film Stew* 网站

The masterpiece of the bunch is the last, wonderful piece by Alexander Payne. Payne is admired here, and apparently in Paris too, for the modern comic classic "Sideways". Here, in the moving and funny story of an American in Paris, he amuses us with the rambles of an ordinary woman, a Denver letter carrier who has been saving for years for this trip and even learned French for it. (Her accent is likably atrocious). Very few filmmakers can get humor as bittersweet and realistic as Payne; he gets it again here.

—— *Michael Wilmington*，*Chicago Tribune*

这个集合中的杰作是排在最后的亚历山大·佩恩导演的那个惊人的片断。佩恩在我们这儿人气很高，在巴黎也是如此，这归因于他那部现代喜剧经典《杯酒人生》。在这个关于一个美国人在巴黎的既感人又逗笑的故事中，他把我们的注意力吸引到一个平凡的女人凯洛身上。她是一个丹佛的邮递员，为巴黎之行做了多年准备，甚至为此学了法语（她的口音糟得可爱）。很少有导演具备佩恩这样现实主义的喜忧参半的幽默感，我们再次领略了这一点。

—— *Michael Wilmington*，《芝加哥论坛》

# Sympathy for Lady Vengeance

# 亲切的金子

**导演/编剧**：朴赞郁（Chan-wook Park）

**主演**：李英爱（Yeong-ae Lee）

　　　　崔岷植（Min-sik Choi）

**片长**：112 分钟

**制作**：韩国希杰（CJ Capital Investment），2005 年

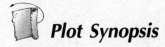

# *Plot Synopsis*

After a 13-year imprisonment for the kidnap and murder of a 6 year old boy, beautiful Lee Guem-ja starts seeking revenge on the man that was really responsible for the boy's death. With the help of fellow inmates and reunited with her daughter, she gets closer and closer to her goal. But will her actions lead to the relief she seeks?

## 剧情简介

美丽的李金子背负着绑架和谋杀一个 6 岁小男孩的罪名在狱中度过 13 年，出狱后，她开始向真正的元凶实施复仇计划。金子和亲生女儿得以团聚，并在狱中好友们的帮助下离目标越来越近。然而，她会如自己所期望的那样从中得到解脱吗？

# *Critique*

*Lady Vengeance* is the conclusion of South Korean director Park Chan-wook's "Revenge Trilogy". Over the span of three films, Chan-wook has examined many aspects of the concept of revenge, including the most lasting: consequences. For many movies, the act of retribution is the point of the film. For Chan-wook, it's the starting point for a larger tapestry.

The first hour of *Lady Vengeance* unfolds like a mobius strip*, skipping randomly through time and occasionally doubling back on itself. Patience is necessary; eventually the pace slows enough for us to catch up. There is a shift in tone during the second half as *Lady Vengeance* turns into a meditation on the ethics of revenge, and the question of whether we ever see things clearly enough to argue that "the end justifies the means". Anyone who has enjoyed the filmmaker's previous works, especially *Oldboy* (which received enough of a widespread U. S. distribution to become a cult movie), will appreciate what this film has to offer. I liked it, but a word of a caution to would-be viewers: *Lady Vengeance* contains violence (some extreme), but it is not an action film. It is deliberately paced, allowing the audience to have time to reflect upon what's happening. And the comedy is of the gallows variety.

— *James Berardinelli*, *Reel Views*

《亲切的金子》是韩国导演朴赞郁"复仇三部曲"的最后一部。朴赞郁通过三部影片考察了复仇内涵的方方面面,尤其是影响最持久的一面:后果。对很多影片来说,补偿性质的行为是落脚点;而对朴赞郁来说,它只是通往更广阔叙述的出发点。

故事的头一个小时展开得像一条没完没了的莫比乌斯带,在时间上任意跳跃,并不时地往回折。观看时耐心是必不可少的,

最后叙事速度终于慢到了可以让我们赶上的程度。影片的基调在
后半部分有所变化，金子开始沉思复仇的是非对错，以及我们是
否有足够理由认为"目的正当就可以不择手段"。任何喜欢该导
演先前作品的人尤其是《老男孩》，（该片在美国得以广泛发行，
并被奉为经典）也同样会欣赏《金子》。我喜欢这个片子，但还
是要提醒那些潜在的观众：《金子》有很多暴力内容（有些甚至
极端暴力），但它不是一部动作片。它有意的慢节奏是为了让观
众有时间反应发生了什么事。而它的幽默背后则是刻骨的仇恨。

— *James Berardinelli*，《旋风景》

Bad news first: The over-stylized nature of the film makes it
much less intense and riveting than Park's last two films. That exhilarating moment in *Oldboy* where Gang Hye-jung is crying on the
subway while a human-sized ant sits at the other end of the train is
gone. Instead, the surrealism of that moment become silly moments
of outrageous humor. It's a switch of tone that is hard to settle into,
but it doesn't hurt the film in the long run. Park uses visual effects
not to create monsters or great armies, but to bring unbelievable
space and depth to his images. The shot of Lady Vengeance at an a-
bandoned school, using a puppy as a test subject for her new re-
volver, enraptures and covers the viewer, and there are at least five
other shots like that.

As in all his films, Park has a special talent with the actors.
Yeong-ae Lee has contagious fun with the character but she knows
that *Lady Vengeance* is a tainted woman with deep emotional scars.
Her quest for vengeance seems to run right along with her need to
redeem herself to be a mother, and Lee has little problem showing
the throbbing heart underneath the dark mind. It's an outstanding
performance. On the other side is the reliably brilliant Choi Min-
Sik as Mr. Baek. Min-Sik has little or no trouble finding the fierce
perversity and formidable evil that Baek is capable of. Although we
hardly see an act of cruelty on screen, it's easy to see him as a pur-
veyor of it.

In the end, it all comes back to Park, a master filmmaker, and his ability to surprise us even when we think we have it all figured out. His talents at blending dark humor and images of unrelenting terror can only be equaled by Todd Solondz and Quentin Tarantino. However, when we look at that last shot of *Lady Vengeance*, her daughter, and her lover standing in the snow (cinematographer Jeong Jeong-hun creates miraculous imagery), there is little doubt that Park doesn't just want us to see this as another *Death Wish*. He wants to get into the black heart of revenge, and his films are testaments to that journey.

*—Chris Cabin, Filmcritic.com*

先说坏消息：该片过于中规中矩使人感觉它不如朴赞郁前两部影片那样扣人心弦。《老男孩》中姜慧姃在地铁中哭泣，一只真人大小的蚂蚁坐在另一头的那种让人兴奋的情景一去不复返了。取代这种超现实的是一种愚蠢的过度幽默。影片基调的转换让人一时难以习惯，好在这没有毁掉整部片子。朴赞郁没有把视觉效果用在制作怪物或庞大的军队上，但却给他的影像带来了不可思议的空间感和深度感。比如金子在废弃的学校里用小狗试验新武器的那个镜头，观众看得目瞪口呆。诸如这样精彩的镜头至少还有五处。

朴赞郁的所有影片都显示出了他在锤炼演员方面的特殊才能。李英爱让角色极具感染力，不过她清楚《金子》刻画的是一个创伤严重、泥足深陷的女人。她要复仇是因为她想通过自救重新做回一个母亲，李英爱接近完美地表现出了她阴郁的灵魂中那颗颤抖的心。她的表演非常出色。再有就是是颇有才华的实力演员崔岷植对白老师的塑造。崔岷植能够轻松地表现出白老师身上的那种激烈的反常和骇人的邪恶。虽然我们在银幕上很少直接地看到那些残忍的行为，但他看起来就像是那个行凶者。

最后，我们再次确认了朴赞郁杰出导演的地位，当我们自以为对一切了然于胸时，他仍有本事让我们感到意外。他那种把黑色幽默注入超级暴力影像的能力只有托德·索朗兹和昆廷·塔伦蒂诺可以与之相提并论。然而，当看到《金子》的最后一个镜头

（金子的女儿和爱人站在雪地中，摄影师延正勋摄制出了奇迹般的画面），我们可以确定朴赞郁并不想让我们再看到一部《猛龙怪客》这样的电影。他想让我们深入到复仇的黑暗腹地中去，他的电影便是对这种追求的一次又一次的证明。

—— *Chris Cabin*，*Filmcritic* 网站

Back in 2004, the Cannes Film Festival jury, led by none other than Quentin Tarantino, awarded the Grand Prix (essentially their second place award the top prize that year went to "Fahrenheit 9/11") to "Oldboy", Korean director Park Chan-wook's bloody and brilliantly mind-bending second part of a proposed loose trilogy of films using revenge as the common theme. (The first part, "Sympathy for Mr. Vengeance" finally appeared in the States after the successful release of "Oldboy".) With "Lady Vengeance", the concluding film of the set, it feels as if Park decided to repay Tarantino for the award by crafting a film that is essentially a feature-length homage to the "Kill Bill" films. It's a nice sentiment but in this case, a simple thank-you note might have been more effective because the resulting film is kind of a disappointment the freshness and ingenuity of "Oldboy" has been replaced with the kind of lazy self-satisfaction that often comes when a unique filmmaker unexpectedly achieves worldwide success and isn't quite sure of how to handle it.

I have no idea if Park conceived of the story of "Lady Vengeance" before or after seeing "Kill Bill" but one cannot deny that the two films have any number of similarities a woman re-emerging after a long absence to deal with duel feelings of revenge and motherhood while tracking down the man who did her wrong, over-the-top violence and a scrambled narrative that only gradually reveals itself over time. The difference between the two films is that while these aspects felt fresh and organic in Tarantino's work, they feel somewhat forced and unnatural here. In "Oldboy", Park told a story that was run-of-the-mill in its broad strokes but unique and ingenious in the details. Here, the storyline is pretty familiar and not even the extreme contortions of Park's screenplay is able to quite disguise that fact—even the seemingly surprising developments in the final reels have a whiff of seen-it/done it to them. More problematic is the way that Park insists on the redemption of his central character without ever really providing any true sense of it this is supposed to be the emotional center of the film but it comes off as shallow as everything else.

"Lady Vengeance" has its virtues it is reasonably stylish and rarely boring (it does drag towards the end like "The Da Vinci Code", this is a film that seems to come to a natural conclusion and then drags things out for another fifteen minutes) and Lee Yeong-ae turns in a fearsomely convincing performance in the lead role. However, the drive and energy that marked Park's previous work is largely absent here it feels at time as if he made the film less because he needed to and more because he told people he was doing a trilogy and felt that he had to make good on his word. Hopefully his next work will contain that drive and energy in a way that will allow him to cash the check that "Oldboy" wrote.

—*Peter Sobczynski, Filmcritic. com*

回溯 2004 年，戛纳电影节评审团（担任主席的不是别人，正是昆廷·塔伦蒂诺）将当年的评审团大奖（戛纳电影节的第二最高奖，当年的金棕榈给了《华氏 9/11》）颁给了《老男孩》，这是韩国导演朴赞郁复仇三部曲中的第二部，一部血腥的心灵极度扭曲的影片（第一部《我要复仇》在《老男孩》的发行大获成功之后也最终进入了美国市场）。作为三部曲的完结篇，《亲切的金子》看起来就像是朴赞郁为了报答塔伦蒂诺，而用一整部长片来向《杀死比尔》致敬。这种情操固然高尚，但这还不如干脆用"谢谢你"来得爽快，因为影片实在让人失望：《老男孩》的新鲜和独创性已经无影无踪，随处可见的是懒惰和自满——似乎一个独特的电影导演意外获得了世界性的成功后，却不确定该怎样处理它。

我不知道朴赞郁构思《金子》的故事是在《杀死比尔》之前还是之后，但不能否认的是二者之间的确有很多相似之处：故事都关于一个女人在长期缺席后为复仇和母爱而复出，都有过多的暴力，叙事晦涩，都是在时间推移中逐渐交代来龙去脉。不同之处是，这些方面在塔伦蒂诺的作品中是新鲜而有机的，在这里却让人感到强迫和不自然。《老男孩》的故事是普遍的共通的，独到和才华体现在细节之中。而《金子》的故事线索则太过熟悉了，即使朴赞郁极端扭曲的剧本也不能掩盖这一事实：就是那看似令人惊讶的结局也在人心里激不起什么波澜。还有一个问题是，虽然朴赞郁坚持把重心放在核心人物的救赎上，但却没有给救赎赋予任何实际意义，这使影片的情感中心和影片的其它元素一样浅薄。

《金子》的优点在于它时尚得有分寸，而且很少让人厌烦（它的结尾发展得确实有点类似《达芬奇密码》，这些电影似乎都要在一个自然的结局之后再拖长 15 分钟出来），此外李英爱把主人公演得非常令人信服。然而，该片基本缺乏朴赞郁以前的动力和能量，你甚至偶尔会感到他拍摄《金子》不只是因为他需要拍，更因为他告诉过观众他在做一套三部曲，并感到他要说话算数地做出好东西来。但愿他的下一部影片能够找回他自己，能够兑现《老男孩》给我们的期待。

— *Peter Sobczynski*，*Filmcritic* 网站

## Note

Mobius strip：莫比乌斯带，因德国数学家 Ferdinand Mobius（1790-1868）而得名。取一片长方纸条，把一个短边扭转 180°，然后把这边跟对边粘贴起来，就形成一条"莫比乌斯带"。从带子的一面出发，沿着带一直走，绕完一圈发现回到的不是起点。可以在带上永无止境的走下去，走过每一点，可无论怎么走都仍在同一面上。

# Sideways

# 杯酒人生

**导演：**亚历山大·佩恩（Alexander Payne）

**编剧：**亚历山大·佩恩（Alexander Payne）
吉姆·泰勒（Jim Taylor）

**主演：**保罗·吉亚玛提（Paul Giamatti）
托马斯·哈登·丘奇（Thomas Haden Church）

**片长：**123 分钟

**制作：**福克斯探照灯公司（Fox Searchlight Pictures），2004 年

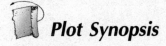

# *Plot Synopsis*

Miles is a failed writer living a meager existence in San Diego as an English teacher. With his career seemingly fading and the fate of a book hinging on a publisher's decision, Miles is depressed with himself and what he hasn't achieved. Jack is a television actor whom some recognize but not many do, as if he were a minor actor who got a taste of success. With his best friend Miles, the two embark on a road trip through California's wine country. Miles wants to give his friend a nice sendoff before married life, while Jack simply wants to have a fling beforehand. As they're both nearing middle age with not much to show for it, the two will explore the vineyards while ultimately searching for their identities.

## 剧情简介

迈尔斯是一个圣地亚哥的中学英文老师，想当作家而不得，生活平淡。他的事业似乎在走下坡路，他想出的书完全依赖出版人的意志，他因此为自己以及自己的失败感到沮丧。杰克是个小有知名度的电视演员，更确切地说，一个浅尝过成功的二流演员。这两个好哥们一起踏上了穿越加州葡萄酒基地的公路之旅。迈尔斯想在老友迈入婚姻牢笼之前好好送行一番，而杰克本人只是想放纵一把。在葡萄园之旅中，这两个人近中年都一无所获的人最终找回了他们自己。

 # *Critique*

Things happen on trips; that's why the road-movie genre, with its radical concentration of means, never seems to tire. An opening to landscape, movement, adventure, and the eternal American desire to drop everything and light out for the territories, the form is both inherently dramatic and supremely flexible. It has served as the basis for crime thrillers ( "They Live by Night", "Bonnie and Clyde"), for violent explorations of the limits of freedom ( "Easy Rider", "Thelma & Louise"), for bruising tests of love and friendship ( "Two for the Road", "Scarecrow"). "Sideways" is one of the last: each man experiences the glories and the horrors of the other's character and is forced, willy-nilly, to look himself in the face in a motel-room mirror.

Payne and Taylor have always made movies about the melancholy middling-to-lower range of achievement and ambition, the near-losers that Americans hate but that so many of us at our most demoralized become. Up until now, the dead-eyed blandness of Omaha, Payne's home town, has dominated his work. He and Taylor have repeatedly satirized the emotional flatness and evasiveness of the place, while treating with tender respect their characters' hesitant, inarticulate yearnings for something more. Together they have created a gallery of memorably mediocre people: the dumb, paint-sniffing but tenaciously enduring Ruth Stoops ( Laura Dern ) in "Citizen Ruth"; the vindictive schoolteacher ( Matthew Broderick) in "Election"; the soured widower ( Jack Nicholson ) in

"About Schmidt". There is, I believe, a quiet but persistent spiritual ethos at the heart of their intention. The blinkered, semi-unconscious sinners stumble toward grace—a moment of clarity, of self-realization. Some of them may even get there.

Payne is a patient and orderly director; he wants character revelation and eruptive moments, and he carefully builds his scenes and gets both, but some of the elements in "Sideways" are no more than commonplace. The jazz score, by Rolfe Kent, plunks along uninterestingly, and when it accompanies the Saab zipping through loamy hills, or plays over a prolonged eating scene, the movie feels like an episode of "Great Getaways". Some of the camera setups are too obvious-the shots of faux—Tudor inns and luscious vineyards come off as conventionally handsome. Payne has finally got himself out of Nebraska—you can feel his limbs warming in the sunshiny beauty of California—but he hasn't come close to developing a visual style that can sweep the audience along. He never breaks free into anything like the startling, brutal lyricism of the French director Bertrand Blier, whose own two-men-on-the-road movies, "Going Places" (1974) and "Get Out Your Handkerchiefs" (1978), were exhilaratingly beautiful, amoral fantasies. Perhaps Payne, given his obsession with emotional inadequacy, can't abandon strict realism. Blier's heroes (Gérard Depardieu and Patrick Dewaere) were thoughtlessly carnal outlaws; Payne's are stunted men who need to grow up, and some of the tone of "Sideways" emerges from the American therapeutic instinct. Still, I fervently want Payne to lift off from the Omaha in his soul.

—*David Denby*, *The New Yorker*

路上总有事情会发生，这是公路片这种形式比较极端的类型电影从不让人厌倦的原因。它向风景、运动和历险敞开，它包容了美国人那种舍弃一切浪迹天涯的不灭激情，它天然地富有戏剧性，又极其灵活多变。它支持过犯罪惊悚片（《以夜维生》、《邦尼和克莱德》），支持过对自由的激烈追逐（《逍遥骑士》、《末路狂花》），支持过对爱情和友谊的严峻考验（《丽人行》、《稻草人》）。《杯酒人生》属于最后一种：两个人都彼此感受到了对方性格中的好与坏，然后不情愿地在汽车旅馆中独自面对着镜中的自己。

佩恩和泰勒向来喜欢把镜头对准那些成就和抱负等偏下的人，那些接近失败的人，那些遭美国人厌恶而我们中的多数又无可奈何地正在变成的人。迄今为止，佩恩的电影中一直笼罩着一种来自他故乡奥马哈的沉闷死气。他和泰勒无休止地讽刺这个地方在情感上的贫乏和逃避，但却以温柔和尊重对待他的人物，尊重他们在迟疑和含糊中渴望逃离的心。他们一起塑造出了一批具有纪念性的小人物：《公民露丝》中沉默卑微但又顽强坚韧的露丝（劳拉·邓恩饰）；《选举》中有报复心的中学老师（马修·布罗德里克饰）；《关于施密特》中酸溜溜的鳏夫（杰克·尼克尔森饰）。我相信，在他们各自的执着中都有一颗宁静坚守的灵魂。这些狭隘的、糊涂的罪人们磕磕绊绊地向一种自我实现的澄澈之境努力迈步，其中有些人或许已经抵达了那里。

佩恩是一位耐心极佳的按部就班的导演。他喜欢让演员在瞬间顿悟和爆发，他小心地调度着场景并蕴育着这样的时刻，然而，《杯酒人生》中的很多元素还是太过平凡了。洛夫·肯特作曲的爵士乐乏味无趣地响着，而当音乐陪他们开着萨博车穿越肥沃的山丘，或者点缀漫长的吃饭场景时，影片看起来就像是一出"胜利大逃亡"。一些机位设置得太明显了，比如对人造都铎式客栈和迷人的葡萄园的取景就美得很老套。费恩在最后终于离开了内布拉斯加，你都能感觉到他舒服地沐浴在加州温暖的阳光下，但遗憾的是他没有发展成一种能感染观众的视觉风格。他不能自由随意地为某事驻足，像野性惊人的法国导演贝特朗·布里叶那样抒情。布里叶的只有两个人在路上的公路片《远行他方》（1974年）和《掏出你的手帕》（1978）则美得让人兴奋，梦幻得超越道德。或许佩恩是因为迷恋情感匮乏这一主题，才不能偏离严格的现实主义。布里叶的主人公（杰拉尔·德帕迪约和帕特里克·迪瓦尔）都是些欠思量的放纵的逃犯，而佩恩的则都是发育迟缓尚需长大的人，而且《杯酒人生》中的某些基调就像是出于美国式的心理治疗本能。无论如何，我诚挚地希望佩恩能把他的灵魂从奥马哈超脱出来。

— *David Denby*，《纽约客》

Nothing much happens in this movie, and then everything happens. There's not a false note here, and the entire supporting cast—Madsen, Oh, Church and Marylouise Burke as Miles's Mother—is uniformly excellent. It rambles along at its own good-natured pace, playing both for laughs and for laments, stretching out a tad too long, but who cares, really? The film's a welcome ramble. Giamatti, as demonstrated in his attention-grabbing turn as comic-book writer Harvey Pekar in "American Splendor", is the master of mopes. His is a mug that registers heartbreak with a downward glance, an imperceptible shift in facial musculature. His Miles is a man whose life is defined by regret, a man who the audience keeps hoping will put down the wine glass and get to living.

—*Teresa Wiltz, Washington Post*

影片中什么事都没发生，然后所有事就都发生了。这里没有一处败笔，所有的配角——迈德森、吴珊卓、丘奇，以及扮演迈尔斯母亲的玛丽路易丝·贝克等都表现得相当出色。它以它自己温和的节奏漫游着，上演着欢笑和悲伤，即使时间有点过长，但谁又在乎呢？影片的这种漫游让人喜欢。吉亚玛提在本片中展现出了令人瞩目的转型（曾在《光耀美国》中扮演漫画作家哈维·贝克），把一种闷闷不乐演得淋漓尽致。他的方式是，用朝下瞥一眼来表达心碎的感受，面部肌肉中流露出一丝难以觉察的转变。他扮演的迈尔斯是一个生活被后悔所定义的人，一个观众一直希望他能放下酒杯，继续上路的人。

—— *Teresa Wiltz*，《华盛顿邮报》

Payne, who adapted Rex Pickett's original novel with his usual collaborator Jim Taylor, has mixed three genres with surpassing skill—the road movie, the relationship drama and the romantic comedy—while the screenwriters and novelist deliver a dead-on, consistently hilarious portrait of a certain classic attraction-of-opposites male friendship.

That friendship between Miles and Jack is so keenly observed and unfailingly well-drawn it may make you wince while you laugh: the seemingly unlikely bond, beloved by writers and filmmakers (mostly, but not entirely male) from Billy Wilder and Neil Simon to the Coen Brothers, between brainy nerd and narcissistic jock-stud.

Giamatti has a priceless spaniel pugnacity and terminal exasperation that convey here, as sharply as in "American Splendor", the real dilemma and comic anguish of an American intellectual/outsider. Church, in a career-altering performance, keeps us laughing or smiling constantly while making Jack the prototype of the aging California Casanova *.

They make their characters come so thoroughly alive on screen because they and the writers, unabashedly, give us good and bad sides. We see Miles conning and robbing his mom and Jack manipulating nearly every half-plausible bedmate he meets. We also see their mutual sometime tenderness, generosity and humor.

— *Michael Wilmington*, *Chicago Tribune*

在对雷克斯·平克特原著小说的改编中，佩恩和他的御用编剧吉姆·泰勒用非凡的技巧融合了三种类型片：公路片、友谊剧和浪漫喜剧。一种经典的具有互补性的男性友谊被他们用精准幽默的方式描绘了出来。

影片尖锐地观察着并无穷无尽地展现着迈尔斯与杰克之间的友情，让你在笑的时候心里一惊：这种惹人烦的书呆子和自恋的花花公子的微妙组合多么像作家和电影导演，比如比利·怀尔德与尼尔·西蒙或科恩兄弟之间。

吉亚玛提演出了一种骨子里的好斗和恼怒之气，其激烈程度不亚于《光耀美国》，这是美国知识分子兼边缘人所特有的尴尬和哭笑不得的痛苦。而丘奇在这场具有演艺生涯所具有的转型意义的表演中让观众从头笑到尾，他演的杰克背后的原型则是上了年纪的加州浪荡公子哥。

他们让人物彻底活在了银幕上，他们（以及背后的作者）能够大胆地毫无保留地把善恶美丑统统展现在我们面前。我们看到迈尔斯操纵和掠夺着自己的母亲，看到杰克调戏着他遇到的所有有上床可能性的女人。我们也看到他们偶尔向对方流露出的温柔、慷慨和幽默。

— *Michael Wilmington*，《芝加哥论坛》

> **Note**
>
> Casanova：卡萨诺瓦（1725-1798），意大利冒险家，以所写的包括自己许多风流韵事在内的《自传》而著称，以后成为风流浪子，好色之徒的代称。

# A Very Long Engagement

# 漫长的婚约

**导演**：让·皮埃尔·热内（Jean-Pierre Jeunet）

**原著**：塞巴斯蒂安·雅普里索特（Sebastien Japrisot）

**主演**：加斯帕德·尤利尔（Gaspard Ulliel）

奥黛丽·塔图 Audrey Tautou

**片长**：133 分钟

**发行**：华纳兄弟（Warner Bros.），2004 年

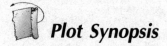

# *Plot Synopsis*

Five desperate men shoot themselves in order to be relieved from the horrifying frontline at the Somme, in WWI. A court-martial decides to punish them by leaving them alone in no-man's land, to be killed in the crossfire. Then all hell breaks loose and they all die. Or not? One of these men's fiancée, a young girl who can't walk since age 3, receives information that makes her suspect his boyfriend might have gotten away alive. So she embarks in a painful, long and often frustrating ordeal to find out the truth.

## 剧情简介

一战时的索姆河战役，五个绝望的人为了离开恐怖的前线而开枪自残。军事法庭判决把他们流放到无人地带，在双方交火的地方自生自灭。厄运压头，他们是生是死给人们留下了一道谜。其中一人的未婚妻，一个从三岁时就再也不能走路的女孩，收到一些消息使她怀疑她的男朋友还活着。于是她踏上了一条痛苦、漫长，不断遭受挫折考验的寻觅之路。

## Critique

"A very long Engagement" is Jean-Pierre Jeunet's first film since the glorious "Amelie". You can still feel the balmy effect of that previous movie, and, to some extent, that's part of the trouble.

"Engagement", after all, stars "Amelie's" Audrey Tautou. She plays, once again, a headstrong, courageous and highly romantic hero searching for her only true love. And for the second time, the audience is treated to strange-looking characters and a sort of omniscient whimsy about the whole thing.

This time, however, more and different things are asked of us. It's set on a bigger canvas, for one. And there's a deeper dose of realism, for another. The story's set during World War I, when trench duty, unyielding mud, senseless slaughter and insane commands from the dysfunctional French leadership are routine. Conditions are so awful that many soldiers intentionally maim their hands so they'll be discharged and saved from almost certain death. When five wounded soldiers—among them, the sweet, fair-haired Manech—are accused of this cynical act, they are commanded to march to the front and take their chances in no man's land. It's their commander's grim sense of poetic justice.

Jeunet, as always, pushes the eccentric/quirky factor whenever possible. Mathilde, for starters, has a pronounced limp resulting from polio, and she plays the tuba. There's a dog with a flatulence problem, and we meet a postman whose daily, skidding arrival at Sylvain's doorstep becomes a comedic motif.

It's a pleasure to watch Jeunet's direction. (He also made "Delicatessen", "The City of Lost Children", and the wonderfully nonformulaic "Alien: Resurrection". ) There's a scene involving a zeppelin, moored inside a makeshift hospital building and facing an imminent explosion, that is a fantastic, suspense-filled spectacle. And details of the battlefront, which we return to often, are etched with staggering detail.

But unfortunately (or perhaps fortunately), movies tend to thrive on simplicity and focus; novels are freer to maneuver in whatever direction or directions they please. In its zeal to honor Sebastien Japrisot's popular book ( "un long dimanche de fiancaille" ), "Engagement" simply disappears inside its own enormous, intricate and ambitious design. And the emotional effect (which came so effortlessly in "Amelie") is surprisingly muted. It could be that two or three viewings would help the movie emerge, so one could effortlessly differentiate the characters and their plotlines, and see the beautiful big picture. But for this one-time viewer at least, Jeunet's movie is a game of great singles* inside an overextended ballgame.

—*Desson Thomson*, *Washington Post*

《漫长的婚约》是让·皮埃尔·热内继辉煌的《天使爱美丽》之后的第二部作品，你仍能从中感受到《爱美丽》那种温暖的感觉，不过在某种意义上，这也给该片带来了麻烦。

《婚约》的主演仍然是"爱美丽"奥黛丽·塔图，她又一次扮演了一个一心要寻找唯一真爱的勇敢任性、超级浪漫的女主人公。影片再一次呈现给观众外表举止怪异的人物和一种笼罩在一切之上的魔幻氛围。

然而这一次，影片对观众的要求更多，而且不同。其一，它的故事背景更广阔；其二，它的现实意味更浓厚。故事发生在一战期间，法国高层统治无道，到处都是泥泞的战壕，麻木的屠杀，荒唐的命令。在一种绝望的情形下，很多士兵弄残自己的手以便逃脱必然的死亡。五个受伤的士兵（其中之一便是可爱的金发马奈克）被指控犯了这种叛逆行为，他们被流放到前线的无人地带去，生死由天。这是司令做出的残忍而浪漫的裁决。

热内一如既往地驱动一切可以驱动的古怪/离奇元素。玛蒂尔德，作为驱动人，因为小儿麻痹症拖着一条明显的瘸腿，她吹奏大号；一只肠胃胀气的狗；一个邮递员每天以急刹车的方式非常喜剧性地来到塞尔文门前。

热内导演的电影总能让人赏心悦目（他的作品还有《黑店狂想曲》、《童梦失魂夜》，以及非常有想象力的《异形4》）。比如《婚约》中那个失陷在医院大楼中时刻都会爆炸的飞艇就是一个富有悬念和奇思异想的奇观。还有常常闪现在我们面前的前线，它充满了令人吃惊的细节。

可惜（或许也是幸运），电影总是倾向于简化和集中，而小说则可以自由地向你想去的各个方向漫游。塞巴斯蒂安·雅普里索特的同名畅销书值得我们向他致以诚挚的敬意，而影片《婚约》却简单地消失在它种种庞大、复杂和艰巨的设计背后。原本在《爱美丽》中表达自如的情感效果在此竟然默然无声。这部电影你大概需要看上两三遍才能明白究竟，才能不费力气地辨别出人物和情节线索，才能没有负担地欣赏美丽的大画面。而对那些一次性的观众，热内的电影就像是一场扩张过度的棒球赛中的一垒打比赛。

—*Desson Thomson*，《华盛顿邮报》

If you've seen "Delicatessen", "City of Lost Children" or "Amelie", you know that French director Jean-Pierre Jeunet has pioneered a whimsical filmmaking style that relies on fast-cutting, visual non-sequiturs and slightly surreal, computer-animated backgrounds.

He's currently the hottest director in Europe. The first two films made him the darling of critics and the great white hope* of French cinema, and "Amelie" —a huge star-making vehicle for Audrey Tautou—was one of France's biggest worldwide box-office hits ever.

With his new film, "A Very Long Engagement", he joins forces with Tautou once again and puts his distinctive style to the service of a genre that does not seem immediately suitable to it: an epic romance set against the backdrop of World War I.

And, truth be told, it's a rough fit of style to subject. Indeed, we spend a good deal of the movie uncomfortably uncertain of where it's going, and unsure if it's at all serious about its weepy romance. Jeunet's tongue often seems perilously close to his cheek*.

And yet, his extraordinary visuals keep us riveted throughout, his story is progressively compelling, his star is as irresistible as a hot fudge sundae and his movie gradually sneaks up to deliver a considerable emotional wallop.

Yet, bizarre as it is, the movie works amazingly well as a historical epic. It's packed full of dazzling period detail and such awesome re-creations as Paris' Place de la Opera in 1920 ( half real, half computer-generated) and its long-vanished Les Halles market ( all real).

"A Very Long Engagement" also finally comes together to be a touching love story and showy star vehicle. It's not as strong a role as Amelie, but Mathilde's faith and determination are immensely appealing, and Tautou's special magic carries the movie all the way.

　　　　　　　　　　*—William Arnold*, *Seattle Post-Intelligencer*

　　你要是看过《黑店狂想曲》、《童梦失魂夜》或《天使爱美丽》就会知道法国导演让·皮埃尔·热内是魔幻电影风格的先驱。其特点是快速剪切、打破现实逻辑的视觉造型，以及略微超现实的电脑特效背景。

　　目前他算是欧洲人气最高的导演。前两部电影让评论界对他青眼有加，使他成了法国电影的希望，而《爱美丽》则使奥黛丽·塔图一举成名，并成为法国电影史上的全球票房最高的影片。

　　在新作《漫长的婚约》中，热内再度联手塔图，并把他的个人风格向类型化的方向发展，虽然他似乎还没马上适应这个题材：一部以一战为背景的浪漫史诗。

　　说实话，这是一部风格和主题搭配牵强的影片。我们确实感到在很长的篇幅中，它有一种让人不快的不确定感——既不确定影片的走向，也不确定是否应该把它催人泪下的浪漫当作真正严肃的事情。看起来他常有心口不能一致的危险。

然而，影片非凡的视觉表现力从头至尾地吸引着我们，它的故事越来越有强度，它的主角越来越有感染力，最终，影片累积起了强大的情感漩涡。

因此，虽然它有些古怪，但仍不失为一部令人称赞的史诗。它充满了令人眼花缭乱的历史细节，不可思议地重现了1920年的巴黎歌剧院广场（一半实景，一半电脑合成）以及消失已久的阿莱市场（全部实景）。

最终，《漫长的婚约》综合了动人的爱情故事和主人公的魅力秀。虽然玛蒂尔德不如爱美丽那样深入人心，但是她的信念和决心深深地打动了我们，而且塔图的个人魅力从始至终地牵动着我们的神经。

——*William Arnold*，《西雅图邮讯报》

"Engagement" is a lavish spectacle with an all-star cast and a gargantuan budget (at least by French standards, $57 million, largely supplied by America's Warner Brothers). Yet, even though it's obviously intended for a mass world audience, it's neither condescending nor crass. It's a magical film which manages to transport and rivet us in the same highly-imaginitive, breezily playful way "Amelie" did, while also drenching us in the horror of war: France's World War I battlefield miseries and tragedy.

When we think of the best French cinema, we usually conjure up small, personal films done by auteur directors. But Jeunet, it seems, is an auteur who likes to play with bigger toys, "the world's largest electric train set", as Orson Welles once described big studio moviemaking. With the help of his impish-faced star and a great large cast, he strikes a giddy balance between comedy and terror, romance and incandescent action, between the demands of his huge canvas and his intimate emotional subject.

Jeunet performs a classic cinematic conjuring trick here, the kind French artists like Jean Renoir and Marcel Carne once managed regularly. Like Jean Paul Rappeneau in this year's other big, lush, French war entertainment "Bon Voyage", he balances film artistry and crowd-pleasing entertainment. Luckily, like Manech, he has his private angel, Audrey Tautou.

*— Michael Wilmington, Chicago Tribune*

　　《婚约》是一场由明星阵容和超级预算（按照法国电影的标准，5700 万美元的确不低，主要由美国华纳兄弟公司投资）所支撑的视听盛宴。不过虽然它有明显的大众诉求，但它既不刻意讨好也不粗制滥造。它像想象力充盈、风格轻快的《天使爱美丽》一样让我们激动和投入，又让我们身临其境地体验到了战争的恐怖，体验到一战期间法国战场上的苦难和悲剧。

　　每当提到最优秀的法国电影，我们通常想起来的都是作者导演的小制作的个人作品。不过热内却是那种喜欢玩大玩具的人，就像奥逊·威尔斯曾经形容大制片厂的电影制作是"世界上最大的电动火车"。在表情顽皮的女主角和大规模的演员队伍的帮助下，他从容地在喜剧和恐怖之间，浪漫和激烈之间，宏大的背景和私秘的情感之间达成了平衡。

　　热内在这里变了一出经典的电影戏法，这些戏法像让·雷诺阿和马赛尔·卡尔内这样的法国艺术家以前经常玩。如同让·保罗·拉佩纽和他今年关于法国战争的鸿篇巨制《一帆风顺》那样，热内很好地平衡了电影艺术和大众娱乐之间的关系。而且他和马奈克一样遇到了自己的幸运天使——奥黛丽·塔图。

*—Michael Wilmington，《芝加哥论坛》*

## Note

　　Single：【棒球术语】一垒打，击球手安全到达一垒的一击。

　　White hope：被寄予厚望者，被支持者们寄予希望能获得巨大成功的人，尤其指初期的竞争者。

　　Tongue in-cheek/to speak one's tongue in one's cheek：舌头没有放正，表示态度不是认真的，心口不一。

# King Kong

# 金 刚

**导演:** 彼得·杰克逊(Peter Jackson)

**主演:** 杰克·布莱克(Jack Black)

亚德里安·布洛迪(Adrien Brody)

娜奥米·沃茨(Naomi Watts)

**片长:** 187 分钟

**制作:** 环球影业(Universal Pictures),2005 年

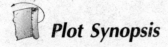 *Plot Synopsis*

Set in the 1930s, this is the story of a young and beautiful actress Ann Darrow from the world of vaudeville who finds herself lost in depression-era New York and her luck changes when she meets an over-ambitious filmmaker Carl Denham who brings her on an exploratory expedition to a remote island where she finds compassion and the true meaning of humanity with an ape Kong. The beauty and the beast finally meet their fate back in the city of New York where the filmmaker takes and displays the ape in quest of his fame by commercial exploitation which ultimately leads to catastrophe for everyone including a playwright Jack Driscoll who falls in love with Ann and plays an unlikely hero by trying to save her from Kong and her destiny.

## 剧情简介

故事背景是上世纪 30 年代，年轻貌美的歌舞圈女演员安·达罗发现自己迷失在纽约的经济大萧条中。在结识了野心勃勃的导演卡尔·德纳姆后她的命运发生了转变。卡尔带她远征探险来到一个荒岛上，岛上的一只大猩猩"金刚"让她生出了同情之心，并发现了人性的真谛。他们的命运再次在纽约相遇，导演借金刚的名气做商业宣传时引发出一场席卷了每个人的灾难。爱上安的剧作家杰克挺身而出，试图从金刚手中夺回安，并拯救她的命运。

 **Critique**

The big guy is back: the same chocolate-doughnut nose, seriously mashed, as if he'd been sleeping face down in the jungle for decades; the matted hair, worn natural as always; the eyes both fierce and plaintive; the heavy-limbed body, though it's stronger than before, and quicker, too. He swings his weight easily, hanging from promontories and thick vines, but he's definitely a wrestler by temperament, taking on three allosaurs—or whatever they are— at once, and flinging them about as if they were barroom thugs. King Kong never really went away. The most familiar of pop-myth creatures, he just seemed, for some reason, to be hiding from us since his last appearance, in 1976, in which he found himself entrapped in a rather cheesy camp-colossal retelling, updated to the (then) present. That movie was a self-consciously jokey story about a greedy oil-company scouting expedition, a Princeton paleontologist (Jeff Bridges), and a ditzy starlet (Jessica Lange), who chatted to the ape as if he were hanging out in her dressing room.

This time, however, the hero is a playwright and screenwriter, played by the long-faced Adrien Brody. A knight of the doleful countenance if ever there was one, Brody is perhaps not quite right as a leading man; in any case, he receives less affection from Ann than the ape does. The first two movies were about an ape who wanted a blonde he couldn't have, and the woman who came to like the big dope; Jackson's version is about an impossible union between partners equally in love with each other. But nothing can compare with the original's strange combination of naïve enthusiasm and knowing lewdness. (When Denham brought Kong and the girl back to New York, and exhibited them in a theatre, he claimed that she had "lived through an experience no other woman ever dreamed of.") There's no place for lewdness—for the jokes and innuendos that movie nuts have been buzzing over for decades—in this new, tender version.

I also missed any equivalent to the enchanted-isle graphics of the first movie. But there's no point, I suppose, in shrouding computer graphics in mist, since we're paying to see what we cannot see in life. The trouble is that Jackson, an exuberant director, fresh from his triumph with the "Lord of the Rings" trilogy, likes to shoot up a storm, and here his exuberance spills over into senselessness. Repeating what Spielberg has already accomplished in the "Jurassic Park" series, Jackson has fallen into a trap. Spectacle must be more and more astonishing or it creates as much boredom as wonder, yet it's not easy, as filmmakers are finding out, to top what others have done and stay within a disciplined narrative; at any rate, our awareness that so little is staged in real space feeds our impatience. Even children may feel that they've seen it all before. This "Kong" is high-powered entertainment, but Jackson pushes too hard and loses momentum over the more than three hours of the movie. The story was always a goofy fable—that was its charm—and a well-told fable knows when to stop.

—*David Denby*, *The New Yorker*

那个庞然大物又回来了：同样的巧克力多纳圈般的鼻子被挤压得严重变了形，好像它趴在丛林里睡了几十年似的；蓬乱的头发，还是那么不修边幅；既凶猛又悲哀的眼神；沉重的身躯——虽然比过去更强大也更迅速。它灵活地运用四肢攀越在山崖和藤蔓上，它还是一个脾气暴躁的摔跤好手，可以一气抓住三只异龙

（或随便什么）甩来甩去，像对付酒吧里的混混一样。其实金刚从来没有离开过我们。这个流行神话中最家喻户晓的怪物，在1976年最后一次现身后似乎出于某种原因隐居了起来，大概是当时它发现自己遭到了最粗制滥造、哗众取宠的重拍。那是一部自顾自地兜售滑稽和玩笑的电影，故事的主要角色是一家远征考察的贪婪的石油公司，一个普林斯顿的古生物学者（杰夫·布里奇斯饰），一个缺乏头脑的小演员（杰西卡·兰格饰），她和金刚聊天的感觉就像金刚是挂在她更衣间的什么东西。

然而这一次，影片真正的主人公是由长脸的亚德里安·布洛迪所扮演的剧作家和电影编剧。布洛迪拥有一张想象中的骑士的忧愁面容，或许他并不十分适合做主角；不管怎么说，他还没有金刚更能让安激动。在前两部电影中，金刚爱着一个自己得不到的金发美人，而这个女人渐渐对这个大笨蛋生出了好感；杰克逊的这一版则是一对平等相爱却没有可能性的恋人。不过，什么都比不上最初的那种天真的热情与世故的放纵之间奇异的结合。（当德纳姆把金刚和女孩带回纽约在剧院中展览时，他声称她"体验着一种其他的女人想都没想过的生活"）而这新的更温柔的一版影片没有给放纵留下任何空间（因为影迷们对此开了几十年的玩笑和冷嘲热讽）。

此外，我觉得该片中的荒岛景象也不及第一部那样梦幻迷人。当然我认为这不能责怪电脑动画，我们本来就是付了钱来看现实生活中看不到的东西。问题在于杰克逊，这个刚刚从《魔戒》三部曲的辉煌中走出来的精力旺盛的导演喜欢把什么都往大了做，这次终于过犹不及。《金刚》是在重复斯皮尔博格在《侏罗纪公园》系列中已经实现的成就，这使杰克逊陷入了迷失。奇观一定是要么越来越让人惊奇，要么越来越惹人烦。而电影制作人发现，既想超越前人同时又保证叙事的合理性并不是一件容易的事。无论如何，离开现实空间太久让我们失去了耐心，甚至小朋友都觉得它没有一点新鲜的东西。这个《金刚》是浓墨重彩的娱乐，但杰克逊用力过度，并在3个多小时的片长中丢失了叙事动力。电影故事向来就是愚人的童话，这也恰恰是它的魅力来源，但这个故事要讲得好，并能在该停的地方停下来。

—*David Denby*，《纽约客》

Spectacular, clumsy, hilarious, ludicrously self-indulgent, terrifying and far too long, Peter Jackson's remake of the 1933 classic is a monster in every sense. Throwing economy to the winds, Jackson has staged the romance between struggling actress Naomi Watts and her giant gorilla as tragedy on a Shakespearian scale. It doesn't always work, but when it does, King Kong really is the eighth wonder of the world.

The original Kong lasts for a trim 100 minutes. In this version, it takes nearly that long before we even get to meet the title character. First we spend some time in a thrillingly recreated 30s New York, and then the film gets stuck in a boat for simply ages with obsessed movie director Carl Denham and his crew. This interlude, marred as it is by portents of doom and clanging dialogue, is a bit of a trial.

Finally, Kong makes his entrance, and he's worth the wait. Jackson's team has created a marvellously expressive, menacing and tragic beast. In a film stuffed with superb performances—Watts, in particular, is wonderful—it's the monkey who deserves the Oscar.

—*Paul Arendt*，*BBC*

奇观，笨拙，喧哗，可怕，滑稽的自我陶醉，过长的篇幅——彼得·杰克逊对 1933 年经典的重拍在任何方面都是一个怪物。在烧钱的同时，杰克逊将挣扎的女演员娜奥米·沃茨与她的大猩猩之间的浪漫爱情提升到了莎士比亚悲剧的高度。这不见得总是有效，不过一旦成功，金刚就真的是世界第八大奇迹了。

第一部《金刚》整整 100 分钟。而这一版我们看到 100 分钟时几乎还没见到片名中的"金刚"。我们先是看到对 30 年代纽约的惊人再现，然后看着电影导演卡尔·德纳姆和他的团队长时间困在一只船上，这段被厄运的征兆和嘈杂的对话所填充的间歇实在对观众是一种考验。

终于，金刚出场了，他值得我们等待。杰克逊的团队创造了一个表情异常丰富，极具威慑力的悲情野兽。在一部演员表演可嘉（尤其是沃茨的表现）的影片中，最该得到奥斯卡的是这只猩猩。

—*Paul Arendt*，*BBC*

What do you do after creating the multiple Academy Award winning "The Lord of the Rings", arguably the greatest film trilogy of all time? Well, if you're Peter Jackson you immediately jump behind the camera and direct "King Kong", a film that became a classic when it stunned audiences back in 1933.

Jackson has been obsessed with this "beauty and the beast" story since he was a child and saw the original film flickering across his black and white TV at home in New Zealand.

He was so taken with the movie that the budding filmmaker tried to make his own version when he was just 12 years old using his mother's donated old fur stole for Kong. The top of the Empire State building was made out of cardboard and the New York City skyline was painted on a bed sheet. Unfortunately, this epic was never completed, but the desire to make a film about "King Kong" continued to burn in Jackson's heart.

After becoming a full-fledged filmmaker and making the critically acclaimed "Heavenly Creatures", he tried again to get "Kong" made in 1996, but Hollywood wouldn't bite.

After the huge success of the "Rings" trilogy, Hollywood would probably have let him make a movie about a phone book.

He chose to return to his childhood dream and make " King Kong".

In a word, Jackson's "King Kong", is spectacular, awesome, phenomenal and breathtaking. OK, so I can't boil it down to one word.

*—Paul Clinton, CNN*

拍完了《指环王》，这部赢得了数项奥斯卡奖，并无疑是史上最宏大的电影三部曲之后，你会做什么？如果你是彼得·杰克逊，你就会立刻跳到摄影机后面执导摄制《金刚》，一部早在 1933 年就震撼过观众的电影经典。

杰克逊在童年时代就迷上了这个"美女与野兽"的故事，当时他还是在新西兰家中的黑白电视上观看了最初那版电影。

在对影片的痴迷中，这个萌芽中的电影制作人试图用他妈妈的毛皮围巾扮金刚来拍一部自己的版本，当时他才 12 岁。帝国大厦的顶部用硬纸板做成，纽约的地平线则画在一张床单上。不幸的是，这部史诗从来没有完成，但是拍摄《金刚》的愿望则在杰克逊的心里生根发芽。

在杰克逊成为一名名副其实的电影制作人并拍出了受到评论界肯定的《梦幻天堂》后，他在 1996 年再次试图拍《金刚》，但是好莱坞并不买帐。

在《魔戒》三部曲获得空前成功后，好莱坞大概要请他拍一部关于一本电话簿的影片，而他则选择拍《金刚》来实现童年的梦想。

总之，杰克逊的《金刚》是壮观的、可怕的、非凡的、惊人的。哎呀，我实在难以用一句话来总结它。

*—Paul Clinton, CNN*

# Capote

# 卡波特

**导演：**贝尼特·米勒（Bennett Miller）

**编剧：**丹·福特曼（Dan Futterman）

**主演：**菲利普·塞默·霍夫曼（Philip Seymour Hoffman）
　　　鲍勃·巴拉班（Bob Balaban）
　　　凯瑟琳·基纳（Catherine Keener）

**片长：**114 分钟

**发行：**索尼经典（Sony Pictures Classics），2005 年

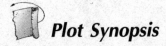 *Plot Synopsis*

In 1959, Truman Capote, a popular writer for *The New Yorker*, learns about the horrific and senseless murder of a family of four in Holcomb, Kansas. Inspired by the story material, Capote and his partner, Harper Lee, travel to the town to research for an article. However, as Capote digs deeper into the story, he is inspired to expand the project into what would be his greatest work, *In Cold Blood*. To that end, he arranges extensive interviews with the prisoners, especially with Perry Smith, a quiet and articulate man with a troubled history. As he works on his book, Capote feels some compassion for Perry which in part prompts him to help the prisoners to some degree. However, that feeling deeply conflicts with his need for closure for his book which only an execution can provide. That conflict and the mixed motives for both interviewer and subject make for a troubling experience that would produce an literary account that would redefine modern non-fiction.

## 剧情简介

1959 年，《纽约客》的知名作家楚门·卡波特得知堪萨斯州的霍尔库姆发生了一起一家四口被谋杀的惨案。故事的素材激发了他的灵感，于是卡波特和助手哈珀·李远赴小镇为他的文章做实地调查。随着了解的深入，他决定扩大写作规模，使之成为他最伟大的作品《冷血》。为此，卡波特开始仔细深入地采访凶手们，尤其是佩里·史密斯，一个安静、善言辞、有着不堪回首的过去的人。在写作过程中，卡波特对佩里产生了同情，并为此在一定程度上帮助了他。而同时，他想完成书的愿望又使他矛盾地期待死刑的到来。在对被访者和题材的矛盾心理中，卡波特的写作不啻于一场煎熬体验。而其文学成就却将重新定义现代的写实文学。

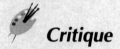

# Critique

On November 15, 1959, while luxuriating in abundant literary and social success in New York, the young Truman Capote was called to an unexpectedly spartan test. On that day, in Holcomb, Kansas, two ex-cons looking for money and thrills murdered four members of the Clutter family on their farm. A few weeks later, Capote, who had been eager to expand the boundaries of journalism, went to investigate the case for The New Yorker. Whatever his ambitions, Capote was an odd man for a police-blotter job. He was born in 1924 in New Orleans, and grew up in Alabama, Connecticut, and New York, where he went to the Trinity School for a while and worked briefly as an office boy at this magazine. For years, many readers (and, in particular, writers) have wondered how this habitu of Le Pavillon and La C te Basque, with his high, thin, goose-quill voice and his floating palms, could possibly have gained the trust of the straightforward men and women of rural Kansas. In "Capote", which stars Philip Seymour Hoffman, the writer, Dan Futterman, and the director, Bennett Miller, satisfy that curiosity. "Capote", which draws extensively on Gerald Clarke's 1988 biography, is devoted almost entirely to the five years in which Capote lived and wrote "In Cold Blood", an assignment that became a four-part series, a best-selling book, and a literary classic. Small-scaled and limited, "Capote" is nevertheless the most intelligent, detailed, and absorbing film ever made about a writer's working method and character—in this case, a mixed quiver of strength, guile, malice, and mendacity.

Moviegoers who have followed Philip Seymour Hoffman's supporting work in such films as "The Talented Mr. Ripley" and "Cold Mountain" sensed that he had a lot more to give, and here it is. As the cinematographer, Adam Kimmel, moves in close, Hoffman's Capote looms up like some strange Rushmoric* outcropping-heavy-domed skull, golden hair, pink skin, double-peaked upper lip, owlish glasses, and blue eyes that occasionally peer directly at the bruised ego and longings of the person in front of him. Hoffman starts with the physical and works inward to the soul. He's only a few years older than Capote was when he went to Kansas, but his thicker features seem to forecast the coarsening of face and body and the spreading spiritual rot that afflicted the writer in the years after the book came out. As Hoffman plays him, Capote is an actor, too: a wounded personality who remade himself; a public figure capable of facing down scorn. Holding forth at parties with cigarette and glass in hand, he dispenses rancorous gossip in a way that cuts off any possible life beyond his perfect sentences.

The filmmakers work intimately, with an easy, unstressed understanding of such things as Capote's homosexuality and the fervent solicitude that his friends felt for him—solicitude mixed with jealousy, exasperation, and dismay. No doubt people will pick at inaccuracies in the portrait and say, "That's not Truman", but "Capote" is Truman enough—and an image likely to make any writer grimace in recognition. There are some oddities: Harper Lee's character is a little fuzzy, and the filmmakers turn William Shawn

(Bob Balaban), the editor of *The New Yorker*, into an aggressive force who pushes the plot along. For the record, Shawn was not in the habit of demanding the bloody details in stories about murder, or of rushing off to the Midwest to keep his writers company at executions. Finally, the filmmakers' suggestion that Capote never recovered from the death of Perry Smith, or from the success of "In Cold Blood", strikes me as doubly sentimental. Capote was ultimately done in by alcohol. Yet, however one interprets it, the finale is acrid: the chronicler of death triumphs, and then has nowhere to go but to his own inglorious end.

—*David Denby*, *The New Yorker*

　　1959 年 11 月 5 日，纽约文艺圈和社交界的宠儿、年轻的楚门·卡波特遭遇了一场意料之外的严峻考验。当天，在堪萨斯州的霍尔库姆，克拉特一家四口在自家的农庄被两个犯有前科的前来抢劫和找刺激的歹徒所残杀。这件血案刺激了一直想拓宽新闻界限的卡波特，于是他前往事发地为《纽约客》搜集材料。无论是什么动机，他做这种警局记录员的工作看起来都很古怪。卡波特 1924 年生于新奥尔良，长于阿拉巴马、康涅狄格和纽约，他在纽约三一学校呆了没多久便去《纽约客》做小工。很多年以来，很多读者（尤其是作家）不明白这样一个纵情享乐、嗓音尖细、举止轻飘的人怎么就能赢得堪萨斯乡下那些憨厚的居民们的信任。在影片《卡波特》中，主演菲利普·塞默·霍夫曼，编剧丹·福特曼，导演贝尼特·米勒令人信服地填补了这一疑问。《卡波特》很大程度依赖于格拉德·克拉克写于 1988 年的传记，它把篇幅几乎全部集中在卡波特写《冷血》的那五年。《冷血》由最初的报刊文章最终发展成了一个分四部分写就的畅销书和文学经典。而《卡波特》虽然是有限的小制作，却是对一个作家的写作方式和性格最睿智，最细腻，最动人的演绎，这个"卡波特"不可思议地集勇气、狡诈、恶毒和谎言于一身。

看过菲利普·塞默·霍夫曼在《天才里普雷先生》和《冷山》中拔头彩的表演的影迷们都感到，他能给的比我们要的还要多，此处亦然。当摄影师亚当·金梅尔将镜头推近时，霍夫曼的"卡波特"就像是拉斯摩尔山的那些奇诡的浮雕一样呈现在银幕上——沉重的头颅、金色的头发、泛红的皮肤、有两个尖儿的上唇、猫头鹰式的眼镜，蓝色的眼睛偶尔直勾勾地凝视着眼前的人，看穿他的自尊心和他的渴望。霍夫曼的表演从肢体出发，然后向灵魂深入。霍夫曼比去堪萨斯时的卡波特大不了几岁，但是他深邃的面容似乎能够预示出卡波特在《冷血》出版后心力交瘁、神形俱毁的痛苦。霍夫曼在演卡波特，卡波特在演自己：一个受过伤害而重新做人的人，一个能够震慑住各种轻视和不屑的公众人物。他手夹香烟和酒杯在聚会上高谈阔论，将那些恶意的流言消于无形，将任何可能的生活都阻隔在他漂亮的言辞之外。

影片拍得很私秘，并以放松的、心照不宣的态度对待某些事，比如卡波特的同性恋身份，比如朋友们对他的强烈感情——在关心中还混杂了说不清的嫉妒、恼怒和沮丧。不怀疑人们会挑出人物刻画的某些不精确之处说"这不是楚门"，但是《卡波特》已经足够"楚门"了——它塑造了一个可能会让很多作家不得不皱着眉头承认的楚门。影片也有一些失实之处：哈珀·李这个角色面目模糊，还有《纽约客》的编辑威廉·肖恩（鲍勃·巴拉班饰）在片中被处理成一个推进情节发展的激进力量。而事实上，肖恩并没有这种追逐谋杀案中血腥细节的习惯，也没有急杀到中西部陪他的作者一同经历死刑的场面。影片在最后暗示卡波特再也没有从佩里·史密斯的死或者《冷血》的成功中恢复过来，这双重地震撼了我。卡波特最终死于酗酒。不管人们怎么诠释，这个结局都够辛辣：一个死亡之神的记录者最终逃无可逃地结束于自己不体面的死亡。

—David Denby,《纽约客》

That intertwined trajectory of creation and destruction is at the heart of the severe film, almost like a diagram of the primal Faustian bargain: The artist grows so much and gains so much, achieves immortality, really—and it only costs him his soul.

"Capote" gets at the writer's ethical dilemma: Real people and their lives are never as tidy as a good story, and they must be nudged, shoved, manipulated to get with the program. Every writer of long-form nonfiction faces this issue; he also needs the cooperation of people his book will be unkind to, and so the manipulations are creative, as are, in his interior life, his justifications.

Throughout the long writing (close to six years) of "In Cold Blood", Capote plays these games with a grandmaster's finesse, even when they become clouded by emotional engagement, possibly even love. He falls for one of the killers, a forlorn and embittered loser named Perry Smith. Yet even as he loves the poor wretched thing that Perry is, he must use him, first to find out what it is that enables a man to put a 12-gauge muzzle to the head of other humans and pull the trigger—four times! —and second, for the killer's account of the event, which he knew would form the climax of his book and make it great.

So he seduces Perry at least metaphorically and guides him by offering and withholding love, by enabling the young man's fantasies of specialness and, cruelest of all, by denying the nature of the book he is writing, even to the point of lying about what the

book's title will be. He also knows something more terrible: His
book will be better if Perry swings at the end of the Kansas
hangman's rope. He needs that scene.

Stories of ambition— "Champion", "What Makes Sammy
Run" —usually turn on a sociopathic hero, following men without
consciences who backslap, then backstab (the same backs) their
way to the top without a qualm. "Capote" revises this formula; the
point it makes, and almost as a dish of justice served hot, is that all
this cost Capote everything. He did what he had to do, he wrote
what he had to write, and he was left with fame and fortune—and
plenty of nothing. It ignores theories of alcoholism as disease. Instead it treats alcoholism as a symptom of a deeper soul rot.

*—Stephen Hunter, Washington Post*

创造和毁灭之间的纠缠是这部冷峻影片的核心，这几乎就是
浮士德与魔鬼之间最初达成的那份契约：艺术家真地成长了很
多，收获了很多，他从此不朽——而得到这些唯一的代价是他的
灵魂。

《卡波特》触及了作家的道德两难：现实中人和他们的人生
从来不可能像一个好故事那样洁净无尘，他们必须被鞭策、被强
迫、被操纵，才能使事情得以进行。每一个长篇纪实文学的作者
都要面对这一问题。因为他也需要那些将会被他无情书写的人的
合作，因此这种操纵应该是巧妙的、行之有效的，就像他内心的
理由一样。

在《冷血》的长期写作中（接近 6 年），卡波特以大师的手
法玩弄着这种游戏，虽然他也有情感介入的困扰，甚至爱。他情
不自禁地爱上了其中的一个名叫佩里·史密斯的凶手，他是个遭
遗弃的、苦难深重的失败者。可即便是他爱这个可怜人，他同时

也必须利用他——首先他需要知道是什么原因可以使一个人用12号口径的枪口对着别人的脑袋扣动扳机——而且是4次！其次，他需要凶手把事件的过程讲述出来，他知道这将会是书的高潮，并使之成为伟大的作品。

于是他引诱佩里（至少是在修辞上），他若即若离地用爱来引导他，让他幻想自己是特殊的，最残忍的是他对佩里隐瞒了正在写作的书的性质，甚至对书名都撒了谎。他心里还藏着更可怕的想法：如果佩里能最终死在堪萨斯州的绞架上，他的书将写得更好，他需要这一场景。

凡是关于野心的故事，比如《冠军》、《什么使萨米跑起来》，通常都有一个反社会的主人公跟着一个缺乏道德感的人暗地里打点应酬，然后没有一丝不安地为了爬上顶端而扫清障碍（同样是暗地里）。《卡波特》改写了这个规则，它的意义在于高举了正义的大旗——卡波特为此付出的代价是他的一切。他做了必须做的事，写了必须写的书，以此赢得了名誉和财富，而其实一无所获。影片没有把酒精中毒当成疾病来对待，而是把它当作灵魂从深处腐烂掉的象征。

—*Stephen Hunter*，《华盛顿邮报》

> ## Note
>
> Rushmoric：Rushmore，美国"国立拉斯摩尔山纪念馆"，俗称美国的"总统山"，位于美国南达科他州皮德城郊区，以山的轮廓为依托刻着美国四位总统的浮雕（美国第1任总统乔治·华盛顿，第3任总统杰斐逊，第16任总统林肯和第26任总统西奥多·罗斯福），是世界上最大的人面雕刻群。